Social Theory, Sport, Leisure

Social Theory, Sport, Leisure offers a clear, compact primer in social theory for students needing to engage with the application of sociological perspectives to the study of sport and leisure. Written in a straightforward style and assuming no prior knowledge, the book offers a fresh and easy-to-read overview of sociology's contribution to sport and leisure studies.

Ordered chronologically, each chapter:

- focuses on the work of a major social theorist and their most influential ideas;
- provides helpful historical and biographical detail to set the person and their thinking in contemporary context;
- identifies questions in sport and leisure on which the theory can shed useful light;
- considers how the ideas can be, or have been, applied in the study of sport and leisure;
- works as a self-contained unit, enabling students and lecturers to use the book flexibly according to their needs.

Written by an outstanding sociologist of leisure and sport, this intelligent yet jargon-free textbook enables students to get to grips with a wide range of important concepts and understand their diverse applications. As such, it is essential reading for any course designed to explore the place and meaning of sport and leisure in society.

Ken Roberts is Emeritus Professor of Sociology and Research Fellow at the University of Liverpool. He has also contributed to sport and leisure teaching at the University of Chester for over twenty-five years. He is a founder and honorary life member of the Leisure Studies Association, past President of the International Sociological Association Research Committee on Leisure, and past President of the World Leisure Organization's Research Commission. His books have been used on sport and leisure courses for forty years.

'This is the best introduction to understanding sport and leisure sociologically for foundation year undergraduates, from the sociologist who established the field of leisure studies.'

John Horne, *Professor of Sport and Sociology,*
University of Central Lancashire, UK

'This book makes an enormous contribution to the study of sport and leisure. In his thoughtful, reflective and thorough way, Ken Roberts opens a door for a range of new studies by offering a profound examination of sociological theories and their contribution to these fields. Scholars and students will no doubt treasure this book in their reflection on and inquiry into current issues.'

Atara Sivan, *Associate Dean, Faculty of Social Sciences &*
Professor, Department of Education Studies,
Hong Kong Baptist University, China

'This is an outstanding and crucial book for any students wanting to understand sport and leisure through the lens of sociological theory. Roberts writes in a clear and engaging style, showing the reader exactly how different theories and theorists can be used to make sense of sport and leisure.'

Karl Spracklen, *Professor of Leisure Studies,*
Head of the Research Centre for Diversity,
Equity and Inclusion, Leeds Beckett University, UK

'For those of us whose background in sociology is limited, Ken Roberts has produced an invaluable resource. He offers a concise review of the seminal lines of sociological thought, which facilitates easy access to them; shows how they interrelate; and offers insights on how each of them have been, and potentially could, enhance our understanding of leisure behavior. It is relentlessly positive in perspective, emphasizing the potential contributions of each of the lines of thought, and resisting the temptation to promote some at the expense of others. When I entered this field in the late 1960s, Ken Roberts was one of the small number of academics who were pioneering the study of leisure. I can think of nobody else in the field who is as well-equipped to produce this resource. It is written in his usual lucid prose in a highly readable style. In my view, it is an instant classic in the field and will be as relevant in 20 years' time as it is today.'

John Crompton, *University Distinguished Professor,*
Regents Professor, and Presidential Professor for
Teaching Excellence, Texas A&M University, USA

Social Theory, Sport, Leisure

Ken Roberts

Routledge
Taylor & Francis Group

LONDON AND NEW YORK

First published 2016
by Routledge
2 Park Square, Milton Park, Abingdon, Oxon OX14 4RN

and by Routledge
711 Third Avenue, New York, NY 10017

Routledge is an imprint of the Taylor & Francis Group, an informa business

British Library Cataloguing-in-Publication Data
A catalogue record for this book is available from the British Library

Library of Congress Cataloging in Publication Data
Names: Roberts, Kenneth, 1940- author.
Title: Social theory, sport, leisure / by Ken Roberts.
Description: 1 Edition. | New York : Routledge, 2016.
Identifiers: LCCN 2015042823| ISBN 9781138936720 (hardback) |
    ISBN 9781138936737 (pbk.) | ISBN 9781315676661 (ebook)
Subjects: LCSH: Social sciences—Philosophy. | Leisure—Social
    aspects. | Sports—Social aspects.
Classification: LCC H61 .R595 2016 | DDC 300.1—dc23
LC record available at http://lccn.loc.gov/2015042823

ISBN: 978-1-138-93672-0 (hbk)
ISBN: 978-1-138-93673-7 (pbk)
ISBN: 978-1-315-67666-1 (ebk)

Typeset in Scala
by Swales & Willis Ltd, Exeter, Devon, UK
Printed in Great Britain by Ashford Colour Press Ltd

Contents

chapter 1

Introduction

Auguste Comte (1798–1857), a Frenchman, coined the term 'sociology', and is therefore generally regarded as having founded the subject which since then has been the home of social theory. Because sports and all other leisure activities are social inventions, sociology is their natural academic home. Nearly all our modern sports, and many other modern leisure activities such as the holiday away from home, were invented in nineteenth-century Europe, in countries that were becoming industrial and urban. Sociology was born in response to, and as attempts to explain, these social transformations. However, it was over one hundred years after Comte's death in 1857 before sociologists collectively began to study any leisure activities. This neglect of leisure was not peculiar to sociology. None of the social sciences paid significant attention to 'frivolous' pastimes before their economic importance was recognised, which was towards the end of the twentieth century. By then the most advanced economies were becoming post-industrial, and leisure goods and services were increasingly important as sources of employment and contributors to countries' trade balances. Hence the explosion of student numbers and courses with leisure, recreation, sport, media, tourism and events in their titles. All these courses expect an input from sociology, including its theories about the character of the societies in which sport and the rest of leisure are located. The problem is that from Comte onwards hardly any of the major social theorists wrote anything about any kind of leisure. Even so, this book will show that the theories can be made to speak about sport and leisure. They can be used to find answers to questions that sport and other leisure scholars are already addressing, and to pose entirely new questions.

Sociology and its social theories

Auguste Comte founded sociology in the sense of coining the word, which literally means the study of society or societies. Coining the word, and the word itself, became important in creating an identity for a new kind of social thought. Comte's own theory was soon rejected, but his ideas about the mission of sociology, its overall character and scope, governed its development in Europe until the 1930s. Comte's sociology was to differ from earlier social thought because sociology's methods would be scientific. The nineteenth century was an age when the prestige of science was ascendant. Science was responsible for the remarkable progress that was continuing in transportation, manufacturing and the arts of warfare. Comte expected sociology to earn the same status, and to unleash equivalent progress in the management of social change.

Comte's sociology, in his own terms, was to study social statics and social dynamics, what we now call social structure and social change. It was to establish laws of history that would account for the changes that were under way in France (Comte's home country) and the rest of Europe in the nineteenth century, and explain how to ease the birth of the emerging economic, political and social orders. Comte was born in the aftermath of the French Revolution (1789–1793). In 1799, during Comte's infancy, Napoleon Bonaparte, an army commander, took charge of the revolution, was declared Emperor (of the French Empire) in 1804, and then led the country into a series of ultimately unsuccessful military campaigns which were supposed to spread French republicanism and the ideals of the revolution (liberty, equality, fraternity) throughout Europe. The Bourbon monarchy was restored in 1814, but throughout Comte's adult life there were continuous rumblings of discontent among the people of France, and in 1830 and 1848 there were failed attempts to repeat the revolution of 1789. The foundations of France and other European societies were shaking. Comte's sociology was to explain what was happening, to identify what was driving the changes, and to reach conclusions on how the changes should be managed.

Comte was keen to keep sociology separate from what he called 'social physics', what would now be called social statistics, gathering data on rates of fertility, marriages and deaths, housing, health and other conditions in industrial factories, mines and cities. Comte's insistence that sociology should have grander intellectual ambitions was to cripple the subject's development in Europe for a century. Researching conditions in industrial towns and factories, measuring the incidence and seeking the causes of poverty, crime and other social problems, became a separate endeavour which was linked closely to social and political reform movements. When it became the base of an academic subject, this was called 'social administration', a title subsequently dropped in favour of 'social policy'.

In America sociology developed differently from the 1870s onwards. It studied social change in the nation. This subject became a popular student choice, and from the 1890s spread rapidly throughout universities across the USA. In Europe sociology was an academic weakling until European and American sociology converged and European sociology embraced Comte's social physics, which was after the Second World War. Until then European sociology comprised theories about the course of history and the general character of the latest modern societies. The subject did not sink any academic roots until Emile Durkheim (1858–1917) became Europe's first professor of sociology at the University of Bordeaux (France) in 1895. The subject then began to spread to universities in other European countries, but the spread was extremely thin. Sociology was taught at the London School of Economics from 1905, and nowhere else in Britain until the end of the 1930s. The discipline was then reconstituted. American and European sociology converged. In Europe the subject embraced Comte's social physics, grew in popularity rapidly, and soon became part of the standard university offer. As sociology grew, its scholars began to special-ise in the family, education, crime and so on, and it was as part of this process that the study of sport and other kinds of leisure became sub-disciplines among sociology's numerous specialisms, albeit very minor sub-disciplines until the 1990s. Sociologists at the time of the subject's great expansion, between the 1940s and 1960s, had to decide which theo-ries from the nineteenth and early twentieth centuries they wished to retain in the discipline which was to be presented to new cohorts of students. Comte was not among these theorists. The choice of 'founding fathers' or 'classical theorists', as they became known, comprised Emile Durkheim, Karl Marx (1818–1883) and Max Weber (1860–1920). These, along with the American sociologist Talcott Parsons (1902–1979), who studied and devel-oped a synthesis of European social theories, are the scholars, the classical theorists, who feature in Part I of this book.

Durkheim and Parsons held academic posts as sociologists. Max Weber was an academic, but his job title was economics. Karl Marx, like Comte, did not have an academic career. Auguste Comte was secretary to a French aristocrat who, in effect, was Comte's patron. At that time Europe's intellectuals were not necessarily based in universities. They were as likely to be clergymen as academics, or persons with independent means, or they were supported by wealthy patrons. Comte realised that his own career belonged to an era that was drawing to a close. Karl Marx shared this belief. His main patron was Friedrich Engels (1820–1895), who was from a German family with wealth made from the manufacture and trade in textiles. Some eighteenth- and nineteenth-century social theo-rists held academic posts, but not in sociology. In the eighteenth century they would most likely have been called moral or political philosophers, to which the subject political economy was added during the nineteenth century. Theorists who were claimed by sociology during the twentieth century had not necessarily regarded themselves, or been regarded by contemporaries, as practising sociology. Politics, economics, sociology, law and history began to separate as distinct modern disciplines only during the 1890s, and this separation continued gradually until the 1930s. As already explained, some nineteenth-century intellectuals were based in universities, but others had independent means or wealthy patrons, or non-academic occupations. Thomas Malthus (1766–1834), whose essay on population commanded widespread attention throughout the nineteenth century, was a clergyman. He argued that human populations tended to increase in geometric progression (doubling then doubling again), whereas food supply rose only in arithmetical progression (by an identical unit in successive time periods). According to Malthus, this meant that population growth had to be held in check by famine, pestilence or war. This future could be avoided only if humans exercised sexual restraint, which Malthus considered unlikely. Malthus's ideas enjoyed huge credibility throughout the nineteenth century, when Europe's economies were expanding but poverty persisted. Then, from the late nineteenth century, Europe's populations began to practise birth control, and Malthus's theory was forgotten. Malthus was not claimed among the founders of sociology. Apart from having been proved wrong, his intellectual ambitions were too narrow.

All the theories claimed as part of sociology's history offered explanations of how societies had changed throughout human history. Some claimed that human thought had been the change driver. This was the view of Auguste Comte and his contemporary Georg Hegel (1770–1831), the eminent German philosopher. Comte believed that human thought had developed through three stages (his Law of Three Stages). A theological stage when events were explained as the work of fire spirits, wind spirits and so on had been followed by a metaphysical stage when explanations were in terms of abstract forces such as natural law or the will of God, which was being followed by a scientific stage where explanations were in terms of laws of cause and effect. Comte's view was that the scientific era had begun in the natural sciences and would conclude with the development of sociology. Comte was enthusiastic about the future. He expected sociology to become the new religion. Science replacing religion was a common expectation among nineteenth-century intellectuals, fuelled by battles between churchmen and scientists, over astronomy during the fifteenth, sixteenth and seventeenth centuries, then about evolution in the nineteenth century, and science appeared to be winning all these battles. Leonard Hobhouse (1864–1929), the first professor of sociology at the London School of Economics, believed that moral evolution had been the historical change driver. In the earliest societies people had followed specific moral rules that governed behaviour towards particular categories of persons such as family members. Hobhouse believed that the eventual outcome of evolution

4

would be general ethical principles that applied to all humanity. Hobhouse's ideas were forgotten during the mid-twentieth-century reconstitution of sociology, but today, with the United Nations having created courts which claim worldwide jurisdiction, it appears that Hobhouse may have read history correctly. However, like Comte's Law of Three Stages, Hobhouse was dismissed as mistaken. It was Max Weber's more sophisticated account of the role of ideas in history that was incorporated into the reconstituted post-1945 sociology.

In the nineteenth century theories of evolution were among the big debates and advances in the natural sciences. Eventually it was the theory of Charles Darwin (1809–1882) that triumphed. Evolution was said to be the outcome of struggles for survival between different plants and animals, and the specimens within species that were born with innate advantages were said to be the most likely to survive and eventually to become the dominant type. Many nineteenth-century social theorists argued that societies had evolved in a similar manner. The nineteenth century was the period when scientists were dividing humanity into different races. It was also an age of empire-building. Europeans (most of them) had no doubt that they were innately superior to other races. This is why social anthropology, a subject that spread alongside empires and studied 'primitive people' and their simple societies, aligned not with sociology, but with anthropology, which studied the physical differences between different sections of humanity. Ludwig Gumplowicz (1838–1909), who was based in Krakow (now in Poland, but part of Austria at the time), argued that the driver of social evolution had been a struggle for supremacy between different races. Arthur de Gobineau (1816–1882), a French aristocrat, agreed, and he also identified (or invented) an Aryan race. These contributions have been airbrushed from most histories of sociology, but they, alongside Comte and Hobhouse, would have been part of the curriculum on pre-1939 courses in Europe.

A different explanation of social evolution was offered by Herbert Spencer (1820–1903). He was the son of a Derbyshire clergyman and started his working life with a railway company, then became an independent scholar earning his living from books, journalism and lectures. He argued that all species had evolved from simpler to more complex types because complex organisms were always the stronger, the best able to survive. Spencer (not Darwin) was the first to use the expression 'the survival of the fittest'. He was also the first to liken societies to biological organisms such as animal bodies. Spencer was a polymath, an expert on everything, an intellectual type that has now become extinct. He became an international intellectual celebrity, invited to lecture in the USA, and his advice was sought by the Japanese government when the country was seeking to modernise in the late nineteenth century. Adam Smith (1723–1790), a Scottish moral philosopher, had already drawn attention to the advantages of a division of labour within businesses (enabling workers to specialise in the tasks to which they were best suited), and also to the progressive force of the 'hidden hand of the market' and how the pursuit of individual self-interest led to greater all-round prosperity. Spencer argued that a broader division of labour, across all parts of a society, strengthened its chances in the struggle for survival. Unfortunately for Spencer's legacy, his ideas were incorporated into Emile Durkheim's more comprehensive account of the progressive division of labour, and it was Durkheim who became recognised as one of sociology's founding fathers. Durkheim also had the advantage of being a dedicated sociologist rather than a polymath, and he was not only employed as a sociologist, but became Europe's first professor of sociology in 1895. Spencer could not compete with this CV.

For Georg Hegel (1770–1831), a battle between ideas had been history's change driver. Hegel rarely features in histories of sociological thought, though he has as strong a claim as Gumplowicz and de Gobineau, for whom the change driver was a struggle between races. For others, as explained above, the struggle was between simpler and more complex social organisms. Karl Marx and his collaborator and patron Friedrich Engels (1820–1895) had a different view: the change driver had been conflict between groups within societies. According to Marx and Engels, the protagonists were classes defined by their relationships to the means of production. This thinking cut across the previous assumption (too obvious to need defence) that societies were weakened by internal strife. Max Weber (1864–1920), a generation later, added that there could be classes in addition to owners and workers, and that conflict could also be about status and sometimes the pursuit of power for its own sake. These ideas earned Marx and Weber their reputations as classical social theorists.

Max Weber had German contemporaries who made lasting contributions to sociological thought. They included Ferdinand Toennies (1855–1936), who contrasted traditional *Gemeinschaft* societies where life was governed by 'natural will' that expressed instincts, habits and convictions, and where social relationships were emotional and co-operative, with *Gesellschaft* societies which were governed by rational will, where social relationships were contractual and impersonal, individualism ruled and life was competitive (Toennies, 1887). Georg Simmel (1858–1918) was another contemporary who first became famous internationally for his essay on the metropolis and mental life (Simmel, 1903), but has attracted renewed interest in the twenty-first century because he also wrote about the 'financialisation' of goods, services and social relationships (Simmel, 1900). Toennies and Simmel did not become ranked as major classical social theorists, not because their ideas were rejected, but because their theories were narrower in scope than those of Durkheim, Marx and Weber.

Part II of this book deals with successors to the classical theorists. The criteria for inclusion in Part II are necessarily different than those in Part I. Durkheim, Marx and Weber were declared founding fathers of sociology and classical theorists long after their deaths when it was decided that their ideas should be kept alive. Their successors are either still living or too recently deceased to apply an equivalent test. They are selected as major social theorists because their ideas have been and are still being used in most of sociology's sub-disciplines, and sometimes in other subjects also. The exception is Norbert Elias (1897–1990). He is included because he does feature in the work of contemporary sports scholars, though rarely anywhere else.

Most of the successors in Part II have continued the classical agenda in offering reinterpretations of history, but a difference is that since Max Weber, social theorists have not attempted to explain the entire span of human history, but have restricted themselves to changes in Europe since the Middle Ages. Those who have offered such reinterpretations are Norbert Elias, the 'critical theorists' in Chapter 7 and Michel Foucault (1926–1984). Others are included in Part II for having offered a different 'analytical' type of theory. They begin with Talcott Parsons, who is in Part I because he became the bridge between pre-1939 European and American sociology, and also between the classical and successor theorists. Parsons endorsed Spencer's and Durkheim's view that the central trend throughout history had been a progressive division of labour, and that the explanation was that complex societies were stronger than simpler societies. He also offered an analytical theory, a set of inter-related concepts that can be used in the study of any society at any time and in any place. Symbolic interactionism, and the work of Pierre Bourdieu (1930–2002), are also analytical theories.

Part III deals with theories that are still being developed in the present. They continue the classical agenda in addressing the course of history, but here history begins in the late twentieth century. The theories are about the character of the latest modern age, in which virtually all spheres of life have changed during the absorption of new information and communication technology (ICT). 'Post-industrial', 'globalisation', 'neo-liberal', 'knowledge economy' and 'information age' are further keywords that help to define this new era.

The second 'present' chapter is about the latest versions of modernisation theory which are about the post-1989 world in which capitalism has become global. This has inspired a resuscitation of claims that throughout the world all societies are now on a common 'modernising' trajectory. 'Resuscitation' applies because 'one common trajectory' was the view in classical nineteenth-century theories of social evolution, and in development theories (the rest catching up with the most economically advanced societies) and an alleged convergence between capitalist and communist systems driven by a common 'logic of industrialism', that were propounded from the 1950s to the 1970s.

None of the theories in this book are presented in order to perform a demolition job. Each chapter tries to make the strongest possible case for the theory or theorist(s) that feature.

Sport and leisure studies

The case for sociology as the natural home for studying sport and leisure may be overwhelming on purely intellectual grounds, but this is not where sport and leisure first sank academic roots.

Europe has been the main source of social theories about the ever-changing modern age. Comte and his successors had a rich heritage from which to draw and on which to build. Europe was the continent of the Renaissance and the Reformation, then the Enlightenment which produced political and moral philosophers such as Thomas Hobbes (1588–1679), John Locke (1632–1704), Jean-Jacques Rousseau (1712–1788) and Immanuel Kant (1724–1804). American sociology produced theories as necessary to understand contemporary America. There was neither need nor opportunity to explore a long historical trajectory, but America was decades ahead of Europe in developing sport and leisure as academic disciplines.

In the case of sport, this is due to its uniquely elevated role in America's colleges. Most modern sports were invented in England, the world's first industrial nation, then spread throughout the world, but not in the USA. Sport is just one example of American exceptionalism. The country invented its own modern sports – its own version of football, and baseball, to which ice hockey and basketball were added. England's secondary schools (all private at that time) and universities were the sites where most of England's modern sports were invented. It was similar in the USA: the colleges were the main sites. However, America was different, in that from the outset college sports became major spectator events, covered by the media. Subsequently, American colleges that have sought fame through success at sports have offered sports scholarships to attract talented young athletes. These colleges have been ports of entry to careers in professional sport, and the pools from which the USA's Olympic squads are drawn. Sports studies developed within the colleges' sports departments, which are expected to be income generators for their institutions. The costs of sports scholarships and other expenses can be recouped many times over by income produced by spectator events. The original, and still major, issues for sports researchers have been how to identify, coach and train talented young athletes, and how to win on the field, rink or court.

Leisure studies was also born in the USA. By the end of the 1930s America had around a thousand colleges with courses that trained leaders for work in recreation services within the public and voluntary sectors (Pangburn, 1940). By the mid-twentieth century America had a large and diverse system of tertiary education within which it was much easier to create niches for new subjects, such as the study of sport and leisure, than in Europe's less numerous, more elitist, more traditional universities. Leisure studies courses and departments were created in America from the 1950s onwards by merging and building upon existing physical education, recreation leadership and outdoor recreation syllabuses (Samdahl, 2010). In the USA leisure scholars have always maintained stronger connections with the country's leisure services than with any other academic discipline. Right up to the present day, the USA's leisure scholars have not formed a scholarly association, but since 1978 have held their main series of meetings, the Leisure Research Symposium, within the annual conferences of the National Recreation and Parks Association (Henderson, 2011).

Modern sports were first invented in England's secondary schools and universities, but they were played for enjoyment and integrated into curricula for educational purposes (health, fitness and character-building), not as spectator events or to prepare pupils and students for careers as professional players. Sport first became an academic subject within UK higher education as a specialism in teacher training at colleges which offered this option. They were preparing students to teach, not for careers as sport professionals or Olympic competitors. However, teacher training programmes that offered the physical education option were often the base from which broader sport and leisure studies courses were introduced from the 1970s onwards. Leisure studies was then spreading from America into Britain, but a difference was that whereas in the USA sport studies had a separate academic base, in Britain it was often at the heart of leisure studies programmes. The incorporation of these subjects into UK higher education occurred during a period of expansion in student numbers which created scope for new subjects. It was also at a time (albeit towards the end of the era) when sport and other leisure services were becoming part of the welfare state, and this was creating new voluntary and public sector jobs in sport and other leisure services. Leisure studies subsequently spread into Australia and New Zealand, then more thinly throughout the rest of the world, always in the same contexts of growth in higher education and jobs in the leisure industries. However, since the 1970s most of the growth in the leisure industries has been in the commercial sector, and most growth in spending has been by private consumers rather than public authorities. Even so, in the late twentieth century this led to further increases in the number of sport and leisure courses (which, as explained below, have tended to splinter) and students studying these subjects. However, the essential point at this stage is that neither sociology nor any other established social science was the base from which sport and leisure were developed as research and teaching specialisms in either North America or the rest of the world.

Following sport and physical education, media studies was the next specialist academic 'leisure' subject that was created in response to the growth in importance of the media in people's lives and as sources of employment. Since the mid-twentieth century tourism has been among the world's fastest-growing industries, and is now one of the world's largest. The academic response has been the creation of tourism studies. Leisure and sport courses have tended to splinter. There are now many micro-specialisms – sport tourism, therapeutic recreation, youth sport and dark tourism (to Second World War extermination camps and suchlike). 'Events' is one of the latest micro-leisure specialities into which the rest of leisure has sometimes been collapsed. Every theatre performance, every sport fixture, every festival can be treated as an event that needs to be marketed and organised, though the courses invariably focus on the biggest events, the sports mega-events – the Olympics and the FIFA World Cup – which all countries hope to attract.

Throughout these developments sociology has been a contributor to the curricula, but the host departments have tended to pick the most useful aspects, especially 'social divisions', for explanations of why participation varies by social class, age, sex, religion, ethnicity and so on, and how to boost participation among under-represented groups. Tourism studies wants inputs relevant to the imaging and marketing of place, and how to target specific market segments such as countries whose outward tourists spend the most money per day. Although sociology invariably contributes, the courses have tended to drift away from the social sciences and into management or business schools, or in the case of sport, into health faculties.

Sport and leisure studies have drawn selectively from sociology and also from psychology. In the 1950s, 1960s and 1970s they embraced Abraham Maslow's theory about a hierarchy of human needs. Maslow (1943, 1954) had argued that once basic survival needs (physiological and safety) had been met, people would prioritise higher-level needs (belonging, love and esteem), and would eventually seek self-actualisation. Its scholars were keen to present leisure as where self-actualisation could be achieved by everyone. Later on, leisure studies embraced Mihaly Csikszentmihalyi's (1990) theory about optimal experience, which he called 'flow'. This was experienced when individuals' skills were stretched to the utmost and their attention was absorbed totally in accomplishing a task. Again, leisure was offered as where everyone could achieve regular flow. More recently leisure scholars have been keen to demonstrate how leisure activities can enhance 'well-being', which includes physiological and mental health, and can also be given economic and social dimensions (see Haworth and Hart, 2007; Haworth et al., 1997). At present these composite measurements are being evaluated as possible alternatives to economic indicators, especially gross domestic product (GDP), as measurements of social progress.

Leisure scholars have also developed their own theories. In the 1970s Stanley Parker (1971) offered a theory about work–leisure relationships in which the meaning of leisure was seen to depend on how people experienced their work. The Canadian sociologist Robert Stebbins (1992, 2001, 2005) has developed an analytical theory which distinguishes between casual, project-based and serious leisure. Leisure scholars have constantly developed theories about the character of the current or soon-to-be societies in which leisure will play a larger and stronger role than ever before. These efforts were begun by Joffre Dumazedier, a French sociologist, in the 1960s (Dumazedier, 1967, 1974). However, up to now none of the theories generated within sport and leisure studies have been mainstreamed into any of the social sciences.

Maybe there is no problem. Sport and leisure scholars can bunker down. They can market themselves on the basis that they produce and teach knowledge that can be put to practical use in the various leisure industries. However, this must concern sociologists, whose subject rests on the premise that the parts of any society can only be properly understood in the context of the whole. The constant sub-division of knowledge leaves even the most highly educated mystified about the significance of what they know and what they do.

Preamble

This book does not berate sport and leisure scholars for an alleged myopia. It is sociology that needs to reach out. This is the aim in all the following chapters. Since its reconstitution and expansion between the 1940s and 1960s, sociology itself has splintered. This has not been planned, but has simply happened as the sheer volume of output has forced scholars to specialise. It has become impossible for any sociologist to keep abreast with research across the entire discipline. Sociologists now specialise in sport, tourism, leisure, consumption, everyday life, the media, health, the family, crime, education, societies in different parts of the world, and many other slices of their discipline's subject matter. Many sociologists now work (as teachers and researchers) in multi-disciplinary units which are dedicated to youth studies and management, and this list includes sport and leisure. Social theory itself has tended to become a specialism, the concern only of sociologists whose specialism is social theory. This is dangerous because only theory can hold sociology together, which it must if sociology's founding premises are correct: that the parts of any society can be properly understood only in the context of the whole, and that the past is part of the present. Research methods will not hold sociology together because the discipline has no methods that are not used elsewhere, and there are no methods that all sociologists use.

So this book is reaching out to sociologists and students who specialise in sport and leisure. It is not aimed primarily at students on sociology courses. The treatment of the theorists and their theories is likely to be too perfunctory for their needs. Each chapter highlights just the main points of the theory that is introduced. It then illustrates, but does not offer an exhaustive account of, how the theory has been and can be used in sport and leisure studies. Another feature of the book is that it presents a brief biography of each theorist and his (there are no females) historical context. Theories become easier to understand alongside the times, lives and social contexts in which they were produced.

The classical theories were produced in the nineteenth and early twentieth centuries in European countries that were undergoing industrialisation and urbanisation alongside demands for democratisation. Their successors have tended to take a longer-term view, treating the changes in nineteenth- and early twentieth-century Europe as parts of modernisation processes that had begun by the sixteenth century. The theories about the present do not replace earlier theories. Globalisation, neo-liberalism, ICT and the shift of employment from manufacturing into services have not erased history. The older theories continue to highlight features of the societies in which they were produced that persist into the present. The theories may suggest answers to questions that sport and leisure scholars are already addressing. They always pose additional questions.

PART I
The classical theories

chapter 2

Emile Durkheim (1858–1917)

Introduction

In the 1880s and 1890s Emile Durkheim was a young Frenchman with a mission, seeking to have sociology recognised and established as an independent science, equal to all the other sciences, and thereby trans-form intellectual life in France and beyond (see Durkheim, 1895). These were huge ambitions which Durkheim had remarkably fulfilled by the time he reached the age of 40.

Durkheim did not write about sport or any other leisure activity, but his social theory demands attention from all sport and leisure scholars. When anyone claims that any use of leisure will benefit everyone – that everyone's well-being will be enhanced, that an entire community or nation will be drawn closer together and that the group's prestige will rise – they implicitly assume that Durkheim's theory of society is correct. So sport and leisure scholars need to understand the theory and the many criticisms it has attracted. If the critics are correct, we must become suspicious of claims that everyone will be a winner and that there will be no losers in any lei-sure project, whether it is a successful bid to host an Olympics, subsidising high culture or spreading more active leisure throughout a population.

Durkheim was a dedicated sociologist, and became Europe's first professor of sociology when appointed to the post at the University of Bordeaux (France) in 1895. His aspirations for sociology were similar to those of his French predecessor, Auguste Comte: to establish a science of society which, among other things, would account for the entire course of human history. Durkheim's objections were that Comte's methods had not been truly scientific, and that his theory about the main force that drove history forward (the development of human thought) was mistaken.

Durkheim's historical driving force was the division of labour, the creation of forever more specialised social institutions and roles which made people more inter-dependent and thereby bound them together. He believed that, once in motion, the division of labour became a self-perpetuating process (Durkheim, 1893).

Durkheim succeeded where others had failed. He invented a complete sociology – a theory which accounted for the main direction of historical change, the main features of earlier and modern societies, and a set of methods for their investigation. Both the theory and the methods remain alive today. So who exactly was their inventor?

Career

Durkheim was born in 1858, and grew up in Lorraine, a region of France that bordered Germany until annexed by Germany following the Franco-Prussian War in 1870–1871, when Durkheim was age 13. He lived in troubled times, which continued beyond his own lifetime. Lorraine and its neighbouring region Alsace are now in France, because Germany was defeated in the twentieth century's two world wars.

Durkheim's family was Jewish: his father, grandfather and great-grandfather had all been rabbis. Emile Durkheim became non-religious, but this did not lead to a break with his family or the Jewish community. In fact, most of Durkheim's academic collaborators throughout his career were Jews. Durkheim must have been sensitive to his Jewish descent and connections. Anti-Semitism was widespread in Europe towards the end of the nineteenth century, and between 1894 and 1906 France was convulsed by the Dreyfus affair (as it became known). Dreyfus was a Jew and a French army officer who was accused and convicted of passing military secrets to Germany. He spent two years on Devil's Island before doubts about his conviction led to his return to France, though he remained in captivity until 1906. By then it had been established that the military hierarchy was aware of Dreyfus's innocence and had concealed the guilt of the real offender (who was not Jewish). France was divided. Had the military hierarchy acted honourably in order to protect the French nation's reputation? Or was this a case of outrageous discrimination and injustice? Durkheim must have felt affected by these events: his wife was a Dreyfus. However, there is no evidence that Durkheim personally experienced discrimination on account of his Jewish origins and collaborators.

Although he was the son of a rabbi, Emile Durkheim was given a conventional French academic education. After *lycée*, in 1879 he attended the Ecole Normale Supérieure in Paris, where he became interested in social science. He also became frustrated because at that time social science was not taught in higher education in France. Throughout the nineteenth century and beyond, whether human behaviour could be studied and explained scientifically was controversial. As a post-graduate, Durkheim spent two years in Germany, where they did teach social science. He could read and speak German, Italian and English, and became familiar with the work of Herbert Spencer. On returning to France, Durkheim taught at *lycées* while working on his dissertation, which became his first book, *The Division of Labour*, published in 1893. The favourable reception of this book led to Durkheim's appointment at the University of Bordeaux, where he became Europe's first professor of sociology in 1895, in Europe's first university sociology department. By then Durkheim was publishing his second book, *The Rules of Sociological Method*, a textbook on how to conduct sociological investigations in a modern society (Durkheim, 1895). This was followed by *Suicide*, which was intended to illustrate and demonstrate the remarkable results that could be achieved using Durkheim's methods (Durkheim, 1897). By then Durkheim was attracting a group of followers, and sociology was a growing subject in France. In 1898 these pioneers established Europe's first academic sociology journal, *L'Année Sociologique*. The subject was soon spreading to universities in other European countries, especially Germany, where social science was already firmly established. In 1905 sociology was introduced at the London School of Economics. The young man with a mission had succeeded. Durkheim's own career prospered, and he became a professor at the Sorbonne in Paris in 1902. There was never any doubt when the description was conferred (after the Second World War) that Durkheim would be recognised as one of sociology's founding fathers. Durkheim's last major book, on religion, was published in 1912.

It helps us to understand Durkheim's sociology if we appreciate his concern about the state of France during his lifetime. Since the French Revolution which began in 1789, France had experienced continuous constitutional instability. Britain's nineteenth-century history was very different. Its period of chronic constitutional instability had been in the seventeenth century. After a civil war, the execution of Charles I in 1649, a period as a republic (1649–1660), the restoration of the monarchy in 1660, the overthrow of James II in 1689 and the succession of William and Mary of the House of Orange, then the Hanoverian succession in 1714 when Queen Anne (the sister of Mary of Orange) died without leaving an heir, the position of the monarch was settled: he or she reigned, but did not rule. Subsequently, during the nineteenth century, it was possible to extend the franchise in stages, first to the property-owning urban middle classes, then to successive sections of the working class. There were tumultuous reform movements, mainly the Chartists (1838–1858) and violent incidents, including the Peterloo Massacre (on St Peter's Field, Manchester) in 1819, when the cavalry charged a crowd of 60,000–80,000, resulting in 15 deaths and injuries to 400–700, but compared with the rest of Europe, change in Britain during the nineteenth century was evolutionary rather than revolutionary. The USA, the other major country that was industrialising and urbanising from the closing decades of the nineteenth century, did not have a feudal heritage which needed to be overthrown.

France had an entirely different nineteenth-century history. Napoleon Bonaparte, an army commander, took control of the revolution in 1799, had himself declared Emperor in 1804 and led France in a series of ultimately unsuccessful military campaigns. Subsequently, the Bourbon monarchy was restored, but following attempted revolutions in Paris and other cities in 1830 and then again in 1848, France had lurched between republic, monarchy, then republic again. Like other north-west European countries, France began to industrialise and urbanise, and was building an overseas empire, but this was alongside constant battles within France between republicans and monarchists, and a partly cross-cutting and partly linked battle between secularists and those who wanted to retain an intermesh between church and state. This was in the context of continuous (at least simmering) border disputes with Prussia (Germany after 1871).

Throughout the nineteenth century Britain was the safe haven to which Europe's monarchs and aristocrats, and revolutionaries who feared for their lives at home, could flee. A third French republic had been established following defeat and loss of territory in the Franco-Prussian war of 1870–1871, after which Frenchmen had battled against Frenchmen as government forces wrestled control of Paris and other cities from local communes. The central problem that Durkheim addressed in all his work was how to achieve and maintain solidarity in a complex modern society.

The division of labour

Durkheim agreed with Herbert Spencer that the division of labour, a movement from simple to complex societies, had been the master trend in history. He also agreed that the division of labour enabled societies to become more productive and more powerful, and that this trend was not purely economic, but a general historical movement which also, for example, separated economic production from the family, removed governments from the detailed regulation of economic life and separated justice systems from government. However, Durkheim did not agree with Spencer that the survival of the fittest – competition that led to the strong eliminating or absorbing the weak unless the latter changed – had been the principal driving force. He did not believe that the main historical driving force had been competition for dominance between races, nations or states. A Durkheimian view would be that the division of labour will lead ultimately to the unification of humanity through bonds of inter-dependence.

Durkheim argued that as the division of labour progressed, social solidarity was maintained in different ways. Simple societies, where people led very similar lives, were said to be knit together by a powerful *conscience collective*. People shared common ideas about how they all ought to behave. The entire society would be outraged when its rules were broken, and retributive punishment would match the level of outrage, thereby enforcing a 'mechanical' kind of solidarity. As the division of labour progressed, the *conscience collective* was said to weaken, though without ever becoming wholly extinct. According to Durkheim, the division of labour itself then became a source of 'organic' solidarity. People would perform their specialist roles to the best of their ability because they knew that others depended on them. In turn, they realised that they themselves depended on other people performing their roles competently and reliably. Unlike Adam Smith, Durkheim did not believe that self-interest alone was sufficient to keep a society strong and healthy. Self-interest had to be complemented by a sense of inter-dependence with a moral dimension. When rules were broken, the punishment of the guilty party was restitutive; he or she had to make good any damage that had been done.

Once in motion, Durkheim believed that the division of labour became a self-perpetuating process. Each step weakened mechanical solidarity, which would require a further division of labour to boost organic solidarity. What set this process in motion? It was impossible to provide an answer grounded in historical evidence. It could have been drought or famine, or threats from external enemies. However, Durkheim believed that the most likely and common first cause would have been population growth, which required a division of labour in order to produce enough to sustain a growing population, which in turn weakened mechanical solidarity and set history in motion.

If one type of solidarity could be replaced smoothly with another, how did Durkheim explain the chronic instability in nineteenth-century France? How did he account for the crime and industrial conflict that were becoming widespread as European countries became urban, capitalist and industrial? Durkheim's answer was that the division of labour could take abnormal, pathological forms – forced, anomic and egoistic:

- A forced division of labour was said to arise when people were placed in roles for which they were unsuited. Durkheim believed that the normal outcome would be for people to opt for roles, or to be allocated to roles, that matched their capabilities and inclinations. This was how Adam Smith (1776) had envisaged the division of labour boosting productivity. People would be able to specialise in tasks for which they were best suited. Otherwise, Durkheim recognised that people would become discontent, motivation would sag, and risks of conflict, protest and rebellion would escalate.

- An anomic division of labour was said to be likely in times of rapid and major social change, when people's obligations and entitlements became unclear and there was a collapse of social norms. Anomie is a state of normlessness, the absence of any clear rules. According to Durkheim, anomie might spread in times of economic crisis or war, but it was equally likely when standards of living were rising or when lives were being dislocated as people moved from rural villages into industrial towns and cities.
- Egoism was said to occur when, although there was a normative order which regulated most people's behaviour, some just could not perceive how they fitted in. Egoists were unclear about their own obligations towards others and what they could expect from them.

In offering these explanations of instability and social breakdown, Durkheim encountered, and his ideas continue to encounter, waves of opposition. Critics argue that what Durkheim treated as abnormal and pathological are in fact normal features of urban, capitalist societies. Durkheim's model of society treats integration, cohesion, consensus and stability as normal. His critics prefer to start with a model of society in which different groups have different, conflicting interests, in which one group profits at the expense of others, where many are obliged to play roles in which they encounter more frustration than satisfaction, where neighbours are knit together neither by shared norms nor inter-dependence, where the distribution of rewards is widely perceived as blatantly unfair, and where egoistic behaviour – maximising private interests – is better rewarded than altruism. Supporters of Durkheim counter-argue that his model should be treated as a benchmark against which deviations can be identified then explained, not a representation of how things really are. Durkheim realised all too well that the France in which he lived was not a perfectly integrated and cohesive society.

Social facts and sociological methods

Durkheim's mission was to establish sociology as an independent subject, equal in status to all other sciences, and he believed that this required sociology to have a unique subject matter on which sociologists, and they alone, were the recognised experts. Durkheim was probably mistaken. Biologists and psychologists both study human perception and memory without diminishing the credibility of either discipline. However, Durkheim's sociology was to be distinct from all other subjects in studying social facts – patterns of behaviour across a population which could change, but which tended to persist over time and could remain stable throughout a population being completely replenished by births and deaths. Birth rates, death rates, marriage rates and crime rates are examples of Durkheim's social facts. Durkheim believed it was self-evident that these rates could not be explained as outcomes of the independent wills and decisions of thousands of individuals. Rather, Durkheim contended that social facts had the power to force themselves onto members of a population, and this power arose from the moral force created by mechanical and/or organic solidarity. In Durkheim's view, explaining a rate (of births, crime and so on) was an entirely different problem from explaining which individuals gave birth and committed crimes. He argued that explaining a rate did not require delving into individuals' minds. This could be left to psychology. One set of social facts was to be explained through their relationships with other social facts. Thus sociology was to be an independent, self-contained discipline. We should note that Durkheim did not intend sociology to be separate from the study of economics and politics. Sociology was to be *the* social science. Durkheim lived in a period when the boundaries between these subjects (and law and history also) were still unclear, and they would remain so during the inter-war years of the twentieth century. Until then, no one who practised sociology believed that the subject could be restricted to the parts of society that remained when the economy, government and law had been extracted.

Durkheim chose to study suicide because he believed that since suicide was generally regarded as one of the most individually motivated of all acts, demonstrating its susceptibility to sociological treatment would be a powerful illustration of the effectiveness of his methods. For this research Durkheim used official records of causes of death, and he was able to show that suicide rates varied between populations. He found that suicide was more common among Protestants than among Roman Catholics, and less common among the married than among people who were living singly. Both relationships were said to be explicable in terms of the strength of the bonds that knit people into their societies. Those living in families benefited, and Catholic congregations were said to be relatively communal, well integrated and cohesive compared with Protestant faiths, which were more individualistic.

Durkheim argued that there were different types of suicide, distinguished by their different causes, which overlapped with his different pathological forms of the division of labour:

- Egoistic suicide occurred when individuals were adrift from social bonds, as when separated from their families by divorce or the death of close relatives.
- Anomic suicide was said to occur when social bonds were weak, as in Protestant as opposed to Catholic communities.
- Altruistic suicide was said to be due to social solidarity being too strong, resulting in individuals sacrificing their lives in the interests

of a group. They could be applauded as heroes or martyrs. Jesus Christ is an example, and there have been many subsequent martyrs in Christianity and Islam. Military campaigns usually produce heroes who risk and sacrifice their own lives from a sense of duty. Such acts may be applauded, but if everyone acted in these ways a society would disappear. In his *Rules of Sociological Method* Durkheim argued that certain levels of crime and other forms of deviance had to be accepted as normal because a society that suppressed all deviance would also prevent innovation and progress.

'Suicide' did not identify a type that corresponded with Durkheim's 'forced' division of labour.

Critics have queried the accuracy of the suicide statistics on which Durkheim relied. Families (where present), and especially Catholic families, were likely to have tried to persuade doctors to attribute a suicidal death to some other cause, and Catholic doctors may have been particularly amenable. Even so, Durkheim's study of suicide illustrates the method of enquiry that he was proposing for sociology. This method has subsequently become a standard part of the discipline's arsenal of research techniques. Nowadays, Durkheim's social facts are called variables, and investigators are able to use more sensitive statistical techniques than were available to Durkheim in establishing the strength of relationships between variables. The use of Durkheimian methods, exploring the relationships between social facts (or variables), has become increasingly common as large data sets have multiplied in number, and as it has become possible for these data sets to be accessed from remote online workstations. A difference today is that sociologists do not try to exclude all psychological processes from their explanations. Durkheim was aggressively sociological, maybe unnecessarily so, but he believed that the subject's acceptance depended on it being a self-contained science, and the psychology of Durkheim's lifetime from which he wanted to keep sociology apart was different from the psychology of today. In the late nineteenth and early twentieth centuries psychology was preoccupied with what were then believed to be innate mental dispositions, such as levels of intelligence and criminality.

As noted above, Durkheim's intention was that sociology should incorporate the study of economic life and politics. Adam Smith (1776) had believed that the pursuit of self-interest and the common good could be reconciled by 'the hidden hand of the market'. As also noted above, Durkheim disagreed: he believed that economic life needed to be embedded and morally regulated by a wider social order. Similarly, he believed that a political constitution could work only with such embedding. Societal cohesion depended on all members of a society feeling that everyone was being fairly treated and rewarded. Social facts could impose themselves on people only because these facts had a moral dimension and force. Some twenty-first-century dilemmas in the European Union (EU) amply illustrate the problems that arise when politics, the economy and people's sense of moral obligations and entitlements become out of kilter. Citizens may be less willing to fund welfare payments to migrants from another EU country than to migrants from different regions in their own countries. Nations that share a currency (the euro) may not be willing either to pool their debts or to surrender their elected national governments' rights to govern national taxation and public spending.

Religion

Durkheim was not the first non-believer (nor was he the last) to take a keen interest in religion. Part of the fascination is always that others retain beliefs that appear untenable in a rational and scientific age. People have remained willing to die for their beliefs. Missionaries and their funders continue with efforts to convert non-believers and those who adhere to 'false' religions. There are still countries, usually Moslem countries, where apostasy (abandoning the faith) is a capital offence. It is also the case that non-believing sociologists, including Durkheim, have first suspected then concluded that religion has played a vital social role by acting as a meta-phorical form of glue, binding people together. This poses the problem of what happens when people abandon faith. The nineteenth century was the age of the great battles between science and religion, mainly about the theory of evolution. The victory of science and the eventual decline of religion seemed inevitable to those on the side of science. What, if anything, would replace religion? Comte's answer had been science itself.

Durkheim wanted to grasp what lay at the core of religious beliefs and practice. What were the basic, elementary features of religion? He decided that the best way to address this question was to examine the religion of Australian Aboriginals, whose societies were believed to be the simplest still surviving, the closest to the beginning of the evolutionary chain. Durkheim assumed that their religion would be 'basic', from which the core features of all religions could be most easily identified. It is now accepted that Durkheim's reasoning was flawed. During Durkheim's career social anthropologists were discovering that 'primitive' societies were not as simple as Europeans had assumed. These societies typically had extremely complicated family and kinship systems which social anthropologists spent their entire careers trying to understand. There were rules and customs stipulating who could and who could not marry, the value and types of gifts that should be exchanged, and obligations towards different categories of kin. It is the modern family that is relatively simple. Likewise, social anthropologists were discovering that 'primitive' people subscribed to complex cosmologies explaining the origin of all things and how worldly affairs were governed. Durkheim himself did not confront these problems because he never visited Australia. He relied entirely on reports of traders and missionaries. Social anthropologists (cultural anthropologists in North America) had conducted studies in Africa, among Pacific Islanders and among indigenous Americans, but not in Australia. Durkheim was undeterred, but before dismissing his work we must bear in mind that investigators can draw wrong conclusions from valid evidence, and it is possible for conclusions to be correct even if the assumptions that guided the collection and interpretation of the evidence are suspect.

Durkheim's conclusions were as follows:

- He decided that totemism was the most basic form of religion and the core of all religions. A totem is a sacred object. This may be a totem pole, a cross, a remnant of a garment, a book, an animal or the remains of a saint. Any object can be totemic. It becomes totemic by virtue of its sacredness. Sacred objects are set apart from everyday profane life. Sacred objects are held in awe. They must be approached respectfully and handled with care, if at all.
- Durkheim proceeded to argue that the associated rituals were more important than the details of religious belief. Rituals draw together the members of a society, who gather and physically or metaphorically prostrate themselves before a sacred object.
- Durkheim then argued that the real object of worship was the society itself. The totem represents the society, and by participating in rituals the members of a society experience the reality of the society to which they have to submit. Periodic rituals reaffirm and reinforce the power of a society. Durkheim argued that such rituals were especially important in times of threat, whether from attack and invasion or drought. Rainmaking ceremonies could not actually make rain. The participants might fear, and even realise, that their worship would not move sacred forces. Nevertheless, the rituals could reinforce solidarity and hold a people together throughout difficult times. Similarly today, even non-believers attend church services to celebrate births, marriages and deaths. Wider populations do so in times of national emergencies and disasters. Why? They find that the rituals draw them together and make them feel better. The rituals amplify their joy or bolster their resilience, depending on the occasion.

If Durkheim's account of the significance of religion is correct, what happens in a secular age? Church attendances were declining in Europe throughout the nineteenth century. Durkheim had no firm answer to 'What happens next?' Comte had proposed that science would replace religion.

Durkheim toyed with this idea. One problem is that scientific knowledge and its experts are not held in awe, but are constantly being questioned. Monarchs, presidents or flags and national remembrance/celebration days might take the place of religion. Could sport act as a modern quasi-religion? Durkheim himself had greater hopes for 'professional' associations. He was a socialist of the syndicalist type who envisaged industries and enterprises being run by associations of employees. Members would be bound together 'mechanistically' and bound to other associations 'organically' (Durkheim, 1928, 1957). Durkheim also attached great importance to education (Durkheim, 1922, 1925). He was always a professor of education and sociology. This is because, at that time, a principal function of universities in France was to educate future teachers: France had introduced universal elementary education. Even if university graduates did not become teachers, it was considered desirable that qualified experts should be able to teach their subjects to others. Durkheim believed that schooling was important. Home education could not be an adequate substitute. It was in school that children first learnt to subordinate themselves to a group larger than their families. He also advocated placing national history at the core of the curriculum. Young people needed to know and respect their shared history. Durkheim was a patriotic Frenchman.

Durkheim's books on these topics of employment and education were first published posthumously, compiled and edited by colleagues from (possibly unfinished) manuscripts and drafts of lectures. Durkheim died in 1917 during the First World War, in which his son had been killed in 1915. He died knowing that his own mission was still incomplete, and that France had still not solved the problem of establishing then maintaining solidarity, which had been *the* central issue in all his books. Nevertheless, Durkheim offers a complete social theory which accounts for how societies have evolved over time, the characteristics of the latest modern societies, and how they are to be investigated. This body of theory proposes some answers, but it is equally important for the criticisms it has attracted and the questions it leaves unanswered.

Applications in sport and leisure

Some of the following sentences will be repeated in subsequent chapters. The sole changes will be the names of the theorists. Durkheim did not write about sport or any other leisure activity. He might have done so. He lived during the time when most of our present-day sports were being invented and when a fellow Frenchman, the Baron de Coubertin, was organising the first modern Olympic Games in Athens in 1896. Durkheim lived during the period when the modern holiday for industrial workers was being invented. However, very few social scientists paid any attention to any leisure activities until these became important in national economies, trade balances and as sources of employment, which was towards the end of the twentieth century. Until then, serious intellectuals did not concern themselves with 'frivolous' pastimes; doing so would have diminished their academic credibility. However, there were always exceptions which should be of interest to all social theorists. These have been 'the arts', such as painting and classical music, which in Durkheim's era (and before) enjoyed the patronage of the rich and powerful. However, Durkheim did not engage as a social theorist with either the increasingly popular modern uses of leisure of his day or the classical arts.

Even so, we can still ask whether Durkheim's theories can be applied to sport and leisure, and we immediately find that there are numerous ways in which Durkheim's theory fits trends in and features of sport and leisure which were under way in the nineteenth century and which are present today. All told, Durkheim's theory is more easily mapped onto sports and other leisure practices than any of the other theories in this book. This is the theory that sport and leisure scholars can embrace most easily, but for reasons given below, they should proceed with caution. The easily applied parts of Durkheim's theory are as follows:

1 Participation rates in most leisure activities are excellent examples of Durkheim's social facts: stable or changing slowly over extended time spans.
2 The creation of new sports, sport clubs and associations, hobby and arts clubs, and youth movements in the nineteenth century are examples of the ongoing division of labour.
3 Team sports are examples of the advantage of allowing players to specialise. The most effective way for a team to play is not for every player to try to do everything, but to distribute them into specialist positions. Also, team sports illustrate the pitfalls of a forced division of labour (players in the wrong positions), an anomic division of labour (taking the field without a game plan) and the egoistic division of labour (each player performing to earn personal glory rather than for the good of the team). We can see how the failure of a sport team, or any leisure club, may not be due to personal deficiencies in the membership, but to poor organisation.
4 Sports teams, drama clubs and other leisure associations illustrate how the inter-dependence that accompanies a division of labour fosters a sense of moral obligation – not to miss practice sessions, and to perform to one's very best abilities. The special satisfactions that arise from achieving more than any participant could achieve alone reinforce the moral order which requires all to use their special talents in the interests of a group.

5 All voluntary associations, which may be based on sports, arts, crafts, hobbies, or volunteering in the interest of a deserving or needy cause or group, create webs of inter-dependence, social bonds, whereby members of a society become morally obligated to one another.

6 Shared leisure can create powerful 'mechanistic' bonds. Fans' devotion to their sports teams has a religious character. The stadium and the shirt become totemic objects. The principal attraction of drinking parties, betting pools and ocean cruising usually has less to do with the activities themselves than the group solidarity, the communality that is experienced (see Bancroft, 2012; Guillen et al., 2012; Lusby et al., 2012). Sport teams need competitors to play against. This is acknowledged by the 'Old Firm' of Glasgow Rangers and Glasgow Celtic, the bitter rivals who each gain strength from the presence of the other. Such inter-dependences should counter-balance mechanical solidarity within clubs with organic inter-dependence, though the latter sometimes seems overwhelmed by fan rivalries.

7 Tourists who visit and respect other people's 'sacred' objects, which may be exhibits in galleries or museums, buildings or landscapes, and who return home with photographs and souvenirs which rekindle sentiments experienced at the time of visiting, can be seen as binding humanity into a single moral community (see MacCannell, 1976).

Durkheim's theory fits sport and other types of leisure in all the above ways, but with one qualification and then a major problem. The qualification is that shared leisure may bind populations, but does the formation of scores of tightly knit groups for different leisure activities fragment a society? One might argue that it is only complementary producer roles, not different consumer/leisure interests, which can create the mutual inter-dependences that generate organic solidarity. So is the net effect of leisure to bolster or to weaken social order? A great deal of sport and leisure has not been split off from but remains within families (whose members play sports and other games and watch television together). Most schools and colleges make some provisions for students' leisure, and some businesses cater for some of their employees' leisure interests in sport, fitness gyms and social clubs. All these are examples of how leisure can bind, and also how it simultaneously divides.

It is possible to read Durkheim as confirming commonly claimed benefits of sport and other leisure activities, and explaining how these benefits arise. One might say that Durkheim offers a social theory which confirms what members of sport and leisure groups already knew or wanted to believe. At a micro-level, Durkheim's theory explains the advantages of the division of labour within sports teams and other leisure groups, provided that members can use their special capabilities, appreciate each other's contributions to a common effort, and indeed, how all their contributions are indispensable, thus nurturing moral bonds and obligations. Similarly, Durkheim can be read as confirming the ability of representative sports teams and cultural groups to boost the prestige and solidarity of a school, business, neighbourhood, city or country.

The big problem arising from the easy fit between Durkheim's theory on the one hand and sport and much of the rest of leisure on the other is that in sociology, the home of modern social theories, Durkheim encounters far more criticism than endorsement. Durkheim is a theorist of consensus and integration. He treats order and solidarity as normal, arising mechanically from shared beliefs or organically from inter-dependence. Other theories treat order and stability, in so far as these are maintained, as the result of one group subjugating others. Sport and leisure, and the claims routinely made for them, then become an apparent veneer concealing the uglier underside of the societies of which they are a part. Durkheim will be attractive to the many sport and leisure scholars who are enthusiasts, willing to act as spokespersons for the activities they study, but can the immediate attractions of Durkheim survive the counter-claims of revival theories?

In the nineteenth and early twentieth centuries representatives of the various sports and hobbies, which at that time were all organised by voluntary associations, formed a recreation movement which lobbied governments for facilities, financial support and politico-moral endorsement. Numerous forms of leisure, based on different tastes and interests, and serving different client groups, gained strength by uniting, recognising what they shared in common. Leisure today is different. It is mostly commercial. Leisure businesses cater for a wider variety of tastes – in music and television programmes, for example. Sports compete for market shares. Each can prosper at the expense of, and ideally by eliminating, its closest rivals. These issues are not in Durkheim's books, but today the issues are raised only when we bring in Durkheim. He was a man and theorist of his own time, like all of us. Durkheim's division of labour, like that of Adam Smith (but not Herbert Spencer), was primarily in the economy. Lack of social solidarity for Durkheim meant higher rates of crime and suicide, risks of defeat in war, and the fragility not just of governments, but French constitutions. In the twenty-first century we find that the division of labour has continued, and one outcome has been a splintering of the tastes and lifestyles that are catered for outside our workplaces. If these trends dilute macro-solidarity, the outcomes may include rising crime and suicide rates, but will probably not include military defeat and the collapse of governments. Solidarity can be maintained in alternative ways. However, one outcome could be greater reluctance to fund universal social services – health care, education, roads, railways, pensions and energy security, plus sport and other leisure services – out of taxation.

part i: the classical theories

Another outcome may be a shortage of volunteers, not for high-profile, experience-of-a-lifetime events such as the Olympic Games, but for day-in, year-out, low-profile voluntary work. In 2010 incoming UK prime minister David Cameron promised to create a big society. This idea became a big flop. Are leisure trends implicated? Durkheim's books do not contain answers, but sport and leisure scholars need to bring in Durkheim in order to raise these questions.

Conclusions

Durkheim will always be regarded as a major social theorist because he introduced social science into French universities and established Europe's first sociology department at the University of Bordeaux in 1895, from where the discipline and the study of modern social theories spread throughout Europe. Durkheim's immediate influence was massive. He drew upon earlier ideas about the advantages of the division of labour, especially the ideas of Adam Smith and Herbert Spencer, then added that as well as being more productive and making societies more powerful, the division of labour replaced an older 'mechanical' solidarity with a new 'organic' solidarity. Chapter 3 will explain how Durkheim's theory of the division of labour was incorporated as the 'functionalist' part of Talcott Parsons's theory, which became the world's most influential social theory of the mid-twentieth century.

Parsons and Durkheim have subsequently fallen from fashion in preference for theories which explain order as an outcome of one group successfully subordinating others. Yet Durkheim remains the social theorist who justifies the claim that supporters of sport and other forms of leisure make routinely: that their favoured activities can be equally beneficial for all. Students of sport and the rest of leisure need to understand Durkheim's theory. They must feel able to defend the theory, or if rejected, become critics of the win–win benefits claimed for the kinds of leisure they study.

chapter 3

Talcott Parsons (1902–1979) and structural functionalism

Introduction

Talcott Parsons occupies an important place in the history of modern social theory, and not only because he was the world's most famous living sociologist between the 1930s and 1970s. He acted as a bridge between classical pre-1939 European social theory (exemplified by Durkheim) and post-1945 sociology. He also made a key contribution to the convergence between the rather different versions of sociology that had developed in Europe and North America.

Since the 1970s Talcott Parsons has become sociology's forgotten (and usually misunderstood) man. The structural functionalist theory, with which his name will forever be associated, is reborn every autumn for each new generation of students, only to be quickly and ritualistically slaughtered. Thereafter Durkheim may disappear, along with Parsons. The latter did not like being called a functionalist. He preferred to be known as an action theorist. The reasons for this, as well as the reasons why the functionalist label has stuck, will become apparent as we proceed. Parsons's view was that all sociology is necessarily functionalist in the mathematical sense: that is, examining how change in one part of a system – in our case a social system, a society – leads to changes in other parts. Unfortunately Parsons was not noted for his lucid prose, and very little of his considerable output continues to be read. However, his theory deserves to live on because it can be used, and can prove extremely useful, in sport and leisure studies. In fact, it is a contender as the most useful among all the theories in this book. Durkheim is the more easily applied, but arguably Parsons wins on outcomes. Parsons's is a theory within which all sporting and other leisure practices can be located. His theory does not stop at inviting us to identify the functions performed by sport and other uses of leisure. It is Parsons's theory alone that explains why leisure is necessarily ubiquitous, why it is found everywhere, and why it cannot be compartmentalised into a clearly separate block of leisure time or leisure places. There is leisure in families, in schools, in workplaces, in political parties as well as in sport clubs, drama societies and so on. Parsons's theory invites us to ask what difference it makes whether leisure is here or there. Parsons's theory also explains why some people's leisure involves work-like tasks and obligations. However, we must begin by understanding how Parsons became so prominent and influential in mid-twentieth-century sociology.

Career

Talcott Parsons is another theorist from a religious family who became a non-believer, like Herbert Spencer and Emile Durkheim before him. Parsons's father was a Congregational minister in Colorado Springs. Talcott Parsons studied sociology, psychology and biology at Amherst College, where he became aware that European sociologists had developed a type of theory that was absent from the subject in North America.

The history of the subject in the USA dates from 1875, when the first course bearing the name 'sociology' was taught at Yale University. As in Europe, American sociologists were interested in social structure and social change, but America did not have any Middle Ages, so the changes they studied were those that were in process in America in the late nineteenth and early twentieth centuries. This was a period during which America was absorbing immigrants into its expanding cities. The University of Chicago became the main centre for teaching and research in sociology, and the city of Chicago itself often acted as the source of material. American sociology was far more successful than sociology in Europe in attracting students and publicity. Even so, Parsons became interested in the European version of sociology, so as a postgraduate he visited the London School of Economics (LSE), the only place in Britain where sociology was taught at that time. From LSE he was directed to Germany, where he became particularly well acquainted with the work of Max Weber (see Chapter 5), and also learnt about the works of other European social theorists. However, it was Max Weber's work, mostly still unpublished even in German at the time of Weber's death in 1920, that Parsons himself began to translate and brought to the attention of American and other English-speaking scholars.

Parsons returned to America and was appointed to the economics department at Harvard University in 1927, then transferred to the sociology department when it opened in 1931. He became head of this department, remained there for the rest of his career, and trained numerous graduate students who went on to become prominent American sociologists. They included Robert K. Merton, probably the most eminent American sociologist among the immediate post-Parsons cohort. It was these disciples who made Parsons the best-known and most influential living sociologist of the mid-twentieth century.

Talcott Parsons's first book, *The Structure of Social Action*, published in 1937, was a review, and an attempted synthesis of European sociological theories. Parsons built on this initial synthesis in books and papers published between the 1940s and 1970s (for example, Parsons, 1951, 1966; Parsons and Smelsner, 1956). Parsons's work was wide-ranging. His sociology had porous boundaries. He collaborated with scholars from economics and cybernetics, and with Freudian psychologists. He was not just a functionalist, though he became known as *the* principal functionalist sociologist. Parsons saw himself primarily as an advocate of 'action theory', which he drew mainly from Max Weber, but combined the social and historical dimensions of action with psychoanalysis. However, at that time, in the 1950s and 1960s, it was the symbolic interactionists (see Chapter 8) who were being treated as *the* action theorists in sociology. Talcott Parsons was given the functionalist slot. Yet Parsons was not just a functionalist. He believed that he had solved the problem of combining structure and agency in sociological analysis. 'Structure' is composed of social facts, in Durkheim's terms, which impose themselves on individuals, or to use terminology developed subsequently, behaviour is explained in terms of the structure of actors' situations. 'Agency' treats actors as behaving purposefully, exercising choice. Parsons claimed to have reconciled these two kinds of explanation with his concept of 'voluntaristic' action.

Parsons's theory

The social system

Parsons's social theory incorporates Durkheim's (and Spencer's) view that the main historical trend has been a progressive division of labour, and that the explanation is that this makes societies more productive, more powerful and better balanced. To this Parsons added that the division of labour has been along functional lines, creating sub-systems each of which concentrates on one of the functions in Figure 3.1. Because he considered the division of labour to be progressive, Parsons believed that Western

Adaptation	Goal attainment
Integration	Latency and pattern maintenance

Figure 3.1 Parsons's social system

capitalism, which separated the economy from politics, would prove superior to and outlast Soviet communism.

Parsons's theory is an analytical scheme that identifies essential functions that must be addressed and resolved if any society is to endure. First, any social system must adapt to its environment, meaning that it must have an economy to procure the resources it needs and that delivers outputs in return. Second, a social system must have procedures for setting goals, and rules stipulating how these goals are to be pursued. In other words, the social system needs a political sub-system. Third, a social system must have integration procedures to enforce its rules, meaning, in practice, a justice system – police, courts, penal institutions. Finally, there are latency and pattern maintenance, both said (by Parsons) to be performed primarily by the family. Latency is the release of emotions, drives and frustrations that are created or suppressed by other sub-systems. Pattern maintenance is the socialisation of personalities as required to play roles in other sub-systems.

The idea is not just to decide in which 'box' to place sport, tourism, gambling or anything else. This misunderstands Parsons. Functional analysis may involve asking, 'What is the function of crime, inequality, sport, religion and so on?' This is how Durkheim 'solved' the problem of religion, but these are not Parsonian questions. Parsons's model of society is composed of systems and sub-systems (groups and organisations). Sport, crime and all other social processes and kinds of events may occur within any sub-system. Sports may be managed by businesses that are part of a society's adaptation sub-system (the economy), or sports teams may be run by schools, churches or dedicated member-based non-profit clubs. The division of labour proceeds at successive levels. As noted above, the Parsonian view is that separating an economy from a political sub-system is more effective than merging them, and the West's eventual victory in the Cold War may now be cited in support. Thereafter an economy is likely to split into many different firms operating in many business sectors. Each firm will be a social sub-system which must adapt (obtain resources from its environment and deliver outputs in return). It will need a government (probably a board of directors), methods for rewarding and disciplining workers, then some way of addressing latency functions for which it may rely entirely on break times, or on families providing sufficient outlets, or on workers using organisations that cater specifically for people's leisure, or it may create its own social club or give staff access to a similar outside facility. Our firm, if it is a large enterprise, will divide itself into many departments, each of which may split into several workgroups, and each of these sub-systems will need an economy, political leadership, methods of enforcing its formal or informal rules, while for latency the staff may go out occasionally (or frequently) to the theatre, to play a sport or for drinks after work. A sport club will need an economy and so on, and after its serious business of playing matches, the players may enjoy time-out in a bar. Some members of the sport club will be 'working' for the club in 'political' and administrative roles. In a family there is likely to be a division of labour, with someone as the main 'breadwinner' while another member enforces discipline and arranges family chill-outs. Leisure and sport can be anywhere and everywhere. They can be part of an economic sub-system, a political sub-system and a justice sub-system. Actors in any of these groups may form themselves into a sports team, go for a drink together, and may even go on holiday together. Meanwhile, in the latency and pattern maintenance sub-systems life will not be all fun and games for everyone.

The cultural system

Parsons's theory also recognises a cultural system which contains beliefs, knowledge and values. This is everywhere. It pervades all social sub-systems, though specific institutions (religious, educational and cultural) may be responsible for maintaining the culture. The cultural system ensures consensus: that everyone speaks the same language, agrees on outcomes that are desirable, and the methods for achieving these outcomes that are right and proper. Parsons identified a series of 'pattern variables' of the either/or type. There are four sets of alternatives:

- particularism versus universalism – treating an object (a person or event) as a unique case or as an example of a general class;
- affectivity versus neutrality – emotional involvement as opposed to detachment;
- quality versus performance – valuing something (a person, an action) for its own qualities or for its usefulness;
- diffuseness versus specificity – relating to all or just one aspect of an object, event or person.

These pattern variables enable the characteristics of any culture to be described, and they describe the dispositions that govern the goals and means that can be adopted in all the sub-systems that share a common culture, thereby enabling sub-systems to operate harmoniously.

As societies evolved and the division of labour became more complex, Parsons believed that cultures would shift from the first to the second

part i: the classical theories

named of the pairs listed above. He is associated far more closely with his theory of the social system because his pattern variables have rarely been used. Investigators who compare different cultures and sub-cultures have usually preferred to treat each society's or each ethnic group's particular beliefs, knowledge and ideals as unique cases. In terms of Parsons's pattern variables, their approach has been particularistic rather than universalistic. Alternatively, they have used simpler dichotomies: Max Weber's distinction between the traditional and rational (see Chapter 5) or Jürgen Habermas's distinction between instrumental and communicative thought, speech and action (see Chapter 7).

The personality system

Parsons's theory also includes a personality system. A society's culture, including the prescribed choices from the pattern variables, must become part of members' personalities, which is said (by Parsons) to be achieved primarily by socialisation within families. Thereafter socialised actors will 'voluntaristically' observe the rules and will sometimes break the letter while keeping within the spirit of the rules in whatever roles they play in any of a society's sub-systems. Cohesion is achieved not, as in Durkheim's theory, by social facts 'imposing' themselves on individuals or by everyone being aware of how others depend on them and how they in turn depend on others (organic solidarity), but through the operation of a common culture and the appropriate socialisation of a society's members. Parsons was able to draw upon psychology, which had made great strides since Durkheim's lifetime. Parsons's special liking was for Sigmund Freud's psychoanalysis.

This view of the members of a society learning the required orientations to action through socialisation, initially in most cases in their families, was never distinctively Parsonian. Parsons simply reconciled what was already psychological and sociological orthodoxy with the rest of his theory. This is why his reputation became and remains associated with his structural functionalist theory or model of the social system.

Criticisms and responses

During his lifetime Parsons became famous as much for the volume of criticism his work attracted as for the size of his following:

- His theory was criticised for being too abstract, bearing no resemblance to any society as ordinarily experienced and perceived. To this Parsons could reply that he had constructed an analytical theory, and that his concepts could be filled with evidence.

- Another criticism was that the theory (like Durkheim's) implied that value consensus and integration were normal, to which Parsons could reply that his theory was a heuristic device which enabled consensus and dissensus, functions, dysfunctions and functionally neutral practices to be distinguished. He could also point out that, as a matter of fact, any ongoing society has to be solving adaptation, goal attainment, integration, and pattern maintenance and latency issues, and that exactly how, and with what success, these issues are addressed are proper topics for sociological enquiry.
- Parsons rejected the criticism that his work was ideologically conservative. His own politics were not right-wing (he normally voted Democrat). His theory can be as easily used to criticise as to justify any existing social arrangements.
- A final criticism has been that functional analysis confuses effects with causes. To this, the reply always was and still is that functions (effects) may be part of feedback loops that institutionalise the behaviour.

Critics have always named causal inadequacy as functionalism's Achilles heel. In fact, functionalism proposes adequate causes, but these differ between Durkheimian and Parsonian functionalism. For Durkheim causal agency resides in a *conscience collective* or, as this weakens, in actors' sense of moral inter-dependence and obligation. In Parsons's structural functionalism, causal agency is from within the socialised individual who has internalised a society's culture. Durkheim was a European theorist, aware of a time when entire societies were united by a common faith, and Durkheim was seeking an alternative basis for solidarity in post-Reformation and increasingly secular societies. Parsons was an American theorist. The individual voluntaristic actor is at the centre of Parsons's theory. Functional integration is maintained by rules, set by a political system and enforced by a justice system. Its different versions of functionalism are examples of a transatlantic divide (Martinelli, 2007). Socialism – common ownership, and common economic and social rights as expressions of moral inter-dependence and obligation – has always enjoyed far more resonance in Europe than in America.

The defence of Parsons may be sound in principle, but the use of Parsons's theory in sociological research was never common except in America, and only for a brief period in the 1940s and 1950s. Its better-known uses include the explanation of stratification and inequality as necessary in order to motivate able individuals to fill a society's most important roles (Davis and Moore, 1945), and why deviance becomes inevitable when a society (such as the USA) invites everyone to strive for success but does not, because it cannot, provide the means to enable all to succeed (Merton, 1938). Parsons used his theory to analyse family life, and noted

part i: the classical theories

(predictably) the advantages of a division of labour in which husbands and wives specialised in different roles (Parsons and Bales, 1955). However, the most common and influential use of Parsons has probably been as a framework for (mainly American) sociology textbooks whose successive chapters discuss the role of the economy, politics, the family, American values and so on. Although Parsons started out as a synthesiser of European social theories, the use to which his work was put in North America tended to strip sociology of historical and comparative content.

Functionalism is unlikely to disappear from sociology, if only because it is part of everyday common sense. Practices are explained and justified or criticised on the basis of the outcomes. Sport is said to make players healthy and law-abiding, so investigators are likely to enquire which if any sports have these results, and the amounts of play that the outcomes require. We encounter functionalist explanations all the time, yet Parson's name is rarely mentioned, let alone used, by present-day sport and leisure researchers. The occasional exceptions (Gross, 1961; Pronovost, 1998) have been setting agendas rather than conducting new research or analysing findings. Researchers have preferred to base their work on sport and leisure-specific theories, or to use one or another of the theories introduced later in this book. Yet Parsons raises questions and provides a framework for the answers that are not posed or offered elsewhere.

Parsons can be treated as (almost) the last of the classical theorists or the first of the successors. He is placed among the classical theorists in this book because the functionalist parts of his theory for which he became best known built on the ideas of Emile Durkheim (Chapter 2). Here, Parsons follows the Durkheim chapter even though this may be unfair to Parsons, who would have preferred to be remembered for the Weberian 'action' elements in this theory. Parsons would have preferred to be positioned following Max Weber (Chapter 5).

Applications in sport and leisure

Some Parsonian questions are probably not worth pursuing, namely those that arise from his work on cultural and personality systems. Parsons invites us to ask what values, knowledge and dispositions are built into sport and other leisure activities and are likely to be acquired when these activities are used for child and youth socialisation. However, Parsons is not unique in raising these questions. He is distinctive in inviting investigators to use his pattern variables, but this is an invitation that is likely to be declined: the variables are difficult to operationalise and have rarely been used anywhere. Parsons is also different in anticipating that within a given society the same basic cultures will pervade all sport and leisure activities (the presumption of consensus). No other social theory considers this to be likely.

It is Parsons's theory of social systems that raises distinctive, challenging and interesting questions for sport and leisure scholars. Some of these questions have been investigated, but the relevant enquiries have not been inspired by Parsons's theory and most of the studies have not been by sport or leisure scholars, which means that the findings have lacked an overall theoretical framework which would assemble the leisure evidence systematically, which is what Parsons offers. Parsons's questions are not about 'what' so much as 'where' and 'with whom' sport and other leisure activities are undertaken. We shall see in later chapters that other major theorists imply in their work that 'with whom' and 'where' are likely to be of greater social significance than exactly 'what' and 'how much of it' people do in their leisure. The questions posed by Parsons's systems theory are:

- Does it make a difference to the leisure experience whether the activity is within a leisure-specific group such as a stand-alone sport club or fitness gym, or elsewhere such as in a college or work-based team?
- Does it make any difference to groups formed within the adaptation, goal attainment and integration sub-systems whether or not they make internal provisions for members' leisure?
- Is undertaking unpaid leisure work (administrative roles in sport and other leisure clubs) more or less satisfying than simply being a player or participant?
- Does it make any difference to the leisure experience of players or participants whether the 'work' (administering, organising) is done by paid employees or by volunteers?
- Is paid work in sport and leisure administration different from other kinds of paid employment?
- What difference does it make to the player's, actor's or singer's experience whether they play as an amateur as a leisure activity or as a professional entertainer?

Sport and leisure scholars may be unaware that we can answer most of these questions. In nearly all cases the evidence is not from sport and leisure research, but from investigations where the prime interest has been in work and employment. Answers to 'Does it make a difference?' have invariably been 'Yes.' As yet, the evidence has never been collated to address sport and leisure questions. Parsons's theory of social systems is an ideal collator.

What, if any, are the distinctive features of paid work in the production and marketing of leisure goods and services? We know that the work tends to be the opposite of fun: it can be unusually demanding. Hairdressing is not really a glamour occupation (see Lindsay, 2004). Front-line employees' appearances and demeanour become part of the leisure service. Hotel and restaurant staff are expected to perform aesthetic labour, probably concealing their real feelings about the jobs they are performing (Warhurst and Nickson, 2007). Employees who produce leisure goods including sports clothing may be expected to use and thereby advertise the products in their own leisure time (see Land and Taylor, 2010). Competition for creative jobs in the so-called creative industries (which include film, television, theatre and new media) is intense. Applicants are normally expected to audition in an appropriate manner. Hours of work are long and the pressure is huge when people are in employment. Spells of unemployment are the norm, throughout which individuals must maintain their labour power and contacts (McKinlay and Smith, 2009).

As leisure grows in scale as an economic sector, more and more people are employed in the provision of leisure goods and services. New paid occupations and entire new industries are formed from what were originally purely playful spare-time activities. Computer games provide current examples. Yu-Hao Lee and Holin Lin (2011) interviewed sixteen Asian real-money trade participants in mass multiplayer online games. The eight professionals among those interviewed were selling products (usually avatars) which others could use in games that typically involved battles between armies of humans, or between humans and monsters, or participation in virtual, second life domains. The professionals were experiencing some problems typical of all self-employed workers, like being reluctant to limit their hours of work because they could be losing business whenever they were offline. They also had problems convincing their families and friends that they had real occupations. Sport and leisure scholars can face the same problem! The professionals studied by Yu-Hao Lee and Holin Lin did not go to workplaces. They did not work for recognised businesses. They found it difficult to demonstrate that they were doing proper work and had legitimate sources of income, and therefore had earned a right to their own leisure. All the professionals studied by Yu-Hao Lee and Holin Lin drew a clear boundary between when they worked and when they played the relevant games purely for pleasure, but these boundaries were not visible to their families and friends.

We have seen, because it is demonstrated clearly in Parsons's theory of social systems and sub-systems, that non-commercial amateur leisure organisations (musical groups and sports clubs, for example) need to perform adaptation, goal attainment and integration functions. This is likely to involve a great deal of voluntary labour. How does this differ from other uses of leisure? Rapuano (2009) argues that the public presence of volunteers can obscure the appropriation of profit (by venue providers and equipment manufacturers, for example). However, Stebbins (1992) contends that there are special satisfactions in this type (and other types) of serious leisure.

Pay can certainly change the experience of what, for others, is a leisure activity. Does pay enhance or degrade the experience? Pay carries obligations. Professional sport players need to train and play according to a coach's instructions. The activity may still be intrinsically enjoyable, but it ceases to be purely playful (Roadburg, 1978). We have seen that professional online game players typically prefer to keep their own leisure play more leisurely and separate from the time when they are playing to earn money (Yu-Hao Lee and Holin Lin, 2011).

From the 1960s into the 1980s the work–leisure relationship was a major research topic in the sociology of leisure. The core issue was whether the character of people's jobs and their experiences in employment led to spill-over or compensation in leisure, or neither. Stanley Parker (1971) made a major contribution and became a 'founding father' of the sociology of leisure by discovering extension, opposition and neutrality relationships. He found that extension (work extending into leisure) was most likely when people enjoyed and identified with their occupations and with work colleagues. Opposition (using leisure to do entirely different things) was said to be a reaction to disagreeable work. Neutrality was when work and leisure were treated as simply different, and was said to be typical when people were neutral about their jobs. Parker's research findings were presented and have always been understood as showing how paid work does (or does not) influence uses of leisure, but causality is likely to flow in both directions. Spending leisure time reading work-related literature and in the company of work colleagues must feed back into performance and morale in the workplace. Before the Second World War it became common for large firms to run their own sport and social clubs. Most were closed when television and the motor car changed people's lifestyles. The same has happened to working men's (*sic*) clubs. Spill-over from work into leisure is now most likely to be self-organised by groups of colleagues who use commercial facilities (bars and restaurants, for example). The evidence suggests that if spill-over has become less likely than in the past, this will not be inconsequential for people's experiences either at work or when they are at leisure.

Parsons's theory is the only framework available that will enable sport and leisure scholars to organise all this otherwise disparate evidence into their own coherent body of theory.

What happened to functionalism?

In the mid-twentieth century Talcott Parsons was a mighty social theorist who could not be ignored. In sociology you either had to be a supporter or join the band of opponents. By the 1980s functionalism was struggling for visibility. What had happened? Conflict theories (see Chapters 4 and 5) had become far more influential. Functionalism was overshadowed, but it did not disappear. During its heyday the theory was beginning to splinter. There was a watered-down, neutered neo-functionalism, and this type of analysis remains common, though rarely under the 'functionalist' label, and thereby may escape the critical scrutiny it deserves. There were also spin-offs from functionalism which became specialist genres within sociology – exchange theory and systems theory – but these lack the analytical breadth in the case of exchange theory, and the explanatory power that agency injected into the original, Parsonian structural functionalism.

Neo-functionalism

The main advocates of neo-functionalism have been the American sociologist Jeffrey Alexander (1947–) and the Greek but London-based Nicos Mouzelis (1939–). Both take the view that functionalism has features, not found elsewhere, that are worth preserving. Basically, their versions of neo-functionalism are stripped of explanatory power. What remains is the investigation of the systemic implications of specific practices which may prove to be functional, dysfunctional or functionally neutral, and the identification of how functions that are essential in an ongoing social system are performed (Alexander, 1985; Mouzelis, 1995).

Sport and leisure scholars will recognise neo-functionalism. It is the standard template for much research in these fields. It identifies and measures benefits (personal physical and mental well-being, plus social and cultural benefits) that accrue from particular practices. Recognising the neo-functional character of these accounts is useful. Neo-functionalism insists that all outcomes should be identified, such as sport injuries as well as gains in fitness and health, and that other outcomes which may be dysfunctional or functionally neutral should also be explored. Furthermore, neo-functionalism insists that alternative ways of achieving functional outcomes be considered. Perhaps most important, analysts are forced to acknowledge that its neo descendant is a neutered version of functionalism and is devoid of explanatory power.

Exchange theory

This was developed during the heyday of functionalism. Its main advocates were George Homans (1910–1989) and Peter Blau (1918–2002), both eminent American sociologists. Exchange theory appeals in offering more scope for agency than Parsons's voluntaristic action. It does this by building bottom-up, in contrast to Parsons's grand theory in which the parts of a society are governed by their locations within the whole. Exchange theory starts with the smallest social unit, the dyad, just two people who give and receive from one another under what is postulated as a universal norm of reciprocity (Blau, 1964; Homans, 1961). Such elementary exchanges are said to be the building blocks from which larger groups, organisations and societies are constructed. Exchanges happen because they are functional for all parties. This applies whether the exchanges are between individuals or larger groups. Each party participates because it is in that party's interest to do so. The actors seek to maximise gratifications or, in economists' language, to maximise utility. Power is said to accrue to whoever gains least in the short term. The other party becomes indebted, and the creditor can choose how and when to call in favours. This is said to be how power is generated. It is generated from below rather than imposed from above. Larger systems of stratification are said to be built from unequal exchange relationships.

If a weakness of Parsonian functionalism is causal inadequacy (which can be disputed; see above), exchange theory has the opposite problem. Critics allege that actors are credited with excessive agency. In practice most people play no part in building the macro-systems within which they live. The society precedes each actor. We do not rebuild the societies into which we are born. The reality is more like individuals being confronted by Durkheimian social facts. Exchange theorists need to contend that people acquiesce or renegotiate and change the relationships in which they are involved according to whatever they find most gratifying, but in practice most people have little choice. They must submit to the law and otherwise behave as necessary to function competently as members of their societies. The strength of exchange theory lies in exploring the micro, and its limitations are exposed when faced with the macro.

This balance of strengths and limitations swings strongly in exchange theory's favour when dealing with the minutiae of sport and other leisure activities. Why do individuals socialise on nights out? Why do friendships, usually short-lived, form so quickly and easily within holiday tour groups? Players in sports teams need to co-operate with one another, and they also need opponents to play against. Exchange theory suggests that we can explain all these types of behaviour in terms of the gratifications that accrue to each of the parties. Expectations of future gratifications can explain why relationships are maintained through exchanges of Christmas and birthday cards, telephone calls, and nowadays by email and on interactive websites. Established relationships enable all parties to inform, offer and request. Through their various leisure activities individuals can build extensive social networks. The norm of reciprocity enables those who can give most in the short term to accumulate social capital. The limitation of exchange theory lies in explaining the larger systems from which people acquire the assets with which to engage in exchange. However, this does not diminish the value of exchange theory in exploring how individuals, small groups and wider social networks behave within their given macro-contexts.

Systems theory

If exchange theory takes functionalism down to the most micro-levels possible, systems theory, in the form proposed by Niklas Luhmann (1927–1998), a German sociologist, lifts functionalism to an even higher level of abstraction than Parsons achieved. Luhmann criticises Parsons's theory of social systems for placing too much emphasis on the *social* instead of focusing on features that arise from societies being examples of *systems* (Luhmann, 1997). Social systems are not tied together mechanistically, but according to Luhmann, by flows of information. Since information flows globally, the social system is worldwide but contains sub-systems such as states and organisations. All systems are said to be capable of auto-poiesis, meaning that they are capable of self-correction and reproduction. Autopoiesis differs from homeostasis, in which an organism returns to its former state. Under autopoiesis a new self-correcting and reproducing system can be different from the original. Social systems are said to draw and filter information selectively from their environments (other social systems and the natural environment). They are said to do this in order to meet their systemic needs. Talcott Parsons himself was interested in cybernetics and computer modelling, but did not develop these aspects of his work.

Systems theory remains alive within present-day sociology, but has migrated away from functionalism and has had social substance inserted. Systems thinking is used in theories about a 'network society' that is said to be evolving in the current 'information age'. This is discussed in Chapter 11. Systems thinking has also been incorporated into world systems theory, the site of modernisation theory which is the subject of Chapter 12.

Conclusions

Talcott Parsons played a major role in the twentieth-century development of social theory. He, more than anyone else, engineered the convergence of European and American sociology. This would surely have happened in any case, but in the event, Talcott Parsons was the main driver.

Parsons deserves a prominent place in the roll of social theorists. His version of functionalism needs to be offered to every new cohort of students, and not only in order to be slaughtered. This is the only post-Durkheim modern social theory that treats social order, integration and consensus as normal, or at least achievable. Parsons's and Durkheim's are the only theories that allow any practice – any sport or other use of leisure – to be prescribed as 'good for society'. Anyone who wishes to speak in this way needs to be able to defend Durkheim's or Parsons's version of functionalism. Parsons's theory also focuses attention on the likely significance of exactly where and with whom leisure time is spent and sport and other leisure activities are practised.

Sport and leisure studies today would look very different if, from the 1950s onwards, they had built on Parsonian foundations. This did not happen. As in the 1950s, today's sport and leisure scholars are most likely to find the theory far too abstract, and they now have a wide choice of alternative theories. Yet Parsons remains a ghostly presence because of the still widespread belief that certain leisure practices can be 'good for society', good for everyone. Resurrecting Parsons forces the underlying assumptions to the surface for critical scrutiny.

chapter 4

Karl Marx (1818–1883) and Marxism

Introduction

In a future socialist society an individual would be able to 'hunt in the morning, fish in the afternoon, rear cattle in the evening, criticise after dinner . . . without ever becoming a hunter, fisherman, shepherd'. This snippet is from a collection of manuscripts the young Karl Marx and Friedrich Engels wrote in 1845 and 1846. The collection was first published (in the original German) in 1932 in a book (inappropriately) titled *The German Ideology* (Marx and Engels, 1845–1846). This was all that Marx and Engels ever wrote about leisure, and also about the kind of society that would follow the revolution. It was hardly a useful roadmap for their followers, and it falls far short of a theory about leisure.

However, subsequent Marxists have had a lot to say about sport and leisure. Their basic claim is that all leisure is corrupted by capitalism. Sport and leisure scholars need to engage with the claim that the subjects they teach and research, the activities many of them promote and the careers for which their students are prepared are all fundamentally flawed. This apart, Marxism demands attention from all serious scholars because it became the world's most successful change ideology during the first half of the twentieth century. Marxist regimes gained control of governments in Europe, Asia, Latin America and Africa. Subsequent history may appear to have turned against Marxism, but this appearance will not necessarily last. Marx argued that capitalism was necessarily an expanding system, and in recent decades capitalism has spread into spectator and participant sport, broadcasting and much else. We now have evidence from twentieth-century socialist societies with which sport and leisure under capitalism can be compared. We also have evidence from public and voluntary sector leisure services within capitalist countries, though Marxists would claim that their quality is inevitably compromised by the capitalist context. Another of Marx's predictions that currently looks correct is that capitalist societies would polarise and wealth is being increasingly concentrated in the hands of a tiny fabulously rich elite (Piketty, 2014). The missing part of the Marxist forecast, up to now, is the revolutionary working class. However, we cannot dismiss Marx's claim that capitalism contains inherent contradictions which will eventually bring about its destruction.

The original Marxist theory was the joint work of Karl Marx (1818–1883) and Friedrich Engels (1820–1895). So we begin below with the men whose ideas were to become an 'ism', and not just an academic theory, but also the inspiration of political movements that mobilised millions. We proceed with the original Marxism of Marx and Engels themselves, then how these foundations were built upon by subsequent Marxists, and how the theory has been applied in the study of sport and leisure.

The careers of the founders

Karl Marx was born and raised in Trier, a city in the German Rhineland, close to the present-day Germany–Luxembourg border, but part of Prussia (whose capital was Berlin) at the time. Karl was from a wealthy Lutheran family: his father was a lawyer. There was a Jewish presence in his mother's family tree which became the basis on which Marx was treated as a Jew and communism as a Jewish theory by the Nazis who ruled Germany from 1933 to 1945, but Karl Marx's childhood home was solidly protestant and middle-class. Following *Gymnasium*, in 1835 Karl Marx began to study law and philosophy at universities in Bonn, then Berlin and finally in Jena, where he received his doctorate in 1841. Karl was Dr Marx.

Two important events happened to Karl Marx while he was a student. First, in 1836 he became engaged to Jenny Westphalen, a childhood friend who was four years older than Karl. This was a minor local scandal. The Westphalens were an aristocratic Prussian family (albeit from the lower ranks), so Jenny was marrying 'down'. It was a love match. The couple married in 1843 and had seven children, though only three survived to adulthood. Jenny pre-deceased Karl in 1881. There was nothing proletarian about Karl Marx's social background, or indeed his life as an adult.

Second, while a student, Karl Marx became a revolutionary. He became a revolutionary before he became a Marxist. Becoming a revolutionary while a student was not normal, but neither was it uncommon in Europe at that time. If Emile Durkheim had cause to worry about the instability of

France, Prussia presented the opposite problem. It was still rigidly feudal, ruled by the Kaiser and the aristocracy. There was no elected assembly. The situation was similar throughout Europe in the 1830s. France had restored the Bourbon monarchy. There was an elected assembly, but with only around 100,000 electors out of an adult population of millions. The Austro-Hungarian Empire, ruled by its emperor, extended southwards to the Mediterranean (it then incorporated present-day Slovenia and Croatia), eastward into what is now Western Ukraine, and also included a swath of Poland. This empire's southern and eastern borders were with the (then crumbling) Ottoman Empire. Prussia's eastern neighbour was Russia, ruled by its czar. At that time Poland had been partitioned between Prussia, Russia and Austria. Europe's universities were a source of revolutionaries who wanted to overthrow all these regimes and give power to the people. At that time Britain was seen as relatively advanced, and was a haven for threatened revolutionaries and monarchs alike. Throughout the nineteenth century Britain was progressively extending the franchise. Europe's revolutionaries wanted their countries to catch up.

Marx was scathing towards Prussian intellectuals such as Georg Hegel (1770–1831) who supported and offered justifications for the Prussian regime. When Marx was a student, indeed throughout his lifetime, Hegel was regarded as an intellectual colossus across the whole of Europe. Hegel was a philosopher (a subject which then had a wider remit than philosophy today). Hegel believed that history was driven by the development of human thought (as did Auguste Comte). However, Hegel believed that thought had progressed in a dialectical manner (not through just three stages). According to Hegel, prevailing ideas encountered opposition (thesis bred antithesis). The outcome would be a synthesis which became the new thesis, and this process was repeated, and would continue to be repeated until humanity arrived at absolute truth. Hegel managed to convince himself that this point was fast approaching, and corresponding political arrangements were in place, in the Prussia of his time. These views endeared Hegel to the political authorities in Berlin, where Hegel taught. Marx was among the young students who disagreed profoundly with his contemporaries, the young Hegelians. The young Marx believed that the human condition at that time was characterised by alienation: that people were unable to express their true selves and fulfil their potential. Marx believed that thought and history needed to turn through at least another full cycle. This was the sense in which he became a young revolutionary.

Some of Marx's literary output in the 1840s was serious philosophy. Some was outright political propaganda. After leaving university he became a full-time revolutionary, writing pamphlets and for newspapers and periodicals. While a student, he had already come to the attention of the Prussian police, and this made it necessary for Marx to move, first to Paris, then to Brussels, and in both cities he had the same problem as in Prussia. By the mid-1840s Marx was part of a pan-European network of young revolutionaries. England eventually became his permanent safe haven.

It was through the European network that in 1844 Marx first became acquainted with Friedrich Engels, another young German revolutionary. Engels's father was a wealthy cotton manufacturer. Friedrich was sent to Manchester in 1842, nominally to work for the family business, but really to keep him out of the hands of the Prussian police. In Manchester Engels formed a relationship with Mary Burns (1823–1863), who was from a local working-class family. The couple never married. Both believed that marriage was an institution that oppressed women. This relationship lasted until Mary died in 1863. It was Engels, not Marx, who in this respect lived the life of a revolutionary. Soon after Engels's arrival in Manchester, Mary Burns introduced him to various working-class districts within the cities of Manchester and Salford. Engels was appalled by the squalor that he encountered, and wrote a book about the condition of the working class in England (Engels, 1845). It was probably Engels who convinced Marx that the industrial working class would deliver the revolution that both were seeking.

From this point onwards Marx and Engels became lifetime collaborators, and jointly developed Marxism. In 1848, following several years of economic recession, there were attempted revolutions throughout continental Europe. The network of which they were part invited Marx and Engels to write a manifesto. This has ever since been known as *the* communist manifesto (Marx and Engels, 1848). It must be the world's most read item of socialist literature, and has remained in print in most languages up to the present day. Marx and Engels co-authored this manifesto when they were aged 30 and 28 respectively.

Talcott Parsons, an American social theorist (see Chapter 2), had what we today might consider a normal academic biography: successful track record as a student followed by a university-based academic career. This has applied to all the other American theorists in this book. All the European theorists in this book differ: their lives reflected the continent's relatively turbulent nineteenth- and twentieth-century histories.

From 1849 Marx settled permanently in London with Jenny and their children: a model bourgeois family. They are reported to have lived in (genteel) poverty, supported by Marx's occasional earnings from journalism, gifts from Jenny's family, but mainly by Engels, who became Marx's principal patron. Engels had never completed a university course and always seems to have deferred to Marx's intellect.

During the remainder of his life Marx produced commentaries on political events in Europe, most notably the outcome of the revolution in Paris in 1848 (Louis Napoleon, nephew of Napoleon Bonaparte, was elected president of a second republic in 1848, and had himself declared emperor in 1852), and the fate of the Paris commune which was formed after France's defeat in the 1870–1871 Franco-Prussian war. However, Marx's main long-term project was *Capital*. Marx's main workplace and research archive was the British Museum. *Capital* was originally published in German in three volumes, the first of which appeared in 1867 (Marx, 1867). The last two volumes were incomplete when Marx died in 1883. Engels completed them, and had them published with Marx as the sole named author. Engels's own contributions to Marxism were substantial. He is believed to have been the first to use the Marxist terms 'historical materialism' and 'dialectical materialism', broadened Marxism into a social and historical theory, and wrote the first Marxist account of the family and gender relations (Engels, 1902).

Marx himself left behind a perplexing manuscript that appears to have been set aside incomplete in 1858, then was first published in 1939 with the title *Grundrisse*, though the full translated title is *Outline of the Critique of Political Economy*. The 'book' was first published in the original German in Moscow. The first English-language edition did not appear until 1973 (Marx, 1858/1993). Marxist scholars continue to debate the importance of this 'book'. Was it a rough first draft, subsequently abandoned, of the book that became *Capital*? Does *Grundrisse* clarify Marx's message? These questions matter because *Grundrisse* is the main source of Marx's own thinking on pre-capitalist forms of social organisation and the preconditions for a suc- cessful socialist revolution. In this chapter *Grundrisse* is used to construct a coherent outline of the original Marxism. *Capital* became a different kind of book, focused on the functioning of the capitalist mode of production.

At the time of his death it would have been implausible to suggest that Marx would go down in history as the source of a major academic social theory and as a founder of sociology. Marx never described himself as a sociologist, nor was he described as a sociologist by any contemporary. His main scholarly work was *Capital*, and in the nineteenth century this was regarded as a work of political economy. If Marx was to become a founder of any academic discipline, the obvious one was economics, but modern mainstream economics has other founders and Marxist economics has never been more than a critical tendency. It is the same in politics (the academic discipline). Talcott Parsons did not regard Marx as a sociologist. Marx does not feature in *The Structure of Social Action* (Parsons, 1937).

Karl Marx died before Durkheim's academic career began, but Marx entered sociology later. Until the 1940s Marxism was treated in sociology (if at all) as a political theory and movement – that is, as part of socio- logy's subject matter. It was not recognised as part of sociology itself. This changed during the 1950s, and by the 1970s Marxism was among sociology's most influential theories.

The Marxism of Marx and Engels

Marx's major book, *Capital*, is a detailed analysis of how capitalism works. A key concept is surplus value. Wages are said never to rise much above the cost of reproducing labour power. Therefore living standards are capped at a subsistence level. The difference between this and the market price of the output is surplus value, which is appropriated by the employer. This is regarded as exploitation, but a fundamental weakness or contradiction in the capitalist system is said to be that workers cannot afford to buy everything they produce. Therefore capitalism always needs to expand. It must find new markets and invest to develop new products. Even so, it is argued that the system remains prone to crises of over-production, when firms must close or lay off workers who are plunged into desperate poverty. Subsistence is followed by immiseration. Marx expected that this working-class experience, aided by the theory and propaganda he and others were producing, would inspire workers to revolution, leading to the advent of a socialist era. Marx expected this revolution to occur at any time, probably in England, the most advanced capitalist country in the nineteenth century. He died with his hope and expectation unfulfilled.

The Marxism of the mature Marx and Engels (see Marx, 1979, 1989) claimed that work, not thought, was the most basic, essential human activity. Hegel was wrong. Humans were uniquely able to think, but they needed first of all to apply their thinking to their need to work upon nature in order to survive. In order to do this as productively as possible, people had entered into social relationships with one another (relationships of production). Once people were able to produce a surplus in excess of what was required to meet basic survival needs, it became possible to have a 'class' division between producers and those who appropriated surplus value, who could be slave, land, mine, ship or factory owners. The Marxist view is that there is necessarily an antagonistic relationship between producers and 'exploiting' classes. Intellectuals, priests and journalists will be supported by those who directly extract surplus value only while the former justify and legitimise these arrangements. Thus the ideas of the ruling class tend to become the ruling ideas in every age. This is how Marx is said to have stood Hegel on his head. Thoughts (ideas) were part of the super-structure: it was interests rooted in material conditions that drove history forward.

Marx (and Engels) believed that the dominant relationships of production in any age would be those that were best able to exploit the forces of production (natural resources and the tools to work upon them). They claimed that during every historical era the forces of production were developed to the maximum possible extent within the prevailing relationships of production, but that points were reached when the forces of production were developed in ways that could not be exploited fully within the prevailing relationships. This was said to be a potentially revolutionary situation. The time was ripe for a formerly subordinate class, or a faction thereof, to seize control of the forces of production, reset the relationships of production and move history forward. This is how primitive communism was said to have been superseded by the ancient civilisations, and how these in time gave way to feudalism, which was replaced by capitalism, during which feudal relationships between lords and serfs or peasants were replaced by wage labour (payment according to hours and minutes worked or units produced).

Marx was truly impressed by the forces of production that capitalism was developing. He believed that these forces could allow all humanity's needs to be met. Yet according to Marx's analysis of capitalism, its wage–labour relationships of production condemned the producers (the proletariat or working class) to a miserable subsistence existence. Furthermore, alienation was being intensified under capitalism. Workers did not own the tools with which they worked. They did not own the product of their labour. They were not even in control of their own labour power – when at work, they were required to follow their employers' instructions. Marx hoped that the ideas that he was propagating would help to inspire a revolutionary movement that would lead to the proletariat taking control over the forces of production. Workers would then collectively own the tools with which they laboured, the products of the labour, and they would control their own labour power. Simultaneously, everyone's needs would be met. 'Bread and freedom' have been the twin promises that have inspired millions, and Marxism has assured them that their eventual triumph is historically inevitable.

Marxism since Marx

Marx's journey into sociology, which entailed treating Marxism as a serious (scientific) social theory rather than political propaganda, was posthumous and lengthy. Marxism was not just kept alive but developed following the death of Marx in 1883 and Engels in 1895. Durkheim's work was also built upon, by Talcott Parsons among others, but whereas functionalism was developed as an academic theory, Marxism was developed in political movements that bore Marx's name (see Gouldner, 1971). By the time of Marx's death there were already political parties throughout Europe that described themselves as Marxist. The test of their theory was not whether it was supported by evidence from scholarly research. To paraphrase Marx himself, their aim was not just to understand the world, but to change it. The crucial test of Marxism was to be through *praxis*: theoretically informed action. Marxism was to become the twentieth century's most successful ideology for mobilising populations in movements that transformed their countries.

Marxism-Leninism

One Marxist party, the Bolshevik Party, seized control of the state in Russia in 1917. Its ascent to power was not through the ballot box. The Czarist regime had collapsed following defeats in the First World War. The Bolsheviks, acting as a united group, seized control of the Duma (the elected assembly), transferred power to their own soviets, and proceeded to create a Union of Soviet Socialist Republics (USSR) out of the former Czarist Empire. 'Reds' fought 'White Russians' into the 1920s, and the Bolsheviks emerged victorious.

Russia was not a country where Marxist theory would have led anyone to expect a successful socialist revolution. The revolution was supposed to happen first in an advanced capitalist country, probably Britain. Russia was backward. The bulk of the people were illiterate peasants. However, the Bolsheviks developed their own version of Marxism, which became known as Marxism-Leninism. Vladimir Lenin (1870–1924) was the leader of the Russian Bolsheviks at the time of the 1917 revolution. This version of Marxism continued to be developed under subsequent leaders, mainly Josef Stalin (1878–1953), Nikita Khrushchev (1894–1971) and Leonid Brezhnev (1906–1982). It explained how, in a country such as Russia, a communist party could seize power and exercise a dictatorship on behalf of the proletariat, then lead the society through a socialist phase towards a golden age of communism.

As explained above, Marx and Engels wrote virtually nothing on what should happen following a successful revolution. At the beginning of the twentieth century there were several 'models' of socialism. These included worker co-operatives (syndicalism), consumer co-operatives and municipal enterprises. However, by the 1930s the model favoured by socialist parties throughout Europe was state ownership and control (nationalisation). The Soviet Union implemented this in an extreme form: central ownership and planning of virtually the entire economy by a one-party state, and the one party operated according to 'democratic centralism', meaning that once taken at the top, all decisions became binding at all levels. This version of socialism owed more to Russian history and culture than to Marx, but it gave socialism a global reputation that is difficult to dispel.

Throughout the present-day world, Soviet communism is usually regarded as a failed system. However, there are aspects of Marxism-Leninism and Soviet communism that deserve continued attention without a presumption that the theory and its system were all warts. The Soviet regime claimed that it would prove its superiority by results, and gained considerable credibility through its victory in the Great Patriotic War of 1941–1945 (known as the Second World War in the West). The communist system was supposed to be delivering a superior way of life for its people, and its achievements, as well as its limitations and failures, deserve attention from present-day sport and leisure researchers. Judged against Western yardsticks (GDP per capita, and consumer spending on leisure goods and services) communism failed miserably. However, its supporters could claim to be nurturing a different socialist way of life that would eventually prove superior to anything that capitalism could offer. There were heated debates among Russia's Bolsheviks throughout the 1920s and 1930s about whether the bourgeois family and also bourgeois sports and the arts should have any place in a socialist society. The USSR did not compete in any Olympic Games until 1952, but organised its own Spartakiads. However, before the outbreak of the Second World War the Bolsheviks had decided to restore and strengthen the family, and that they would out-perform capitalism at its own arts and sports. Communism was to do this by opening success to all the talents irrespective of social background, and by the enthusiasm that would be generated when artists and players knew that they were representing societies that were truly their own (Riordan, 1980, 1982). Objective judgement of artistic accomplishment is difficult, but sporting success can be measured in victories in international competitions. We shall examine some of the relevant evidence below.

Marxist critiques of Soviet communism

Although claiming leadership in the international socialist movement, which was thereby divided into communists (who underwent successive splits) and 'democratic socialists', the Russian Bolsheviks never held a monopoly in the development of Marxist thought. There were Marxist critics of Soviet communism. After 1945 most Western Marxists were among these critics, and there were dissident Marxists within communist countries, especially following the expansion of the Soviet bloc into Eastern and Central Europe after 1945. Milovan Djilas, a senior Jugoslav politician, became disillusioned and wrote a book describing the communist rulers as a new ruling class (Djilas, 1957). Djilas then spent several years in prison. George Konrad and Ivan Szelenyi, both Hungarians but living outside Hungary since 1975, claimed that socialist intellectuals had become the new ruling class (Konrad and Szelenyi, 1979). Rather than socialist, most Western Marxists preferred to describe the USSR as state capitalist. Communist elites controlled the state, through which they exercised effective ownership of the means of production, and became the new exploiting class that extracted then distributed surplus value.

Capitalism since Marx

However, the developments in Marxist thought that are of greatest interest for present-day sport and leisure scholars are those that address how capitalist societies have changed since Marx's lifetime. By the 1920s Western Marxists were faced with the failure of the working classes in the most advanced capitalist countries to display the revolutionary consciousness that Marx had envisaged. This has continued to be a major problem for Marxists. How and why has capitalism proved so resilient? All the answers that have been offered involve leisure.

The first answer was offered by Lenin himself. He argued that imperialism, the exploitation of colonies, enabled the core capitalist countries to lift their own working classes out of the dire poverty that Marx believed was their inevitable fate (Lenin, 1939). This view has been endorsed in subsequent Marxist accounts of how so-called developing countries are systematically underdeveloped by the global market economy (see, for example, Frank, 1969).

A second answer to 'Why no revolutions?' concerns the growth of middle classes within capitalist countries. Marx had envisaged a capitalist society polarising into a wealthy bourgeoisie and an impoverished proletariat. Small firms, independent tradespeople and professionals, were either to grow into larger employers or become wage labourers. Traditional peasants would either become agricultural wage labourers or be forced off the land into industrial workforces. However, rather than polarising, from the late nineteenth century onwards capitalist countries had expanding middle classes. Most Marxist sociologists (for example, Wright, 1979, 2000) treat managers and professional employees as occupying contradictory class locations. They are salaried, and in this sense belong in the working class, yet they are required to perform functions of capital, including the control of subordinates. The superior rewards, the share of surplus value, that can be given to this 'officer class' are said to secure their loyalty and simultaneously to enable those below to aspire to ascend instead of mobilising to change the system.

'Hegemony' is the third answer offered by Marxists to 'Why no revolutions?' The term was used by Antonio Gramsci (1891–1937), the secretary of the Italian communist party who was imprisoned in Mussolini's Italy, and while in confinement produced his *Prison Notebooks* (Gramsci, 1971). Hegemony develops Marx's proposition that the ideas of the ruling class become the ruling ideas of an era. Capitalism's institutions, the market and private property, and their outcomes – wide inequalities and booms followed by slumps – are made to appear natural, like the weather and the geographical terrain. Trying to construct alternatives is made to look like trying to override nature. Political parties, education, churches and, crucially, capitalism's mass media are said to combine to maintain hegemony. Clause IV in its 1918 constitution committed the British Labour Party to the 'common ownership of the means of production, distribution and exchange'. It might be thought that it would be easy to persuade workers of the benefits of common ownership rather than a system in which less than 0.1 per cent of the world's population controls most productive assets. However, the Labour Party replaced Clause IV in 1995 with a statement which was compatible with the continuation of capitalism, and then won successive general elections in 1997, 2001 and 2005. This is what Marxists mean by hegemony.

The fourth long-standing Marxist answer to the docility of capitalism's working classes claims that capitalism uses its cultural industries to entertain and lull the masses into acquiescence. This argument was developed originally by members of the Frankfurt Institute of Social Research that opened in 1923. The leading members of the institute were Marxists and also Jews, and they and their institute relocated to New York when Hitler seized power in Germany in 1933. They found the popular culture that was emanating from Hollywood, New York's Tin Pan Alley (the centre of the recorded music industry), broadcast on radio and later also on television, just as oppressive, though of course in a different way, as fascism had been in Germany (see Adorno and Horkheimer, 1977). Later in the twentieth century these arguments were applied to what was by then a much wider range of capitalist consumer industries and cultures (for example, see Baudrillard, 1988, 1998).

There were other arguments, now quietly forgotten, about childhood socialisation in authoritarian, patriarchal, bourgeois families and sexual repression, especially among young people, producing docile adults who were amenable to subordination in capitalist workforces (see, for example, Marcuse, 1955).

After 1945 all these arguments became part of a body of thought querying the extent to which economic growth, so-called affluence and welfare states were really improving the lives of capitalism's working classes. The conclusion drawn by most sociologists was that the improvements had not gone far enough, and it was in this context that many chose to locate their own work within Marxism. It was at this time that the original source of the thinking, Karl Marx, was claimed as a classical social theorist and as one of the founders of sociology. Marx would have chuckled if he had known that his work would become a foundation of a bourgeois social science, and that he would be acclaimed as one of its classic social theorists.

Since the 1970s Marxist theory has experienced downward mobility within and beyond sociology. Regimes self-described as Marxist collapsed in Eastern Central Europe in 1989, and all the new independent states became post-communist when the Soviet Union broke up in 1991. The major Western political parties of the left have moved into the centre. Recent history has not been on Marxism's side. Even so, obituaries have never been warranted.

Capitalism has faced no serious competition since communism ended in Eastern Europe and the Soviet Union. It no longer needs to demonstrate to its workforces that it offers better lives than socialism. The capitalist system has become truly global. A global capitalist class is being formed (see Robinson and Harris, 2000; Sklair, 2001). Simultaneously, capitalism is being financialised. It is regulated by international institutions, not democratically elected national governments. The regulators are the World Bank, the International Monetary Fund, the World Trade Organization, the European Union, and meetings and agreements by the G7/8/20 (governments of the world's largest economies). Inequalities have widened within all countries. National governments have little choice but to insert their countries into the global system by pursuing national economic competitiveness, which means being investor-friendly and offering labour that is appropriately educated and skilled, and also cheap, flexible and cheerful.

Marxist thought has been revived in response to this latest stage in capitalism's development. Marxism is still the theory that claims to have identified the fundamental fault line in capitalism that will eventually ensure its destruction.

Applications in sport and leisure

Although Marx and Engels wrote virtually nothing on what was to follow the revolution, or about sport or any other kind of leisure, it will already be evident that subsequent Marxists have had a lot to say on these topics. Marxism-Leninism claimed to be nurturing a socialist way of life that would prove superior to both the high and popular cultures of the capitalist West (see, for example, Vitanyi, 1981). Western Marxists have accused capitalism's leisure industries of suppressing workers' appetites for radical change. Left to their own devices, they have envisaged workers using their free time in ways that strengthen class solidarity. Hence, they argue, the need for capitalism's ruling class to minimise the scope for 'the devil to make work' (Clarke and Critcher, 1985). Marxists have construed all signs of 'resistance' in working-class youth cultures as primitive forms of class rebellion (Hall and Jefferson, 1976; Willis, 1977). The growth of leisure time and spending in the latter part of the twentieth century led to forecasts of class struggles shifting from production to consumption sites and issues, with workers mobilising to defend public housing, parks, libraries and sports facilities (Castells, 1977).

part i: the classical theories

There are two important points that need to be made. The first is that leisure in a capitalist society will necessarily be functional in the Parsonian mathematical sense: it will be affected by and will have effects on other parts of the social system, and will thus be 'functional' within it. The same will apply to leisure in any type of socialist society. Functionality is inevitable and universal. It is not peculiar to leisure under capitalism or in any other type of society. The second point is that supporters of capitalism are just as able to claim that their system offers superior leisure as are socialists to claim that leisure in their preferred types of workers' states will be better. This dispute cannot be settled by evidence. However, it is possible to establish how and to what extent leisure was different under Soviet communism. It is possible to compare the kinds of sport and exercise that are marketed by capitalist businesses with public and voluntary sector provisions. It is impossible to know what leisure would be like in a socialist system that has not yet existed, but the Soviet regime, although it has become history, offers a benchmark against which to compare leisure in the capitalist West.

The leisure or way of life offered under communism were certainly different (see Roberts, 2009). Much provision under communism was via workplaces – housing, health care, holiday centres, sports and cultural facilities. Children's and young people's leisure was catered for in the Octobrists, Pioneers and Komsomol. Other public facilities always operated under the auspices of the state and communist party. Income inequalities were narrower than under capitalism. Everyone was given access to a common way of life via education, the youth organisations, workplaces and public facilities. The downside was that all kinds of consumer goods were scarce. Queuing was a feature of everyday life. The privileges of the elite were mainly in access to scarce commodities – flats, televisions, washing machines and motor cars (for those who could afford them). Even the elite had less choice than in market economies and in countries where independent (of the state) voluntary associations can exist.

The sports systems in some communist countries were remarkably successful in terms of winning Olympic medals. At the 1988 Seoul Olympics, the last before communist regimes collapsed, the USSR topped the medals table, followed by the German Democratic Republic. Whether the sports system that produced these results was specifically Marxist was always debatable. The system had been pioneered in Nazi Germany. It involved sifting the child population for talent, coaching in elite squads and focusing on a limited number of events. Since the demise of communism the system has been adopted by a number of Western countries, including Australia, France and the UK (but not the USA) (see Green and Oakley, 2001). It has also been adopted by China, which is rising towards the top of the medals tables at successive Olympics. This is a narrow yardstick for assessing which countries do sport best, but it is an example of how sport and leisure scholars can investigate *how* and *why* sport and the rest of leisure have been different under different versions of capitalism and communism.

The Marxism of Marx and Engels was basically about how capitalist societies worked and how they would develop. They argued that capitalism divides people into antagonistic classes – a bourgeoisie and proletariat of course, to which Marxist class theory has added a petit bourgeoisie of the self-employed with and without employees (a class that has not disappeared, but accounts for around 15 per cent of workers in the most advanced capitalist countries), and occupational groups (managers and professionals) who are said to occupy contradictory class locations. Marxist theory leads us to expect leisure differences to follow these class divisions. Marxism-Leninism envisaged class differences in leisure blurring and narrowing as the era of communism approached. Marxist critiques of 'state capitalism' suggest that leisure differences under communism should have been little different than in Western capitalism. These possibilities can all be assessed against evidence.

Conclusions

Some of Marxism's main contributions to social thought only become fully visible when we dispel the fog of all the post-Marx Marxisms. Many of Marx's ideas shattered a consensus at that time, but are now everyday common sense (in sociology). It was Marx and Engels who placed the economy, not ideas or politics, at the centre of their social theory. This went against the assumptions of earlier and contemporary (in the early nineteenth century) moral philosophy, political philosophy and political economy. Marx treated the economy as the base of society. It is Marx and Engels themselves, not latter-day Marxists, who continue to remind us that social theory is crippled when it allows the economy to become the private territory of economists. Marx and Engels are still the original source of what is still one of the most plausible conflict social theories, which are the alternatives to functionalist accounts that treat the main historical trend as a division of labour that has improved life for everyone, and accounts that treat modernisation as the outcome of the gradual spread of scientific thought, once again, bringing benefits to all. For Marx and Engels it was conflict that drove history forward, and their conflict theory maintains that the main conflict has always been between social classes with interests rooted in their different positions in the prevailing economic system. Their historical driver was not a Hegelian battle between ideas – thesis and antithesis – or between races represented by nation states. Marx and Engels's victory with these arguments was so total that making the economy pivotal in sociological explanations is no longer considered specifically Marxist. Today, many Marxist positions are widely accepted without acknowledging their Marxist origins. Sport and leisure researchers recognise that they must always explore class differences. They should also recognise the danger of ever assuming that any policies and provisions can be equally beneficial for everyone, and that we should always ask, 'Functional for whom?'

The original Marxist claim that capitalism is beset with internal contradictions that will lead eventually to its demise has not, and can never be, finally proved to be false. The rejection of communism throughout the former Soviet bloc, and the late twentieth-century global spread of capitalism and (to a lesser extent) Western-type democracy, cannot be treated as the end of history (Fukuyama, 1992). It will always be too soon to pronounce history finished. Capitalism is lasting much longer than Marx and Engels expected. Yet in other respects Marx's forecasts about how capitalism would develop look increasingly accurate, having stalled during the era of communism and mid-twentieth-century social democracy. This applies to capitalism necessarily being an expanding system, and the intensification of exploitation. Capitalism has now spread not only into nearly all parts of the world, but also into economic sectors that were once treated as public utilities in Western Europe (gas, electricity, telecommunications, broadcasting, public transport and water), and into what were previously publicly funded education and health care, social care, some penal services, policing, the military and mainstream public administration. Meanwhile, the proportion of gross national products distributed in wages and salaries has declined, which has led to wider and still wider inequalities in income and wealth (Piketty, 2014; Roberts, 2012). Until the 1990s Soviet communism was the alternative with which capitalism's workers could be threatened, while its existence made it necessary for capitalist businesses to offer their workers superior pay and living standards. The threat has now become history. The West's workers can now be told that they need to compete not only with lower-paid East Europeans, but also with labour forces in the BRICS (Brazil, Russia, India, China, South Africa and other emerging market economies). Hence the stagnation (at best) in real wages and living standards in a 'race to the bottom'.

Sport and other forms of leisure have been part of capitalism's recent expansion. In the nineteenth and early twentieth centuries most provisions for sport and the rest of leisure were outside the capitalist system. Sport was run by voluntary associations. In the first of the modern Olympics in 1896 competitors and organisers alike were amateurs. At that time it was public authorities, not capitalist businesses, that provided playing fields, swimming baths, libraries, museums and galleries. It was not until the late twentieth century, when countries were entering what appears to be an endless age of austerity in state spending, that the management of these once public leisure services began to be privatised. Meanwhile, commercial fitness gyms and sport 'clubs' have opened, and access to a global media audience has attracted capitalism into major spectator sports and events. In the mid-twentieth century nearly all radio and television broadcasting in Europe was public service. Now it is overwhelmingly commercial. Viewers get what they are able and willing to pay for. All these developments have continued with renewed impetus since the financial crash of 2008–2009.

The missing part of Marx's prediction is the revolutionary working class, and the 2008 financial crisis and subsequent recession have not led to a global lurch to the left. Marxists continue to critique how capitalism warps sport (Collins, 2013; Gruneau, 1983; Hargreaves, 1986). Some imagine alienated players and spectators uniting to seize control of their clubs and sports facilities (Carrington and McDonald, 2009). This seems improbable. The revolution, if there is to be one, is unlikely to start in leisure since players, spectators and audiences have the option of exit. Leisure is not work, which – as the young Marx noted – is what is necessary for survival. Players and fans who are dissatisfied with what capitalism offers can retain or form their own clubs and associations. Even so, although mistaken about the timing and the outcome, Marx could still be right in proposing conflict between classes with conflicting interests as the driver of history. He would have been amazed to find that the capitalist class, alternatively known as 'business' and 'private enterprise', has so far been winning its struggles, but this will not necessarily last for ever.

If and when the twenty-first-century working classes mobilise for change, they will not be the classes of industrial manual workers of the nineteenth and twentieth centuries. The version of socialism that inspires workers today is unlikely to be the twentieth-century model of state ownership and central planning and state welfare provisions, certainly not the Soviet version, but this was never the only possible form of a post-capitalist socialist society.

chapter 5

Max Weber (1864–1920)

Introduction

This is the book's most difficult chapter to introduce. Max Weber would probably win a vote among present-day sociologists as the greatest of all the classical social theorists. The problem is that it is impossible to explain why within a couple of paragraphs. Weber's reputation rests on many small contributions rather than one big idea. Durkheim is the theorist of order. Parsons is the synthesiser. Marx is the theorist of class, conflict and imminent revolution. Weber is . . . ? All the other theorists are in this book because they were pro-active thinkers. They had new, original ideas. Weber was different: he reacted to the ideas of others, mainly Marx, his predecessor, and also to contemporary German scholars who were disputing whether a 'science' of society was possible. Weber did not earn fame during his lifetime as an exciting teacher. His work did not attract followers. He is unlike Durkheim and Marx in this respect. Yet all who knew Weber personally agreed that he possessed a ferocious intellect. He was respected, even revered, but I doubt if even his admirers suspected that Weber would outpace all others in his influence on social thought during the second half of the twentieth century. Sport and leisure scholars are typically Weberian in their thinking, probably without realising this because some of Weber's ideas have become the orthodox 'default' positions throughout the social sciences. Briefly:

- Weber is the classical theorist who insisted that people's ideas, beliefs and intentions must be prominent parts of all explanations, which include how people spend their leisure.
- Weber regarded status as an alternative to class as a form of social stratification. This means that it is not necessarily how people earn

their livings; it can be how they spend their leisure time and money through which they form significant social bonds and identities.

- Weber argued that the main thrust in modern history was not an increasingly complex division of labour, but was towards increasing rationalisation, and that this would continue whether the context was capitalist or socialist. He regarded the rise of capitalism not as the prime mover, but as just one of the outcomes of rationalisation. By implication, we should expect a trend towards sport and all other leisure provisions being organised rationally, meaning that they should embody means–ends thinking.

Career

There are similarities between Karl Marx and Max Weber apart from both being German and from prosperous middle-class families. Another similarity is that at the time of their deaths no one could have imagined either becoming acclaimed as a major social theorist and laying the foundations for the future development of sociology. Unlike Marx, Max Weber had a conventional academic career, but never held a post with sociology in the job title until the final year of his life. Also, at the time of his death Weber had published only one book, *The Protestant Ethic and the Spirit of Capitalism* (1905). This would have been regarded as an important book by historians and sociologists, but surely insufficient to build an international reputation as a major social theorist. We shall see below that Weber's reputation as a social theorist was established posthumously, and owes much to Talcott Parsons's visit to Germany in the early 1920s.

Both Marx and Weber had fathers who were lawyers, but Weber senior became a prominent civil servant in the post-1871 unified Germany. Max Weber was from a highly political family, whereas the Marx family was not politically engaged until Karl became a revolutionary. Marx and Weber both progressed from *Gymnasium* (where Weber was a particularly precocious pupil) to university. There the similarities end. Max Weber did not become a revolutionary.

Max Weber's family home was in Erfurt, the capital of Thuringia, in central Germany. His childhood household was not only highly political, but also well connected with Germany's political elite. The Webers were visited frequently by senior figures from politics and government. As well as being a civil servant, Weber senior was an active member of the National Liberal Party, which was Chancellor Otto von Bismarck's strongest ally in the Reichstag. This chamber was elected by adult (age 25 and over) male suffrage, but political power was concentrated in the hands of the emperor/kaiser, the chancellor and other aristocrats (Bismarck was a German prince). Socialist parties were subjected to legal restrictions. Employment in the civil service was not incompatible with being involved in party politics in Germany at that time, provided the party was pro-regime. Just before the First World War Max Weber was part of an unsuccessful attempt to create a new centre-left political party. He had not adopted his father's politics. One of Max Weber's abiding concerns was how to subject the government and state bureaucracy to effective democratic control. Weber senior and Max Weber were not political soul-mates, nor soul-mates in any other sense.

From 1882 Max Weber studied law, philosophy, history and economics, first at the University of Heidelberg, then at the University of Berlin. He qualified as the German equivalent of an English barrister, but did not practise. In 1894 he obtained a post at the University of Freiberg, then was appointed Professor of Economics at the University of Heidelberg in 1896. This was Weber's main career job, but he remained politically engaged throughout. Max Weber was active in German politics, especially just before, during and after the First World War. He came closer to real power than any other major social theorist. Nowadays Weber's politics would be described as centre-left. During the First World War he was drafted into the civil service: this was a way in which personnel of military age were replaced. After the war Weber was part of the German delegation which negotiated the 1919 Treaty of Versailles. Weber died shortly afterwards of Spanish flu, in 1920 at the age of 56.

Making the transition from law to economics was not difficult for Weber. He had specialised in commercial law, and his economics was really economic history. The boundaries between what were later to become the separate academic disciplines of economics, law, history and sociology were unclear at the time. As mentioned above, in 1905 Weber published the book for which he is best known, *The Protestant Ethic and the Spirit of Capitalism*, the only book he published during his lifetime. Weber suffered a mental breakdown in 1898, and coped with bouts of depression for the rest of his life. He withdrew from all teaching from 1903, and did not resume until he was appointed to a sociology post at the University of Munich in 1919. However, Weber had continued his scholarly work throughout his years of depression, and left many manuscripts which were unpublished and possibly incomplete at the time of his premature death.

Weber owes much of his enduring reputation to his wife, Marianne (1870–1954). They were cousins, and married in 1894. Marianne was a published author, feminist activist and a public figure in her own right, but after Max's death she withdrew from public activities in order to concentrate on having her deceased husband's work prepared for publication then published. This work included major books on religion in China and India, and on ancient Judaism, which Max Weber had completed during 1916–1918.

The assimilation of Weber into international sociology must be credited mainly to Talcott Parsons. When he visited Germany in the early 1920s

Parsons met Marianne Weber, who gave him access to Max Weber's manuscripts. Parsons was impressed, and became the translator of the first English-language version of *The Protestant Ethic and the Spirit of Capitalism*. This book, and Parsons's personal recommendations, spread interest in Weber among other American sociologists, some with German origins and language. They were responsible for the stream of Weber's English-language publications that appeared in print for the first time up to the 1960s (for example, Gerth and Mills, 1946). There were the religion books, papers on social science methodology, essays on politics and science as vocations, and an intriguing essay on 'Class, status and party' (Weber, 1922). Weber was seen to have adopted positions on social science methodology and on substantive issues with which many post-1945 sociologists could identify, which is how he came to be hailed as one of the subject's classical theorists and founders. Sociology needed a Weber-type theorist. Otherwise Marxism was the only challenger to functionalism. Weber was embraced as another conflict theorist – a non-Marxist alternative to Parsons – though the latter believed that he had assimilated Weber into his own theory.

Max Weber had a younger brother, Alfred Weber (1868–1958), who also built an academic career. As with Max Weber, Alfred Weber's early work straddled what were to become separate social science disciplines, including economics, sociology and geography. Alfred Weber lived long enough to experience the split of the social sciences, whereupon he opted for economics. We do not know which subject Max Weber would have chosen had he lived another twenty years: probably sociology, but maybe politics. He was regarded as a sociologist by German contemporaries who did hold such posts, but Weber can be claimed equally by the study of politics, law and history as a founder of these modern disciplines.

Max Weber is regarded as having ended the classical European sociology that produced grand, all-encompassing theories accounting for the whole of history. This is because of positions Weber adopted that became generally accepted throughout sociology. Unlike Marx and Durkheim, Weber did not believe that all societies developed along the same evolutionary path. He did not believe that civilisations such as China and India were at some point between simple primitive and advanced Western societies. Also, Weber did not believe that explanations in sociology could take the same form as explanations in the natural sciences. He did not believe that sociology could establish general laws of structure and change. Hence there is no Weberian theory, a model of society, supposedly applicable in all times and places. This makes Weber less coherent and more difficult to digest than Marx or Durkheim, or even Parsons. Weber is treated as a founding father because, as already stated, so many of his positions have become generally accepted throughout sociology.

The Marx–Weber debates

Much of Weber's output has been read as debating with Marx or, more accurately, with the Marxism of Weber's lifetime, which was influential though kept to the margins of German politics. We should bear in mind throughout that Weber was a politically engaged academic, seeking a centre-left position as an alternative to Germany's Marxist (at that time) Social Democratic Party. Weber can be read as contesting, but more usually as qualifying and amending Marxist positions.

In the second half of the twentieth century self-defined Marxist and Weberian sociologists took opposite sides on a series of issues, all important within sociology, and all with implications for the study of sport and leisure. These issues were materialism versus idealism, class and social stratification in modern societies, and the historical trajectory of these societies. It is fair to say that in all these debates the Weberians won in so far as Marxists modified their positions and, in effect, became more Weberian.

Materialism versus idealism

In philosophy idealists believe that ideas govern actions. Materialists believe that actions and ideas are governed by circumstances. Idealism and materialism can be pictured as a continuum, as shown in Figure 5.1. Marx can be placed towards the materialist end, though not at the most extreme point. Weber is on the idealist side of the mid-point. The idealist end is where Auguste Comte (1798–1857) and Georg Hegel (1770–1831) are located.

Comte believed that history was driven through three stages by the development of human thought. Hegel agreed that the ability to think distinguished humanity from other animals. This is why humans have a supra-natural history whereas other organisms have only a natural history. We saw in Chapter 4 that Hegel believed that history was driven by humanity's quest for absolute truth, with which would come mastery over nature. He believed that ideas progressed in a dialectical manner in which existing knowledge was disputed (thesis encountered antithesis), from which a synthesis would emerge which became the new thesis, and this process continued until all questions could be answered and humanity fulfilled its potential (see Singer, 1983). Marx disagreed. He agreed that

Materialism...Idealism
Marx   Weber   Comte
                                                                          Hegel

Figure 5.1 The materialism– idealism continuum

humans had the unique ability to think, but they also had a unique need to think about how to work upon nature in order to procure their livelihoods. Humans could not survive on instinct alone. Thought had to be driven by material necessity. Weber staked out a different (we might today say more evidence-based) position.

There is agreement among archaeologists and anthropologists that the earliest human societies were hunters and gatherers. Populations had to be widely dispersed because one group, most likely a family, needed enough territory to be able to hunt and gather to meet its survival needs. However, there would have been relationships between neighbouring family groups (tribes or clans) because, whether by an inherited distaste for incest or through experience, marriage had to be outside a family if a population was to remain sufficiently strong to survive. There is also agreement that the first great leap forward in human civilisation was the development of agriculture and animal husbandry. Arable and animal farming enabled more people to live within a given territory and also required a division of labour, the beginning of Durkheim's history. It also became possible for farmers to produce a surplus with which societies could create states – rulers who could manage irrigation and other major projects, enforce rules within a society and organise protection against outsiders. Durkheim and Parsons, the functionalist sociologists, imagined that these developments could have occurred consensually. A division of labour served everyone's interests. A population would therefore empower its rulers. Weberians side with Marxists in considering it more likely that one section of a population claimed ownership of the forces of production, extracted surplus value from those who were subjugated, and used part of the surplus value to enforce this subjugation. This class division could have occurred within a given tribe, or one tribe might have enslaved another. Most known early societies practised slavery. Acquiring slaves was one of the objectives of warfare. Marx himself believed that the class division thereby created became the basis for conflict which drove history forward. This is how Marx is said to have turned Hegel on his head. The dialectic was not between ideas, but between classes with opposing material interests.

Fast-forward history to Europe in the Middle Ages. We simply do not know how the first farming societies and states were formed. We can merely decide which account is most plausible given our wider knowledge. We know a lot more about the birth of modern societies. In the Middle Ages land was owned by aristocrats and typically farmed by peasants. There were also manufacturers and traders who worked in or from towns and cities, and usually lived in them. They were burghers, the bourgeoisie. Monarchs and aristocrats encouraged trade because it could be taxed. In the fifteenth and sixteenth centuries improvements in shipbuilding and the art of navigation lengthened the voyages that could be made. Eventually

part i: the classical theories

European traders were sailing to and from the Americas, around the entire coast of Africa, then onward to the Orient. This led to a huge expansion in trade. Shortly afterwards the exploitation of new sources of energy (coal and steam power), allied to inventions in the manufacture and processing of metals and textiles, led to an industrial revolution. The Marxist view is that the wealth they amassed enabled traders and manufacturers to become a new ruling class – a capitalist class. This class pioneered wage labour as the preferred way of employing workers. Marx believed that by creating a working class the bourgeoisie was nurturing its own grave diggers, like the old aristocratic ruling classes who had encouraged trade and manufacturing. Marx believed that eventually workers would act in their material interests, just as capitalists had done in expanding trade and manufacturing. Why did they do this? Marxists believe that we need look no further than their material interests.

Weber felt that this explanation was inadequate. Profit-seeking was not new. Why had there been such an unprecedented spurt of progress in the eighteenth and nineteenth centuries? Why had no other civilisations had industrial revolutions? Weber believed that Protestant religion, more specifically the brand of Protestantism preached by John Calvin (1509–1564), had been a vital catalyst. Two Protestant doctrines were considered crucial: pre-destination (to heaven or hell) and the calling (a person's vocation while on earth). Calvin preached that people could not gain salvation by deeds, or through the intervention of a church, because God had pre-ordained everyone's destiny – a view shared by Mohammed (AD 570–633), the founder of Islam. However, Calvin preached that success in the roles on earth to which people had been called by God was a sign of grace, that those concerned were among the chosen few. Weber argued that an outcome had been a this-worldly asceticism – perpetually anxious individuals who were forever seeking signs of grace by endeavouring to do better in their vocations. In business such people developed their enterprises and could never let up. They had never done enough or earned enough. Amid other favourable conditions (the expansion of trade and technological advances), this Protestant ethic was identified by Weber as the spark that had ignited the expansion of capitalism and all that had followed. In support of his theory Weber marshalled evidence showing that capitalism had developed earliest and most strongly in Protestant rather than Catholic countries, and that within countries the most successful early capitalists had tended to be drawn from Calvinist congregations. However, once a Protestant work ethic had been established, it was easily routinised and could be spread among people of any faith. This was the argument in *The Protestant Ethic and the Spirit of Capitalism* (1905).

Weber was responsible for the insertion of 'action' into Parsons's systems theory, and for persuading virtually all subsequent sociologists that the minds of the actors need to be part of all explanations. During Weber's lifetime there was a fierce debate in Germany about the possibility of applying scientific methods to the study of society. Wilhelm Dilthey (1976) propounded the view of most historians that human behaviour could not be explained in terms of general laws, but needed to be 'understood' and interpreted by grasping the spirit of the age. In other words, it was necessary for historians to get inside the minds of those living at the time. This has remained the orthodox view among historians. Weber sought to show how the orientations of actors could be built into causal, sociological explanations. Weber claimed to be reconciling 'understanding' with causal explanation.

His argument about the necessity of 'understanding' has become mainstream in sociology. Contrary to Durkheim, we no longer believe that actors acquiesce obediently under the force of social facts. Rather, people respond to circumstances according to their definitions of the situation. Marxists have conceded that ideas (and politics) have at least limited autonomy, but are likely to insist that in the final analysis, meaning eventually, people will act according to their material interests. Weberians counter-argue that the working class needed converting to socialism with a set of beliefs that could be a catalyst, like the Protestant ethic. Weberians will credit Marxism with having been the world's most impressive change ideology during the twentieth century.

An effect of conceding that ideas play an independent role in social life is to destroy the search for universal laws of history or anything else. Ideas are simply too variable and unpredictable. It is impossible to predict the new ideas and inventions that will lead to changes in the future. Therefore sociology must limit its ambitions to historically specific explanations of the outcomes of particular mixtures of ideas and circumstances. It is impossible to attach fixed proportions to the power of ideas and circumstances in leading to an outcome. This will always depend on which circumstances and which ideas. These are the types of explanations that sport and leisure scholars, and all other social researchers, should seek.

Class and social stratification in modern societies

Before proceeding with differences between Marx and Weber, it will be helpful to list some matters on which all sociologists – Marxists, Weberians and functionalists – will agree:

- Class inequalities have an economic base. Classes are composed of individuals and households who occupy common positions in the regimes of economic production and distribution.
- These are the most important inequalities in modern societies – Marxists would say 'in all societies'.

- There is a difference between classes as objective phenomena and the subjective aspects of class. People who belong to a class as defined by a theorist may not be aware that they belong to the class in question. Lay people may not agree with a theorist or with one another about which classes exist, or where they and others are located. This need not hinder any theorist from allocating people to an objective class as defined by the theory.
- All sociologists agree that classes may, but will not necessarily, develop from economic aggregates into formations with social, cultural and political characteristics. Classes are likely to become social entities through members being more likely to interact with one another at work, in residential neighbourhoods and through family connections than with members of other classes. This can be the context for the development of class-specific cultures which may include sport and other leisure activities, and also conceptions of the people's interests and general outlooks on life. From there a class may become a political actor.

Marx famously declared that classes are defined by their relationships to the means of production. An implication is that in a capitalist society there will be just two main classes: (1) the owners, capitalists or bourgeoisie and (2) workers, the proletariat. Marx himself realised that the actual societies of nineteenth-century Europe had additional classes. Some were 'feudal relics' – a petit bourgeoisie composed of people who ran and worked in their own businesses, and peasants (plus serfs in some countries). Marx expected these relics to shrink as capitalism developed. The petit bourgeoisie would either rise into the grand bourgeoisie or be forced into the working class. Peasants and serfs would either become self-employed farmers, agricultural wage labourers, or be forced into other industries. Marx and subsequent Marxists have then needed to address 'the problem' of the middle class or classes. These are people who sell their labour power, but place their occupations in the middle class rather than the working class. The original Marxist view was that these middle-class identifiers were falsely conscious, and in time would probably see the error of their ways. However, as we saw in Chapter 4, during the twentieth century it became orthodox (within Marxism) to identify contradictory or ambiguous class situations. These arise when people are waged or salaried, but perform 'functions of capital', meaning that they act as employers would act if running their own businesses. Professionals and managers are the main occupational groups whose class situations are said to be contradictory. The outcome, if and when a revolutionary moment arises, is seen to depend partly on with which side these occupations ally. Marxists treat an economy and the class structure as the base on which other institutions and inequalities are built. So politics, and gender and ethnic divisions, are said to be given their characteristics by their locations in a capitalist society. This is a distinctive feature of Marxism.

Marxist and Weberian views on class share much in common. All the Marxist divisions and processes can be accommodated within Weberian thinking, where they are not dismissed, but join other possibilities. Weber argued that classes are formed in markets, and therefore become important only in societies where markets play an important role – that is, in modern societies. Weber agreed with Marx that a major class division, most vivid in labour markets, is between those who hire and those who sell labour power. However, Weber proceeded to argue that there could be class divisions among workers depending on the types of labour power they were selling (their qualifications, skills and experience). Weber did not believe it was inevitable or even likely that all workers would unite to defend common interests. It seemed more likely that those who were able to do so would emphasise their superior abilities, restrict access to their occupations to the qualified, and seek control over the qualifying process. Weber would have been aware that the first workers' combinations (in England) had been called *trade* unions. They were associations of workers in skilled trades who sought the best possible deals from their employers, but also sought to distinguish themselves and claim superior entitlements to less skilled workers.

Weber did not believe that all societies had been class societies. The 'estates' of medieval Europe (nobles, church, commons) were formed by political rather than market processes. He believed that India's castes were better described as status groups rather than as classes. Subsequent sociologists have been intrigued by Weber's distinction between class and status. Status groups, according to Weber, are defined by the degrees of honour attached to their styles of life. The country set and urban gentrifiers are examples of modern status groups. High culture and sport are both possible bases for status group formation. Status rather than class divisions include those between the 'rough' and 'respectable' working classes, the 'deserving' and the 'undeserving' poor, and home owners and households who rent social housing. Marxists treat status as an aspect of the super-structure, built on underlying class divisions. Weber opens the possibility of status differences acting as an alternative base for social organisation and political action.

We must return to what Marx and Weber had in common. Both were conflict theorists. Their approaches to social analysis assumed that within any society it would be possible to identify groups with different self-defined interests which were liable to bring them into *conflict* with one another. Both Marxists and Weberians regard class as *relational*. Classes are said to be formed and defined by their relationships with each other: employing and being employed, managing and being managed, planning and executing work tasks. All this sets them apart from functionalists, who treat inequalities as reflecting the social importance of different positions. Functionalists treat inequalities as *consensual*, integrating rather than dividing societies. High rewards, whether economic or socio-psychological, are said to express a wider population's gratitude. The system of stratification is treated as *gradational*, and can be likened to a ladder which people ascend or descend on merit. Weber differs from Marx in arguing that there can be class divisions among workers, and that status can be an alternative or parallel base for social stratification which will intersect with class divisions, but cannot be reduced to and seen as simply a reflection of them.

All sport and leisure researchers are aware that in almost every kind of leisure, participation is related to social 'class'. They can do more than continue to repeat this finding. Do all leisure differences coincide with class divisions – that is, people's different positions in the systems of economic production and distribution? Or can we achieve more powerful explanations by recognising status divisions that may be within classes or overlap class boundaries? If the functionalists are correct, we should expect to find inequalities in sport and leisure, different strata doing and spending more and less on the same things. If the conflict theorists are correct, there will be 'more and less', but we should also expect the strata to be doing different things, maybe in different places, and with different co-players.

The historical trajectory of modern societies

Up to the end of the twentieth century Weber appeared closer than Marx to the tide of history, but history has a habit of changing in unexpected ways. None of the classical social theorists predicted the twentieth century's world wars, or the rise then demise of fascism, or that a Marxist party would first win power in Russia. We constantly reinterpret the past to make better sense of a changing present. Weber certainly appears vindicated in rejecting the possibility of laws of history which would enable the future to be predicted.

However, until the 1970s it was Marx, not Weber, who appeared closer to the right side of history. Communism had been spread from Russia into the remainder of the former Czarist Empire, then into East, South-East and Central Europe after 1945. It was spreading in Asia – in China, North Korea and the former French Indo-China (Vietnam, Laos and Cambodia). Post-colonial African countries were developing African versions of socialism. Communism gained a toehold in the Americas in Cuba in 1959, then in Chile in 1970, but this ended when President Salvador Allende was deposed by the military in 1973. Western Europe and North America were developing versions of social democracy with mixed private and public sector economies, overall macro-economic management by governments, and welfare states. These countries could be seen as taking an evolutionary, democratic road to a socialist future.

Since the 1970s history appears to have taken Weber's side. Weberians can claim that history never left Weber's side; rather, attention was distracted by what proved short-lived twists. Weber believed that the main driver of modernisation since the Middle Ages had been rationalisation – an orientation to action and outcomes which were routinised and generalised versions of the 'spirit of capitalism' that was nurtured by the Protestant ethic. Rational action is calculative action. Means are selected because they are the best ways of achieving given ends.

Weber distinguished three broad types of orientation to action and corresponding behaviour:

- traditional, where people are predisposed to follow custom and practice, where their being traditional is an acceptable (to an actor and to others) justification for behaviour, and authorities (monarchs and nobles, for example) are obeyed because their right to command is traditional;
- rational, where courses of action and rules are adopted because they will lead to a desired end; authorities are obeyed because occupancy of their positions has depended on their being qualified for the positions, as demonstrated by their credentials, experience and past accomplishments, or voted into office by legally defined and enforced processes;
- affective, where behaviour is a response to emotions; this is how charismatic leaders can inspire followers by virtue of their exceptional qualities; charisma, as displayed by historical figures such as Jesus Christ and John Calvin, was Weber's potentially disruptive, unpredictable force in human history.

Weber argued that an equivalent catalyst to the Protestant ethic could not have arisen in the Orient, but was possible only within the worldviews, specifically the relationship between God and people on earth, fostered in the occidental 'religions of the book' (Judaism, Christianity and Islam). In practice, the catalyst faith and ethic developed only within Western (Roman Catholic) Christianity. However, this would not prevent other societies adopting Western ways of working, or having such ways imposed upon them by imperial countries.

The outcomes of rationalisation noted by Weber were the ongoing development of capitalism, the rise of science and continuous improvements in technology, impartial rule by written laws applied by independent courts, and the spread of bureaucratic organisation, which Weber believed was the most effective form of social organisation ever devised for marshalling the behaviour of thousands of officers and subordinates in pursuit of an objective. There was a deep pathos in Weber's identification of the main direction of historical change. Weber did not like what he saw lying ahead. He believed that socialism would not reverse, but would extend rationalisation, and in this Weber might be considered vindicated in so far as communism (and fascism also) created near-totalitarian states. Weber believed that bureaucracies could spin out of human control. No single person, not even the nominal head, could know what was happening in every office of a large organisation. Many of those working in an organisation could be ignorant as to 'Why?' To what ends were all their efforts contributing? Even those in top positions could find themselves applying rules without necessarily understanding 'Why?' This was the basis of Weber's worry that the German state could not be subjected to effective democratic control. Weber was equally unenthusiastic about the 'quality of life' (to use a present-day term) that rationalisation was delivering. He believed that excitement and unpredictability were being suffocated. Even the identification of charisma was being routinised. Examinations were becoming the new test of exceptional gifts and talents.

We should note that the functionalist trend towards a progressive division of labour, the Marxist expectation of the continuous expansion of capitalism and intensification of exploitation prior to the revolution, and the Weberian expectation of continuous rationalisation, are not either/or. They are compatibles. All could be correct, but it is also possible that just two or just one could be right in sport and leisure and in other social domains.

Applications in sport and leisure

Ideas matter

All of Max Weber's positions *vis-à-vis* Marxism have implications for, and raise issues for investigation by, sport and leisure scholars. Following Weber, sociologists have accepted that there will always be alternative ways in which actors may interpret and respond to any given situation. Thus the actors' 'definition of the situation' always needs to be taken into account. This has implications for the study of leisure (and everything else). Weberian explanations have to be in terms of how people act given their own interpretations of their situations. This applies to all sociological explanations, but given the relative freedom that characterises leisure, the actors' tastes, aims, preferences and choices should have an elevated importance. A key message from Weber is that actors' subjective states *always* have to be included in accounts of their behaviour. It is insufficient to seek relationships between Durkheimian social facts. We cannot assume that, even in a final analysis, people will act according to their class interests or any other interests that are identified independently by an investigator.

Promoters of all kinds of leisure tend to believe that if people are aware of the relevant activities and the benefits that arise from participation, if given the opportunity they will surely take part. It is never so simple. We might imagine that since it is in their material self-interest, if given the opportunity then people will take sufficient exercise to optimise their health and fitness. However, we know that most people fail to do this. Is this because they are unaware of the health and fitness benefits? No, most people agree that their health and fitness would benefit if they took more exercise. Some may be constrained by time, money or geography (access to facilities) or their lack of relevant skills, but others may feel that their existing levels of health and fitness are adequate to cope with their own daily lives, and that there would be unacceptable opportunity costs in their paid work careers or family lives if they spent more time and money on their own bodily well-being. There will be other explanations in other instances. People and their ideas differ widely. There can be no universally correct answer. Weber stops the search for such universals. Every socio-demographic group and historically specific situation presents a unique problem for sport and leisure researchers.

Inequalities

Weber's definition of class and his distinction between class and status open further issues for sport and leisure scholars where their findings can command much wider interest. Opportunities are missed when answers are prejudged by using just one class scheme. A Weberian scheme will include the classes that Marxists identify plus additional divisions within Marxists' classes of workers, and it will also allow evidence to align with functionalist predictions. If functionalists are correct, differences in leisure practices should be gradational, outcomes of the higher strata being able to do and spend more than others. If the conflict theorists are correct, we should expect members of different classes to be doing different things. So interest will broaden from frequency of participation in and amounts spent on sport or any art form, to which sport, which art, where it is played or viewed, and with whom. If Marxists are correct, we should expect any such differences to coincide with the classes Marxist theory identifies. If the Weberians are right, there could be differences within classes of workers as identified by Marxists, and there is the additional and intriguing possibility of status groups (identified by their typical uses of leisure) forming within or overlapping class boundaries.

part i: the classical theories

Rationalisation

Weber also invites us to consider whether rationalisation, his historical master trend, is evident in leisure. Towards the end of the twentieth century Weber's rationalisation thesis was given a remarkable tweak and endorsement by George Ritzer, an American sociologist. Ritzer argued that Weber was correct in identifying rationalisation as the dominant, long-term modernising trend dating back to the sixteenth and seventeenth centuries, but wrong in selecting giant bureaucracies as the eventual outcome. Ritzer proposed McDonald's, the fast food restaurant chain, as a better example of the late twentieth-century outcome (Ritzer, 1993). McDonald's restaurants look harmless: far less threatening than communist and fascist bureaucracies. Ritzer argues that rationalisation spread first in manufacturing industries and government, then into business services, and in the late twentieth century began to spread into consumer services with the outcome he describes as 'McDonaldization'. A successful service is standardised then applied in every city and every country. The name McDonald's is chosen because the business has acted as an exemplar for other consumer services – not just fast food, but also branded hotels, casinos, holiday packages, health care, cruise ships, fitness gyms, sport stadiums, and even higher education, where standardised 'McDonalidized' modules can be adopted by teachers all over the world, and students can now enrol on MOOCs (mass open online courses). Ritzer envisages, and seeks ways of resisting, an age in which we are able to escape from one 'McDonaldized' site only by stepping into another. As was Weber, Ritzer is gloomy, not enthusiastic, about a modernising trend which, he claims, spreads disenchantment while proving irresistible (Ritzer, 1999).

Conclusions

Unlike functionalism and Marxism, Weber's sociology does not provide a fully coherent set of propositions about the character of all societies. There is no Weberian theory within which sport and leisure might be located. Weber did not believe that social behaviour could be accounted for in this way. This looseness in Weber's work, if justified, becomes a strength rather than a weakness, and explains why all his distinctive positions have become mainstream in sociology. His influence is remarkable given that he published so little during his lifetime. Weber's influence is evident in the work of nearly all the theorists who feature in the following chapters, which cannot be said of Durkheim, Marx or Parsons.

PART II
The successors

chapter 6

Norbert Elias (1897–1990)

Introduction

Sociology would have a founding father, a classical theorist who wrote about sport and leisure, if Norbert Elias qualified as a founder. Elias has advocates for his inclusion. He began his academic career during the inter-war years. He became, and always remained, a European sociologist whose thinking was anchored in that period, the classical age, which (unknown at the time) was then drawing to a close. Elias's sociology was written in the classical style with a long historical scan. The reason for placing him among the successors rather than this book's classical theorists is that his work became widely known only from the 1970s onwards.

Elias was a refugee from Nazi Germany whose career suffered an unusually prolonged interruption. Elias might have become a widely recognised classical social theorist had he been born earlier, or if his early academic career had progressed more rapidly in the 1920s, or if there had been no Nazi takeover in Germany in 1933. We cannot know 'What if . . .?' However, one plain fact is that Elias does not feature at all in most books and courses on modern social theories. He is either a lost, wrongly neglected genius, or grossly overrated by a cult-like following who claim him as at least equal to, if not superseding, Marx, Durkheim and Weber. Many of Elias's advocates are sociologists of sport. He is regarded as an important social theorist within this sub-discipline, but rarely anywhere else in Anglophone countries. This chapter presents the evidence – that is, Elias's social theory. Readers can make their own judgements. However, as in all chapters, here we err, if at all, in making the case for our featured theorist.

We shall see below that Norbert Elias had a highly unusual academic biography. Most of his work was first published, and his reputation began to be built, only after he formally retired from his main career post at Leicester University at the age of 65 in 1962. Until then little was known about Elias beyond his immediate colleagues at Leicester. In the 1960s he became best-known more widely in Britain for the book *The Established and the Outsiders* (Elias and Scotson, 1965). This was a study of a small community on the outskirts of Leicester, fictitiously called 'Winston Parva', which had been enlarged by the construction of two new settlements some twenty years earlier: the newcomers were still not welcomed by 'the established'. At the time this was received as just one of many community studies British sociologists were then conducting. Its distinctive Eliasian qualities were recognised only many years later by scholars who wished to keep Elias's ideas alive. The research was originally for Scotson's MA thesis which Elias supervised. Scotson was a teacher and youth leader in the community that was investigated. Under Elias's co-authorship, the status of the 'outsiders' could be equated with 'less civilised', thus establishing a link with Elias's own major theory. Elias also became known (in a negative way) for his 'lost Young Worker Project', which involved qualitative interviews during 1962–1964 with around 900 young people in Leicester. The interviews remained unanalysed until successors at Leicester University retrieved and made use of some of the material (most recently by Goodwin and O'Connor, 2006).

It was not until 1969 that Elias's main book, his magnum opus, *The Civilizing Process* (Elias, 1939/2000), was first published in English and republished in German, and the author's current reputation began to spread. As already indicated, many though not all Eliasians are sociologists of sport. Elias is one of the very few major theorists (if he qualifies) who did write about sport and leisure, but this was only during his official retirement, which lasted from 1962 until 1990. In 1982 his admirers created the Norbert Elias Foundation (www.norberteliasfoundation.nl), which holds regular conferences and publishes a newsletter and an online journal, *Human Figurations*, but its main project, now completed, has been to publish or republish all Elias's work. The publisher is the University College Dublin Press.

The key terms that always signal Elias's influence are civilising process, and figurational or process sociology.

Career

Norbert Elias was born in 1897 and educated in Breslau, now called Wroclaw, in Poland since 1945, but in Prussia (Germany) before the First World War. Norbert's father was a Jewish textile businessman. Norbert attended *Gymnasium*, then served in the German army during the First World War, but suffered a nervous breakdown and was discharged as medically unfit in 1917. He then restarted his academic career in Breslau studying philosophy, psychology and medicine at the city university, and graduated in 1924 with a DPhil. dissertation in philosophy which was titled 'Idea and Individual'. He then turned to sociology, faced financial problems when his family's savings were eliminated by inflation, and started work on his habilitation dissertation, first at Heidelberg under Alfred Weber (1868–1958), the younger brother of Max Weber. In 1929 Elias moved to Frankfurt's Institute for Social Research (see Chapter 7) with Karl Mannheim, who had unofficially become his main mentor at Heidelberg. Elias's habilitation thesis was completed quickly in 1933 because both Mannheim and Elias realised as soon as Hitler gained power that they would need to build their academic careers elsewhere. Elias's thesis was originally titled 'The Man of the Court' (but is sometimes translated as 'The Court Society'). Its publication was to be long delayed. This was mainly because, on account of his Jewish descent and advocacy of Zionism, Elias left Germany in 1933 (like other members of the Frankfurt School and their institute; see Chapter 7). In the first instance Elias lived in Paris, but from 1935 onward settled in Britain, where he completed an expanded two-volume version of his habilitation thesis which was published in German in Switzerland in 1939, under a title which was translated into English as *The Civilizing Process*, but would probably be more accurately translated as 'The Process of Civilisation'. After 1935 Elias held temporary posts at the London School of Economics, which moved to Cambridge at the outbreak of the Second World War, at which point Elias was interned for eight months (as were all German nationals), though he ended the war working for British intelligence. He obtained his first ever secure academic post at Leicester University in 1954 at the age of 57. He was not influential among either staff or students (except Eric Dunning). In the 1950s in Britain Elias's type of sociology was regarded as 'the past'. The theories of Durkheim, Marx and Weber were being used, but their type of sociology was no longer being practised. Sociologists at Leicester and elsewhere in Britain, as in America, were studying their own society. 'Historical sociology' had become a tiny and unfashionable specialism. In 1962 (aged 65) Elias formally retired, then worked in Ghana for two years. Afterwards he remained in or around the Leicester department until 1978, after which he made Amsterdam his home and continued to be professionally active for the rest of his life. He never married, and retained the lifestyle of a graduate student throughout his later life: always reading, always learning more, always writing. His theory is easy to summarise, partly because Elias never changed his mind. He was not swept along by changing fashions in European sociology.

As explained above, Elias's main book, *The Civilizing Process*, had been first published in German in Switzerland in 1939, then was virtually ignored until it was translated into English and republished in English and German in 1969, after which Elias's profile strengthened and his reputation began to spread, initially in Germany and the Netherlands, where he became an academic celebrity and a much-sought visiting lecturer. He accumulated academic and civic honours. In Germany he was celebrated as an outstanding intellectual who had eventually triumphed despite the progress of his academic career being delayed for over forty years by the Nazi episode in Germany's history. Elias continued to work on books and papers, some published during his lifetime, the rest posthumously, until his death in 1990. By then the Norbert Elias Foundation had been created and his reputation was still becoming stronger and spreading more widely.

Elias's social theory

The civilising process

The Civilizing Process is a history of German society from around AD 800, the era of Charlemagne (742–814), until the end of the nineteenth century, but the focus is on changes since the end of the Middle Ages which accompanied the strengthening of the Prussian state in which Frederick the Great (who ruled 1748–1786) was the great national hero. However, Elias's book is not political history, but about the lives of the German people, especially the upper and middle classes. The book is not about sport, which simply does not feature save for a brief reference to boxing. Like Weber, who had lived a generation earlier, Elias was seeking a trend that could account for as many as possible of the changes in Europe's economic, political and social life since the Middle Ages. Elias claimed that this trend, his 'central theory', was not rationalisation (or the division of labour or the rise of capitalism), but what he called 'the civilising process'. During this period Europeans had increasingly regarded themselves as becoming more civilised, more cultured – more so than their forebears, and much more so than more primitive, often barbarous, people in other parts of the world. Elias was not endorsing the view that Europeans were better, but providing an account and explanation of the changes that were involved, and how and why Europeans started and continued to regard themselves as 'more civilised'.

Elias argued that behaviour had become increasingly constrained and controlled, and that this could be seen in sexual behaviour, table manners, control of bodily functions, toilet practices and forms of speech. The degree of control required to avoid public expressions of repugnance had risen. Personalities had been reshaped accordingly, internalising control and restraint, and generating feelings of shame if a person lapsed into uncivilised conduct. Most of the evidence in The Civilizing Process is from the courts that were created by German princes and other aristocrats who built grand palaces surrounded by ornate, carefully designed gardens in the seventeenth and eighteenth centuries (see Fulbrook, 1991). Within these courts there was an increasing differentiation of ranks, each with a pre-scribed style of dress, courtly conduct, and correct seating and manners at the dining table. Thresholds for experiencing shame and embarrassment were tightened. During this period there was also an expansion of an edu-cated middle class composed of civil servants and court officials, all with prescribed modes of dress and appropriate behaviour towards other ranks. Elias related these developments to the strengthening of the Prussian state, which came to monopolise the use of force and guaranteed order within its territory. Given this context, social life could become increasingly civilised. The process, the spread of civilisation, was seen as starting at the top in the courts of princes and other aristocrats, then spreading out-wards. Those at the top regarded themselves as more civilised than lower ranks. Peasants remained relatively uncivilised.

For readers since 1945 a major problem with the civilising process, Elias's historical master trend, has been that up to the beginning of the twentieth century it was possible to see this process spreading through-out the 'large Germany' which included the Austro-Hungarian Empire, and thence throughout the whole of Europe. Prussia had been a growing and increasingly influential European power, arguably a civilising force, for the previous 250 years. It is far more difficult to map Elias's master trend onto the twentieth century, with its two world wars, the rise then eclipse of fascism and communism, and social trends in affluent Western socie-ties after 1945, when young people began challenging constraints on social behaviour. Therefore, in his later work Elias stressed how civilisation had always been a fragile process, and that there had always been backward lurches (Elias, 2013). Even so, he felt that he had correctly identified the master trend in modern European history. Durkheim's division of labour had occurred within strong states in which people could rely on fellow citizens following rules and behaving towards each other in civilised ways. Max Weber's rationalisation had completely overlooked the emotional control and restraint that were involved. Marx had clearly been wrong. The main trend in Europe since the Middle Ages had been the strengthen-ing of nation states within which citizens were able to lead civilised lives. Revolutions occurred only when states collapsed as in Russia in 1917, or were seriously weakened, as in Germany following its eventual defeat in the First World War. These backward lurches were proving to have been temporary interruptions in the civilising process. However, if necessary, Elias was willing to revise his version of the historical master trend. He attached greater importance to the 'figurational' or 'processual' character of his sociology.

Figurational or process sociology

Elias's sociology is described (by himself and others) as 'figurational', or alternatively as 'processual'. Many sociologists remain unconvinced that this is different from a great deal of non-figurational sociology which explores networks and interactive relationships. However, the key idea is that we cease trying to separate causes from effects. In accounting for the civilising process, Elias did not seek a causal equivalent of Weber's Protestant ethic or Marx's relationships of production. The idea is that all parts of a figuration influence all other parts, and that these processes can stabilise or bring about change throughout a figuration. An Eliasian figuration is a network of inter-dependent human beings. Social life is a process, not a state. Elias likened social life to a dance. A figuration is in constant flux, yet structured. The significance of any practice cannot be established by focusing intensely on that practice, but only by locating it within its figuration. 'Variables' cannot not be properly explained when snatched out of context. Also, understanding the present always requires an understanding of history. It is necessary to examine its emergence in order to understand the present form of a figuration. Leisure and all other practices have to be set within their wider figurations and understood as outcomes of historical development. Furthermore, it is impossible to separate individuals from their societies. A society consists of people. It is impossible to identify separately 'the world out there' and what people think about that world. Each is implicated in the other.

In the 1920s and 1930s Elias was battling against what were to become the dominant post-1945 trends in sociology. He was against 'variable sociology' which seeks relationships between Durkheimian social facts that have been plucked from the figurations where they belong. Elias was vehemently opposed to separating sociology, which dealt with the present, from history. Eliasians lost these battles, which is why Elias himself was a marginal figure during his career in the sociology department at Leicester University between 1954 and 1962, and why those who have kept 'the faith' up to the present day now resemble a religious cult.

Elias was also anti-philosophy, in the sense that he did not want investigations to be based on pre-adopted categories (for example, relationships of production, mechanical and organic solidarity, traditional and rational action). Rather, he wanted sociological terms to equate with the processes that were being studied and how these processes were understood by the actors within a figuration, as in the increasingly 'civilised' court societies of seventeenth- and eighteenth-century German states. In this respect, Elias advocated a commonsense sociology which spoke the language of the people who were being studied. However, Elias himself wrote for fellow intellectuals rather than any wider public, and it was the symbolic interactionists (see Chapter 8) rather than the figurationalists who were to capture sociology's 'writing everyday prose' position.

Applications in sport and leisure

At Leicester University Norbert Elias and some of his colleagues (but initially just Eric Dunning) were quick to claim a near perfect fit between the theory of the civilising process and the development of modern sports in which both Elias and some colleagues had past and present involvements as fans and players. Eric Dunning, who was to become a doyen of the sociology of sport in Britain, was initially Elias's student, then colleague, champion and co-author. Initially, Dunning was encouraged by Elias to pursue his interest in what was then (in the 1950s and 1960s) the sociologically unfashionable topic of sport. Subsequently Dunning persuaded Elias that sport was an excellent example of the civilising process. What became a Leicester group of sports sociologists noted, correctly, that it is far easier to map Elias's civilising process onto the development of modern sports than to apply Durkheim's division of labour and the shift towards organic solidarity, or Weber's rationalisation, or the expansion of capitalism, or conflict between Marxist or Weberian classes or status groups.

Until the 1970s it was only Elias's Leicester colleagues who knew about the civilising process and figurational or processual sociology. Elias's wider reputation at that time was associated with *The Established and the Outsiders* (Elias and Scotson, 1965), and among youth researchers, with the 'lost Young Worker Project'. However, it was Elias's central theory, the civilising process and its applications to sport, that attracted some of Elias's Leicester colleagues. So Elias's social theory was used initially, in post-1950s sociology, in the study of sport. The issues in this chapter concern the theory's value in the study of sport and the rest of leisure, and also whether the theory deserves wider attention and use. This is the reverse of the situation with all the other theorists in this book. The other theories are used elsewhere, so the issue in each of the relevant chapters is what the theories can contribute in the study of sport and leisure. Elias's theory is already widely used in the sociology of sport. Leicester was the main centre where this sub-discipline within sociology (the sociology of sport) flourished until the 1990s, when sport studies became a popular student option and spread into most UK universities. Leicester then became an important source of scholars who took their specialism to other universities, and carried Elias's theory with them.

Applied to sport, the core Eliasian argument is that the progress of civilisation requires individuals to exercise increasing control over their public behaviour. They need to restrain expressions of their true feelings and emotions. Therefore, they need an outlet – a domain that will perform

Talcott Parsons' latency function. Sports seem to mesh perfectly. Whether as players or fans, people can be passionate and relatively unrestrained – hence, Eliasians claim, the late nineteenth-century coincidence of industrialisation and urbanisation on the one hand, and the invention of modern sports on the other. Sports are said to offer the excitement that is missing, that people are required to forgo, in the rest of their lives (Elias and Dunning, 1986). Simultaneously, sports themselves have become more civilised. They are regulated by rules that eliminate, or at least reduce, risks of death or serious injury. Players and fans alike are required to exercise some restraint, and sports are scheduled for times and are confined to spaces that are compatible with industrial and urban life. All this is possible without sacrificing the excitement of sport. All these trends are seen as part of the same changing figuration. Eliasian writers have coined the term 'sportification' to refer to the enhanced importance of sports in modern civilised societies (for example, Pfister, 2007).

Elias's civilising thesis is more rarely applied, but it can just as easily be applied to other leisure activities (see Dunning and Rojek, 1992). Maybe (but see below) sports sociologists have too easily been allowed to capture Elias. They certainly tend to exaggerate the extent to which modern populations rely on sport to inject excitement into their lives. Sport is different from most other leisure activities in the small size of its core of dedicated fans and players relative to the much larger number of lower-key followers. In any case, participation in most sports is not best described as exciting or emotional. Training is usually hard grind. Popular entertainment on screens (large and small) allows viewers to identify with the characters' outrageous behaviour and the emotions they express. Listeners can become fully absorbed in music and allow the sounds and lyrics to express their feelings. On holidays there is the excitement of going to places unknown and being able to switch on holiday identities. The Internet has created opportunities to do this every day. Sport is one example, but leisure offers many other opportunities to 'let ourselves go', always within limits.

However, the big problem with the civilising thesis, whether applied to just sport or the whole of modern leisure, is history. We saw earlier that Elias's civilising trend ran into problems during the twentieth century when Europe erupted in wars and barbarism. In the twenty-first century the world's most advanced and supposedly civilised states have engaged in shock and awe warfare. They have tortured and imprisoned alleged enemies of the state indefinitely without any due process. The Elias thesis can accommodate such developments by treating the civilising trend as constantly fragile and recognising that de-civilising lurches are possible. It has also been possible to argue that the civilising process has always been uneven between countries and groups within countries. Late twentieth-century football hooliganism could be explained (hypothetically) in terms of certain (lower) social strata continuing to behave in ways that the majority no longer found acceptable (Dunning et al., 1988). Researchers were also able to show that hooliganism itself was rule-governed, thus making serious injury and damage unlikely (Marsh et al., 1978). However, to retain credibility, the civilising thesis must be able to claim a long-term macro-trend towards more civilised, emotionally restrained conduct, and therefore a growing need for emotional outlets as supplied by sports and other forms of leisure. Also, to continue to make a major contribution to our understanding of sports and the rest of leisure, the civilising thesis must mesh with continuing major trends and tendencies.

What, if anything, does the Elias theory tell us about the invention of so many new sport competitions since the late twentieth century to satisfy the appetite of 24/7 multi-channel television? The Internet has become a space where any taste can be indulged. Across the whole of leisure it can be argued that, contrary to Elias, the public has become more tolerant of diversity in forms of dress, modes of dancing, the use of alcohol and recreational drugs, and how and where it is acceptable to eat and drink. Wouters (2011) argues that present-day permissiveness, which he calls 'informalisation', is actually more demanding of self-control than was previously necessary. People can spend much time and money in cultivating casual appearances. They are required to remain in control while consuming alcohol liberally. Informalisation might be construed as further evidence of the onward march of the civilising process. However, a theory that is compatible with any development ends up failing to explain anything.

In any case, the historical fit between Elias's civilising process and the development of modern sports was never as close as Eliasians have claimed. The late nineteenth-century spate of sport inventions did not coincide with more detailed rules governing courtly behaviour. It coincided with the enlargement of industrial workforces and urban populations. Behaviour in mines, factories and dockyards was rule-governed, but workplace and urban neighbourhood cultures were unruly. They were not more civilised in the Eliasian sense than the rural communities that they replaced.

Sports researchers who claim to be practising Elias's figurationalism are rarely doing anything of the sort. They invariably restrict themselves to the development of sport figurations, possibly wider leisure figurations, but this was not Norbert Elias's agenda for sociology. Genuine Eliasian figurations extend into all areas of the actors' lives. In a global age, they extend worldwide. The goal, applied to leisure, requires an authoritative grasp of all current and historically relevant features of the societies that are considered. Setting a specific sporting practice within just the current wider sport figuration is insufficient. It may distinguish sociologists from other sports researchers, but it is just currently conventional sociology. All sociology is figurational in the limited sense of setting the events and practices on which it focuses in some wider context.

Conclusions

Eliasian sociology is incredibly ambitious. It is classical, nineteenth- and early twentieth-century European theory. It belongs alongside Comte, Durkheim, Marx and Weber in seeking to grasp and explain the direction of historical change, though following Weber, its ambitions have been confined geographically to Europe, and temporally in going back no earlier than the Middle Ages.

After 1945 sociology changed. It focused on the sociologists' own societies and changes that were occurring in the present. In the 1920s and 1930s Elias was a man of his time. When his magnum opus and main theory, the civilising process, became widely known following its republication in 1969, Elias was a throwback. He was resisting the academic fragmentation that was beginning while he was still based in Germany. In effect, he wanted to retain much of history, and also much of economics and political science, within his brand of sociology. Elias was born too late, and his main work became widely known far too late, for him to become recognised as a founder of modern sociology. His influence tends to have remained within a 'cult' of Eliasians, most of whom focus on sports (Liston, 2011), rather than being widespread throughout sociology (see Gabriel and Mennell, 2011), though he also appeals to others who regret that mainstream social theory has abandoned the ambitions of the classical sociologists. Elias was steadfast. He refused to follow the latest fashions. This is a quality that his followers find admirable.

By the time Elias was appointed to a permanent career job at Leicester in 1954, sociology academics were not expected to spend years on major books about whole societies, or groups of countries and their histories. Support was available only for shorter-term projects such as the community study that Scotson conducted in Winston Parva. The special Eliasian treatment is said by Elias's followers to be evident in how the research related the residents' behaviour to their emotions, as well as the more and less civilised contrast with which the established 'insiders' kept themselves apart from the newcomers, the 'outsiders'. Similarly, the 'Young Worker Project' was intended to identify emotional strains that school-leavers experienced in making the transition into the adult world of work. The failure of the fieldwork to find evidence of any such widespread strains was one reason why a full analysis and report from the project were never completed.

Another of Elias's problems is that many of his ideas have been expressed using alternative terms, and have entered sociology and the study of sport and leisure independently. Sigmund Freud (1856–1939) pre-dated Elias in arguing that the advance of civilisation required instincts (libido) to be subjected to tighter control than in the past (Freud, 1930). Max Weber's concept of rationalisation illuminates how the operations of governments and large business corporations have become more orderly and predictable, and therefore exclude the excitement that accompanies unexpected emotional eruptions. Does the concept of 'figuration' add anything to our ability to treat social systems as networks of inter-dependent and interacting parts, or the progressive division of labour creating functional inter-dependences? Elias offers new concepts: civilising process, figuration and processual sociology. The big question is whether these terms really offer anything beyond what can be known using more familiar (in sociology) concepts.

Elias was not an admirer of Talcott Parsons, but functionalist and figurational sociology share features in common. According to functionalist and figurational conceptualisations, power is generated within a system, network or figuration, exercised with consent, and drains away once consent is withdrawn. There are no Eliasian or functionalist equivalents to the power that arises from control of the means of production, or occupancy of command positions in bureaucracies, which enable one group to impose its will on others. The ongoing process of civilisation depended, according to Elias, on states monopolising violence, which enabled citizens to treat each other civilly, with trust, which was in everyone's interests. This has been a further problem for Elias's advocates. Since the 1950s, with Talcott Parsons and functionalism falling out of favour, there has been a preference for conflict theories which highlight how one group exploits and subjugates others rather than a theory about the spread of civilised conduct by all towards all.

Another of Elias's problems has been that by the time his work was becoming widely known (from the 1970s), he had new competitors for influence in sociology. These have included Pierre Bourdieu (see Chapter 10), whose actors enter various 'fields' equipped with different amounts and types of economic, social, cultural and symbolic capital, and also Michel Foucault (see Chapter 9), a French philosopher whose influence throughout all the social sciences and humanities continues to spread in the twenty-first century. Foucault is the sole scholar since the Second World War who has become a widely acclaimed social theorist by reinterpreting European history since the Middle Ages in ways that open new insights into the present. As we shall see in Chapter 9, Foucault has commanded attention because he offers a startlingly new interpretation of trends since the Middle Ages. Elias may impress, but he does not startle. Elias's supporters need to pause. His main works have now been available for almost fifty years. Why is sport still the sole sub-discipline in sociology within which Elias is likely to feature as a major theorist?

chapter 7

Critical theory, the Frankfurt School and Jürgen Habermas (1929–)

Introduction

Germany has been the main source of the social theorists in this book. It produced Karl Marx, Max Weber, Norbert Elias and the main critical theorists in the present chapter. Ludwig Gumplowicz lived in Krakow, which was part of Austria at the time, and can be regarded as German. Ulrich Beck, who features in Chapter 11, was another German. France is second in terms of producing major social theorists – Auguste Comte, Arthur de Gobineau and Emile Durkheim have already featured. Michel Foucault and Pierre Bourdieu (Chapters 9 and 10) were also French. The USA was the home of Talcott Parsons, source of symbolic interactionism and its main pioneers (see Chapter 8), and also the most recent versions of modernisation theory (Chapter 12). It always assists in understanding a theorist if we understand the national context within which he lived and worked (as noted previously, there are no female theorists in this book). These contexts enable us to understand why Europe and the USA have produced rather different kinds of social theory. Germany and France's position at the core of modern European history is the most likely explanation of their exceptional theoretical productivity.

After the First World War Europe became a continent of nation states, and as the title of the United Nations implies, during the twentieth century the nation state became accepted as the normal sovereign political unit.

Before 1914 Europe was a continent of empires. The Atlantic seaboard nations (Britain, the Netherlands, France, Spain and Portugal) had (and in some cases had already begun to lose) mainly overseas empires. The rest of continental Europe was divided between the Austro-Hungarian, Russian and Ottoman empires, plus Germany. The Austro-Hungarian Empire (ruled from Vienna, and so really Austrian) extended to the shores of the Mediterranean through the West Balkans, and eastward into part of present-day Ukraine. The Ottomans ruled most of the Middle East and, at one time, the Eastern Balkans (Bulgaria and Romania), plus Serbia and present-day Macedonia and Montenegro, Greece and Albania. The Russian Empire had been extended into the present-day Baltic States, most of Ukraine, the Caucasus and Central Asia. The unity of all these empires was threatened throughout the nineteenth century by the rise of nationalism, and overseas empires were shrinking in the face of independence movements. Germany was different among the European nations. German nationalism drew together former separate German states under the leadership of Prussia, and a unified state was formally created in 1871. At the time this was regarded as a small Germany. A larger Germany would have included additional territories with mainly German-speaking populations. An aim of Germany that led to the Second World War was to create a larger Germany. In practice, the already small Germany had lost territory following the First World War. Prior to 1914 there were border disputes between all the European empires, most notably over the status of Bosnia-Herzegovina, which Austria had controversially annexed, and small states needed to ally and gain protection from a larger power. Britain and France formally declared war on Germany in 1914 when German troops marched into Belgium, whose territorial integrity they had guaranteed. The German army was en route for France, which it intended to defeat before confronting Russia. France had a different but equally turbulent modern history. Following the French Revolution in 1789, the country experienced over a century of monarchists confronting republicans and secularists confronting Roman Catholics, all alongside border disputes with the ever-stronger Germany.

During the nineteenth century all the West European countries began to experience industrialisation and urbanisation. So did the USA, alongside massive waves of immigration. This was the 'melting pot' that produced the social theory (symbolic interactionism) in Chapter 8. The 'melting pot' also became the world's strongest power – economically and militarily – and this was the twentieth-century context that became the main source of the modernisation theory in Chapter 12. Throughout the nineteenth century European countries were experiencing demands for the democracy which already existed in America (for white males). European governments were being challenged by pressure from below. In Britain, the nation which led in industrialisation, pressure from below led to a gradual widening of the franchise. This was the context in which Britain became the major source of original modern political thought – utilitarianism, and the philosophies of modern conservatism and liberalism. It was also at the forefront of economic thought. Scotland was the home of Adam Smith (1723–1790), who is regarded as a forefather of modern economics. The Cambridge professor Alfred Marshall (1842–1924) is generally regarded as the founder of the modern discipline of economics, and John Maynard Keynes (1883–1946), another Cambridge don, is widely regarded as the greatest economist of the first half of the twentieth century. France's 150 years of constitutional instability after 1789, when the French Revolution began, was the context in which Auguste Comte and Emile Durkheim lived and worked. The main nineteenth- and twentieth-century debate in Germany was rather different: it was about the character of the centralised German state, in which power, prior to the First World War, was exercised by the kaiser and a class of aristocrats. The young Marx wanted to give power to the people, later to the proletariat. Max Weber wanted to bring the state bureaucracy under genuine democratic control. His progressive politics (in a German context) made Weber a suitable member of the German delegation that negotiated the 1919 Treaty of Versailles.

The Frankfurt School

The Frankfurt School is the name given to the work undertaken at the Institute of Social Research which opened in Frankfurt in 1923. Its leading researchers were Marxists and Jews, and they and their institute relocated to New York after Hitler took control in Germany in 1933. Norbert Elias and Karl Mannheim (who had become Elias's mentor) were at Frankfurt for a brief period, but they were not part of the Frankfurt School. The original members of the Frankfurt School included Theodor Adorno, Walter Benjamin, Eric Fromm, Max Horkheimer and Herbert Marcuse. The institute, and some of its original members, returned to Frankfurt in 1949. The institute formally closed in 1969, but its intellectual legacy has remained alive, principally up to the present day through the work of Jürgen Habermas.

Germany was in crisis throughout the 1920s. The country had been humiliated by defeat in war, the subsequent loss of territory and the reparations imposed by the Versailles Treaty. The entire political class was discredited. Unemployment was high throughout, and in the early 1920s there was a bout of hyper-inflation which liquidated savings held in the national currency. Norbert Elias's family was among those whose wealth disappeared. This experience is said to have made a lasting impact (fear of inflation) on the German national psyche. New political movements were formed – fascist and communist – which marched and fought on the streets. We now know that the crisis conditions were resolved only when the National Socialist (Nazi) Party achieved power in 1933. All dissent was then crushed. Until then, Germany had been a seething hotbed of social and political thought.

The Frankfurt Institute was the main centre for original Marxist thinking. Chapter 4 explained how it seemed necessary to examine how capitalism had changed since Marx's lifetime, to ask why it was proving so difficult to mobilise the working class for socialism, and whether the Bolsheviks were creating a genuine Marxist state in Russia. European fascists were vehemently anti-communist. Their ideology was nationalist, and defended rule by elites that represented the nation. Anti-intellectualism was another feature of fascism, but these movements could draw support from Europe's 'elite theorists', as they became known. These were all Germans and Italians, principally Wilfredo Pareto (1848–1923), Robert Michels (1876–1936) and Gaetano Mosca (1858–1941), who all argued, for different reasons, that rule by elites was inevitable and democracy simply could not work. In this book Max Weber has been placed alongside Karl Marx, but he can alternatively be read alongside the elite theorists: pessimistic, but still hopeful that the German government and state bureaucracy could be brought under democratic control. Throughout this period the ideas of Friedrich Nietzsche (1844–1900) were influential. He had been critical of how trends in nineteenth-century Europe were suppressing the Dionysian (instinctive, impulsive) in favour of the Apollonian (controlled, disciplined) side of human nature, and how this was preventing the emergence of modern equivalents of the exceptionally talented and innovative leaders (the supermen) of the past.

As well as developing Marxist thought, the Frankfurt School was also one European centre for debates about whether objectivity was possible in the social sciences. Vienna was another such centre. Was Marxism objectively more correct than rival theories? Max Weber had argued that science could be value-free, but did this mean it could be objectively true? Immanuel Kant (1724–1804), the revered German philosopher, had argued that all human knowledge about the wider world was 'phenomenal' (things as they appear) and that mind-free knowledge of things as they really are, which he called 'nuomena', was impossible. During the twentieth century Alfred Schütz (1899–1959), an Austrian-born Jew, but living in America from 1935 onward, had been applying this doctrine (known as phenomenology) to the social sciences. As explained above, Karl Mannheim (1893–1947) was based briefly at the Frankfurt Institute, to where he was followed by Norbert Elias, before eventually after 1933 both moved to Britain while most of their Frankfurt colleagues headed for America. While in Germany, Mannheim had become a founder of the sociology of knowledge, which explains how all knowledge, including sociological knowledge, is socially constructed.

critical theory and Jürgen Habermas

Mannheim (1936) argued that different groups, specifically different social classes, would see the world from their own particular standpoints: that the privileged and powerful would be inclined to subscribe to 'ideologies' which justified the status quo, while the poor and powerless would be receptive to 'utopias', which could be religious or secular (such as the future promised by Marxism). Mannheim went on to argue that it was possible for intellectuals to see the world from an independent position, but did this make their knowledge objective? Phenomenologists said 'no': the illusion of objectivity among intellectuals was simply inter-subjective agreement, as among all other social groups. Karl Popper (1902–1994), the Austria-born philosopher of science, but based at the London School of Economics from 1945 onward, argued that what were taken to be true in science were simply knowledge claims (hypotheses) that were so far not disproven. If this was so, the Frankfurt School debated where this left all the sciences and their own Marxist thought (see Connerton, 1976; Held, 1980). These debates did not spread into the UK or the USA during the inter-war years. Political conditions in Britain and America were different, far more stable than in Germany and its neighbouring countries.

The Frankfurt School treated sociology, as it had developed in Europe up until the First World War, as part of an 'Enlightenment project' which had been launched during the 'age of reason' in the seventeenth and eighteenth centuries. The hope of the Enlightenment was that through reason people would understand and gain control over their environments (natural, social and political), and thereby achieve emancipation. Hegel and Comte shared this vision. So did Marx and Durkheim. However, the Frankfurt School concluded that, up until their present time, modern reasoning had become another set of controls over most people's lives. Rather than being liberated by reason and the resulting developments in science and technology, people's lives were being subjected to forever more rigorous and detailed control. This applied to people's lives at work. In addition, governments had been empowered in subjugating their citizens. The Frankfurt School sought a *critical sociology* which first of all had to be self-critical (nowadays we would say reflexive), querying its own assumptions. Their big idea was that a truly emancipatory theory would need to reject instrumental reasoning, the ends–means rational thinking that Weber had identified as the hallmark of the modern world. This use of reason enabled people to be treated as means. In so far as sociology, and Marxism, incorporated this kind of reasoning, the Frankfurt School claimed that these modes of thought were more likely to become instruments of oppression than emancipation. The Bolshevik state in Russia was an example. The Frankfurt School's search for a critical theory was unfinished business when its members dispersed. Subsequently they concentrated on their critiques of capitalism and sought explanations of the appeal of fascism. However, their quest for a critical theory was taken up by a younger German sociologist, Jürgen Habermas.

Jürgen Habermas (1929–)

Jürgen Habermas is a German sociologist/philosopher/historian whose ideas, like Foucault's (see Chapter 9), have spread through all the social sciences and humanities. Habermas was born and grew up in Düsseldorf in a staunchly Protestant household. His father was director of the Cologne Chamber of Industry and Commerce, and a Nazi sympathiser. Jürgen Habermas studied at the universities of Göttingen, Zürich and Bonn. He subsequently held posts at the universities of Heidelberg, Frankfurt and Starnberg (near Munich). During his career he has become a widely acclaimed German intellectual and recipient of numerous academic awards. His work has ranged over numerous topics, including aesthetics, religion, rhetoric and developmental psychology. In Germany he is a public intellectual whose views are reported in the media. The keywords that always denote Habermas's influence are lifeworld, public sphere, and communicative reasoning, speech and action. While a student, Habermas decided that an earlier generation of German intellectuals had failed at a crucial moment of historical reckoning when they acquiesced or became apologists for fascism. Thus Habermas chose to associate himself with German academics who fled from Germany in the 1930s, specifically the group known as the Frankfurt School.

Habermas regards himself as continuing the work of the Frankfurt School. He accepts the Frankfurt School's view that instrumental, means–end rationality is an enemy of true emancipation and that objectivity is a false goal for the social sciences. Habermas subscribes to the consensual version of truth, and locates reasoning in structures of inter-personal communication which produce their own truths. Instrumental speech, reasoning and action are contrasted with communicative speech, reasoning and action. The latter are said to take place in an *ideal speech situation* wherein equals interact with one another for their own sakes. Habermas describes such an ideal speech situation as a *public sphere*.

The Enlightenment is said originally to have created a public sphere for the bourgeoisie, and this is said to have been emancipating at the time. Previously, in feudal times, culture is said to have been 'representational' – magnificent palaces and art collections which were intended to impress all observers. Bourgeois public spheres are said to have been created all across Europe during the eighteenth century, and before that in England, in coffee houses, salons and reading clubs aided by newspapers and journals. These enabled people to exchange views among equals outside the control of the state (and churches). This was new and, at that time, emancipating for the bourgeoisie. This is said to have happened at the start of what is called 'the Enlightenment project'. In a public sphere the participants are said to develop a common *lifeworld* of shared practical and moral knowledge. According to Habermas, these lifeworlds are the sole source of knowledge that can be agreed to be correct, both factually and morally.

From the basis of these lifeworlds people are said to create institutions (political parties, businesses and so on) in which action is governed by 'instrumental reason'. Here, people are treated as means, as commodities, not for their own sakes, but to enable one party to achieve its ends. Institutions owe their legitimacy to their grounding in lifeworlds. This enables people to feel that institutions belong to and are acting for them. However, Habermas argues that institutions, ruled by instrumental reason, are not only able to decouple themselves from lifeworlds and communicative reason, but may actually colonise these lifeworlds – a condition said to characterise present-day societies. Habermas follows the original members of the Frankfurt School in arguing that the capitalist mass media have turned the public into passive consumers. The operation of capitalist mass media is contrasted with the publications that facilitated the exchange of views in the bourgeois public spheres of the eighteenth century. Simultaneously, Habermas argues that welfare states have squeezed the true public sphere. Political debates have become between competing claims for state resources rather than attempts to build a consensus (an agreed version of truth). Political parties have replaced participation with representative democracy. Parties attempt to 'buy' votes with promises to different interest groups. Systems are thereby said to have supplanted or colonised lifeworlds.

The outcomes are said to be individuals who feel anxious and that their lives are meaningless, disconnected from their macro-social contexts, and a 'legitimation crisis' in the entire social, economic and political systems (Habermas, 1962, 1976, 1984). The solution, according to Habermas, is to recreate and enlarge the public sphere through new social movements – for peace, environmental sustainability, gender and race equality, and so forth. Habermas does not accept that the Enlightenment project has failed or run its natural course: it is simply unfinished business. Habermas believes that the only kind of truth that matters is truth established among equals – moral truths and practical truths. He remains optimistic that the world can be transformed into a more humane, just and egalitarian place because of humanity's capacity for reason.

The proper role for an emancipatory sociology, given this analysis, is to embed itself in movements that are rebuilding the public sphere. Habermas's own books are not exercises in this emancipatory sociology. He is a public intellectual who speaks beyond his academic communities, but this is different from practising public sociology. Habermas's emancipatory sociology is for others who will 'do as I say, not as I do'. Habermas is highly erudite, not easy to read, but his ideas have down-to-earth implications for the practice of sociology, and possibly most of all for sport and leisure researchers.

Public sociology

Habermas has always been basically a philosopher, a pure theorist. Public sociology is perhaps best exemplified in the intentions (if not yet in the achievements) of Michael Burawoy. He was educated in Britain, qualified in mathematics at Cambridge University in 1968, went to work as a personnel officer in a Zambia copper mine operated by the Anglo-American Corporation, took an MA and moved towards sociology while in Zambia, and has been USA-based from the 1970s onwards. While gathering material for his PhD in Chicago he was employed as a machine operator in an engineering workshop. Towards the end of the 1980s he was employed in a steel works in communist Hungary. Burawoy describes such periods of employment as 'summer vacation jobs'. In the early 1990s he was employed in a furniture plant in an Arctic region of post-Soviet Russia. Burawoy admits that he has always been regarded as an incompetent worker by shop-floor colleagues, but his methods and output have won applause in sociology.

Burawoy (2005) is a passionate advocate for a particular kind of public sociology. This is very different from what Burawoy calls 'professional sociology', where the audience comprises other sociologists. It is also different from what Burawoy calls 'policy sociology', sometimes conducted for, but always intended to influence, the policies and practices of government departments or other organisations. Ideal-typically, Burawoy's public sociology is practised in a Habermasian public sphere. Participant observation is the core research method. There is free and open dialogue with the subjects, who ideally become partners in both the production and implementation of sociological knowledge. Feminism and anti-racism in the West can be cited as successful examples of new social movements within which this kind of public sociology has been conducted. Future successes may include environmental and peace movements. The working class is still the big challenge for Michael Burawoy, and for sociology more broadly, especially neo-Marxist sociology.

Applications in sport and leisure

Habermas must interest sport and leisure scholars because leisure is the site of so many present-day public spheres. The sites of the eighteenth-century bourgeois public spheres that Habermas discussed included salons, coffee houses and reading clubs. Stephen Mennell (2003) has researched the spread of dining out in public restaurants in eighteenth-century France, and how this was accompanied by public discussions of the merits of different restaurants, restaurateurs and dishes, led by gastro-nomes (experts on gastronomy). These were all discussions among equals, united by a common interest in their own and each other's enjoyment of dining out. Today the number of public leisure spheres has multiplied – bars, cafes, sport clubs and crowds, student common rooms, book fairs, audiences at theatres, music concerts and festivals (see Giorgi et al., 2011; Spracklen and Spracklen, 2012). These are all places where people enjoy 'hanging out', sharing news and views with social equals. These are sites of Habermas's communicative speech and action. Engagement is for its own sake. The rewards are 'intrinsic', and this term is frequently used in definitions of leisure.

Karl Spracklen treats communicative speech and action (in Habermasian terms) as the definitive feature of leisure (Spracklen, 2009, 2011, 2013). He argues that this has been the core, essential meaning and purpose of 'time out' throughout history. However, communicative speech and action are not confined to leisure time and activities as ordinarily understood. Habermasian public spheres can be created within workplaces, in working time, and in schools and colleges. Also, much leisure (again, as ordinar-ily understood) is spent consuming commercially produced goods and services and being passively entertained. Television is still by far the most common use of leisure time. The dominant rationality is instrumental. Communicative speech and action can, but do not necessarily, feature in leisure. Nor are they confined to leisure. Therefore, contrary to Spracklen, they cannot be definitive features of leisure. Spracklen is on stronger ground when he adds that leisure times and spaces have been, and can still be, sites of struggle against the instrumental rationalities of powerful groups – priests, politicians and nowadays also commercial businesses. Marxists, including the members of the Frankfurt School, have noted the interest of modern capitalist classes in encouraging uses of free time that can become sources of profit and which also break up public spheres in which workers might congregate and develop revolutionary ideas. Early twentieth-century trade unions and socialist parties often made provisions for their members' leisure, partly because they believed that shared recreation would facilitate informal and formal radical education (see Snape and Pussard, 2013). The Frankfurt School added that the capitalist culture industry atomised audiences for music and other forms of entertainment, thereby destroying working-class public spheres. However, there are plenty of public leisure spheres that co-exist alongside the capitalist mass media, and which have never been extinguished except under communism and fascism: church congregations, hobby clubs and all the other examples listed above.

Members of the Frankfurt School argued that mass entertainment pacified the working class. Habermas takes up this case, arguing that public spheres have been colonised or vaporised as the public has been split into independent consumers with money to spend on the goods and services of their choice, and votes which can be invested in the political parties and policies they favour. Most people are excluded from conversations about what to produce, how to produce it, what services to provide, and what policies political parties should offer. Thus the emancipation that began when the bourgeoisie was incorporated into the political public sphere has stalled. Habermas may be correct about the stalling, but this will not necessarily be because public spheres have gone. A question for leisure scholars is whether the present-day public spheres they study can become sites of more widespread emancipation from the instrumentalities that dominate economic life and politics.

The eighteenth-century bourgeois classes were small, concentrated in major cities, and they were much wealthier than the urban and rural masses. The salons, clubs and restaurants where they met were also used by members of the political classes. Most present-day public leisure spheres are different. They are simply places where people enjoy communicative speech and action with social equals, sharing news and views. These public spheres are separated from one another by people's diverse leisure tastes and interests. Most of the participants are not wealthy and their public leisure spheres do not create access to politicians or any other powerful groups.

However, as noted above, leisure is not the sole site of present-day public spheres. These still exist in some workplaces the lifeworlds from which trade unions and the socialist parties that they created drew support. Neighbourhoods can also be sites for the formation of public spheres within which tenants associations can be formed and from which residents can organise and campaign to protect local public facilities or open spaces (as in Castells, 1977). Maybe most of the older associations with these roots have either atrophied or become detached from the lifeworlds in which they were born, but as Habermas himself notes, new social movements are still being formed – feminist, Green, anti-war, anti-racist and many others.

The Internet has created new public spaces within which social movements can be born, though tweets, likes and other clicks need to be turned into crowds on streets and squares, or votes in ballot boxes, if they are to make a difference. Sometimes support that is mobilised using older and new media is turned into new crowds and votes for new contenders for political office, and these votes do make a difference. This happened in East and Central Europe in 1989, in Jugoslavia in 2000 (the fall of Milosevic) and in the colour revolutions in certain former Soviet republics (Georgia and Ukraine) during 2003–2005. Young people spilled from music clubs and other leisure sites where they had initially been drawn together, took to streets and squares, and toppled incumbent governments (see Beachain and Polese, 2010; Collin, 2007). All this happened without any significant contributions from any new media. More recently, austerity protests in Greece in 2011 subsequently turned into votes for Syriza. The Arab Spring of 2011 toppled rulers in Tunisia, Egypt and Yemen. The Occupy demonstrations of 2011 have changed nothing yet, but Spain's Indignados demonstrations of the same year produced Podemos, which, like Syriza in Greece, had become a serious contender for power by 2015. Research among Tunisia's young people, whose protests triggered the Arab Spring, and among Spain's Indignados found that the protestors were simply not interested in voting for any of the established political parties. They wanted a new politics. They wanted to be involved in 'conversations' in live meetings and online which would work up a consensus (Castells, 2012; Honwana, 2013). However, Habermas realised that institutions, governed by instrumental rationalities, needed to be created and remain rooted in lifeworlds if participation in free communication between equals was to make a lasting difference beyond the relevant lifeworlds. Otherwise outbursts of discontent lead to nothing more than a reshuffling of positions within existing elites, as following the colour revolutions of 2003–2005. Another of Habermas's contentions is that consensus will be the normal outcome if rational human beings engage with equals in free conversations in a public sphere, but is this likely given existing class, ethnic, gender and other divisions?.

The Frankfurt School began its search for a critical theory by posing Marxist questions. Its members sought the emancipation of the working class. Habermas took up this challenge, and transformed the central issue into how public spheres can be revived, enlarged and lead to wider economic and political emancipation. The questions for sport and leisure scholars are about how the sites and activities they study might contribute:

- They must first ask: Which socio-demographic groups' leisure is most likely to involve participation in public spheres? Is it most likely to be the leisure of young people and young adults who have not yet engaged in new family and household formation? Thereafter, is it most likely to be the upper and middle classes? These classes are now over-represented in virtually all kinds of voluntary associations, including trade unions. Working-class cultural consumption is overwhelmingly via the mass media (Bennett et al., 2009).
- The next question for sport and leisure scholars is: Whose leisure is most likely to involve participation in public spheres where the seriously wealthy, politicians and top corporate executives are present? Is

this the leisure of what Owen Jones (2014) calls 'the establishment'? If so, is the net contribution of sport and leisure to exclude the majority from setting business and political agendas?

- Davide Sterchele and Chantal Saint-Blancat (2015) have described how the Mondial Antirazzisti (Anti-Racist World Cup), an annual tournament held in Italy that takes the form of a carnivalesque sport festival, draws together hard-core football fans (Ultras), immigrants and other informal groups and individuals. The result is said to be a 'liminal' space (on the margins of people's lives and experience, where normal expectations, roles and rules of behaviour are suspended) in which discriminatory practices and stereotypes can be challenged. Sterchele and Saint-Blancat envisage the festival's anti-discriminatory practices and multi-culturalism spinning off into wider contexts. So another question for sport and leisure scholars is: Are such spin-offs from liminal leisure sites more common than such sites compartmentalising their cultures, then allowing participants to return to their normal everyday lives?

- Leisure is not the only base for public spheres which can breed politically efficacious movements. So the final question for sport and leisure scholars is: Which, if any, public leisure spheres are more empowering than other public spheres, where 'emancipation' means more than temporary release from mundane everyday life and instrumental rationalities?

It may stretch credulity to envisage (as in Carrington and McDonald, 2009) professional sports players and crowds seizing control of their clubs and triggering wider revolutions, or the 'resistance' evident in some youth cultures having such outcomes (as envisaged by contributors to Hall and Jefferson, 1976). The theory of Pierre Bourdieu (see Chapter 10) suggests that such outcomes are possible from participation in leisure activities and places, but that much will always depend on the economic and social capital, the wealth and connections, of the participants in a public leisure sphere.

Conclusions

Outside Germany, Habermas has been more difficult to relate to common-place ideas about the course of European history than any of the theorists featured in previous or forthcoming chapters. Durkheim and Parsons speak of societies that are forever becoming more complex, in which people's lives are increasingly different yet inter-dependent. Marxism highlights the division between the rich and powerful and the rest. Weber tells us that the pattern of inequalities is more complex than this, and that throughout history and in the present their ideas affect how people respond in any situation. Weber also describes a world in which life becomes increasingly rationalised – Elias would say civilised, Foucault (see Chapter 9) would say disciplined. Sport and the rest of leisure can easily be seen as incorporated and part of these wider trends and realities, or where people can escape from them. These accounts of where our present-day societies have come from and where they are heading are not difficult to grasp.

For most of his career Habermas seemed to be on a different planet, but not in Germany, where he has been a public intellectual. We need, first, to trace the search for a 'critical theory' to Germany following the First World War. Marxists had to answer why the working class was proving difficult to convince. They also had Max Weber and other 'elite theorists' who all insisted that making Germany democratic required more than abolishing the Kaiser, the titles and political and legal privileges of the aristocracy, and giving the country a formally democratic constitution and elected assembly. There were also debates about the possibility of objectivity which were not confined to Germany. What was different about Germany was that these debates had spread beyond philosophers and into social theory. Habermas took up these debates in post-Second World War Germany. He speaks of and to a society which was progressing as it emerged from the Middle Ages, when trade, industry and a bourgeoisie began to expand and the bourgeoisie was incorporated into public life, but this incorporation was not extended to the working class that industrialism began to create in the nineteenth century. Then came the twentieth century, Germany's role in the successive world wars, and how the country was led between 1933 and 1945. Were the German people misled by malevolent leaders? Or were all Germany's people, their history and culture, somehow responsible? Post-1945 social theorists in other Western countries have not been under the same compulsion to address these questions. Another peculiar feature of Germany in the immediate post-1945 decades was that it was impossible to be an avowed Marxist without being regarded as a likely enemy of the state in the Federal Republic of (West) Germany: the eastern part of the pre-war Germany was then under communist rule and hoping to spread its system westward. So although Habermas defined his own work as taking forward the legacy of Germans who had left rather than remained in Germany after 1933, specifically the work of the Frankfurt School whose members were explicitly Marxist, Habermas never defined himself in this way, was not regarded as a Marxist, and never became a hero of the left. He explained the task that confronted the post-war Federal Republic. This was to resume the Enlightenment project and enlarge the public sphere, so businesses and trade unions were to be regarded as social partners – a vocabulary that was adopted and has been retained in the 'European project' currently manifest in the European Union.

By the late twentieth century Habermas was being understood more widely, and had become fashionable outside Germany. His theory of a 'legitimation crisis' was striking chords across Europe and beyond. There was a widening divorce between the lifeworlds of the people and all big institutions – banks and transnational businesses, and governments. The hitherto major political parties were haemorrhaging members and voters. The clearest current example is the emerging European super-state on a continent where people in all countries identify more strongly with their nations, regions or religions than as Europeans. Habermas speaks to the age of new social movements, now able to form and grow rapidly online, which create new (often transnational) public spheres.

Habermas retains what, to many, appears a quaint faith in humans' common ability to reason, enabling all to become part of a big conversation from which they can create more equal societies which are experienced as just by all and as belonging to all. Self-defined Marxists are likely to argue that this is incompatible with capitalism; heirs to the elite theorists just say 'impossible'. Post-modernists, who regard modernity as a product of the Enlightenment project, declare that the liberation of reason creates multiple realities and agreement only that it is impossible for all to agree.

The issue for leisure scholars is how, if at all, they can relate to these arguments. Are sport and the rest of leisure part of Habermas's enemy, destroying public spheres and creating atomised consumers? Or is leisure where old public spheres can flourish and where new public spheres are able to grow? If so, can sport and leisure be among the forces that create Habermas's just world? Or are sport and leisure empowering only for relatively privileged strata? Are other public leisure spheres fragmenting people by taste and creating 'bubbles' in which enthusiasts can play happily while divorced from real economic and political power?

chapter 8

Herbert Blumer (1900–1987) and symbolic interactionism

Introduction

Erving Goffman (1922–1982) did not invent the term 'symbolic interactionism'. He did not even describe his work as symbolic interactionist, but more than anyone else he was responsible for promoting this kind of sociology. Herbert Blumer coined the term and laid out the rationale for symbolic interactionism, but it was Erving Goffman above all others who generated the excitement that surrounded this new sociology.

Erving Goffman was an American maverick in sociology during the 1960s and 1970s. He broke all the normal rules in sociology, but produced eleven books in a career that lasted little over twenty years and built a glittering reputation. His sociology is commonly described as dramaturgical. Goffman's first book, *The Presentation of Self in Everyday Life* (1959), was about actors coming 'on stage', playing a role and thereby managing to present themselves as they wished to be seen by an audience. Every individual could play many parts in different plays on different stages. Goffman contrasted how people can behave differently when they are front and back stage, and described techniques that they can use to display role distance (this is not the real me) and role identification (who I really am). How did Goffman do it? He never laid out his sources of evidence or the methods he used to analyse his evidence to reach his conclusions, except that he was reported as stating that *The Presentation of Self in Everyday Life* was inspired by observation of the staff in hotels while holidaying/doing fieldwork in Scotland.

All Goffman's books offered new concepts, and the concepts were rapidly adopted throughout sociology. *Asylums* (1961) introduced the 'total institution', in which people spend all their time for a short or extended period. Mental hospitals are examples, as are prisons, the military and boarding schools. *Asylums* explains how inmates become 'institution-alised', dependent on the institution, and may be rendered incapable of adjusting to life outside. *Stigma* (1964) explained how people manage 'spoiled identities' (think of paedophiles and other registered sex offend-ers). *Frame Analysis* (1974) explained how we react according to how we 'frame' a situation or event: for example, whether a comment is a joke or an attack on someone's integrity, or whether the regulation of smoking is a health or a civil liberties issue.

Although Goffman himself made no such claim, his sociology was clearly symbolic interactionist. This social theory was American in origin, but exploded into global sociology in the 1960s, inspiring a series of 'new' sociologies – of education, deviance and organisations. Symbolic inter-actionists have sometimes claimed to be building on foundations laid by Max Weber. This is on account of Weber's insistence that actors' subjec-tive states must be part of sociological explanations. However, the term 'symbolic interactionism' was coined by the American sociologist Herbert Blumer (1900–1987), who said that he was building on the work of George Herbert Mead (1863–1931). Blumer had taken over Mead's lectures at the University of Chicago on the latter's death in 1931. Talcott Parsons had decided that American sociology needed to absorb Europe's social theo-ries, and offered his own synthesis. Up to then European and American sociology had been rather different disciplines.

European and American sociology

Before 1939 European sociology was a failing project. As explained in Chapter 1, Auguste Comte is acknowledged as the founder of sociology because he coined the word. He died in 1857, and he did not leave a disci-pline that was sinking firm roots. In fact, it was not until 1895 that Europe's first university department of sociology opened and its first professor of sociology, Emile Durkheim, was appointed at Bordeaux. Sociology then began to spread, but its growth was neither rapid nor dense. From 1905 onward the subject was taught at the London School of Economics, but nowhere else in Britain until after the Second World War. Most of the soci-ology that was defined as 'classical' after 1945 had been produced outside sociology (most notably by Karl Marx and Max Weber). Sociology did not become the monarch of the social sciences that Comte and Durkheim had intended. In the early twentieth century economics and politics developed more vigorously as independent social sciences. So did history, geography and law.

European sociology was floundering. Its foundations were fragile. This was because sociology had been tied (by Comte) to a unilinear view of historical change, and the evolution of societies was supposedly coupled with the evolution of the human species. Hence social anthropology, the study of the allegedly simple societies of so-called primitive people, became allied with physical anthropology, not sociology, which studied modern people and their societies. Classical sociology was produced in an age when scientists were classifying humanity into different races. Sociology was also given in-built vulnerability by Comte's insistence that it be kept apart from 'social physics' – collecting facts about current populations and their social conditions. Friedrich Engels's research in the 1840s into the condition of the working class in England is the only example of a classical theorist (as a collaborator in creating Marxism) who personally explored the lives of people in the society in which he lived. Durkheim's study of suicide used existing statistics rather than his own original fieldwork. His book on religion was based entirely on secondary sources. Having helped to develop Marxist theory, in his later life Engels took a different, more Durkheimian approach in studying the *origins* of the family and gender relations. Researching current social conditions was left to social reformers, and their efforts became the basis for a separate academic subject that was called social administration in Britain (a title later replaced by social policy), from which classical sociology kept a clear distance. It was economics and social administration, not sociology, that helped to pave the way for the development of social democracies and welfare states in post-1945 Europe. Economics, politics and social administration, not sociology, produced the great public intellectuals of the early and mid-twentieth century.

From the 1870s onward America began to develop a different kind of sociology. Charles Horton Cooley (1864–1929) is generally regarded as the first American sociologist. He is best known for his phrase 'the looking glass self' (we see ourselves as others see us) and for coining the term 'primary group' (face-to-face groups in which all members are known to each other personally, as in families) (Cooley, 1909). William Isaac Thomas is another first-generation American sociologist who coined a phrase with which all subsequent sociologists have become familiar: 'If men define situations as real, they are real in their consequences' (Thomas, 1927). Thomas worked at the University of Chicago, which opened the first sociology department in the United States (and the world) in 1892, and launched the world's first academic sociology journal in 1895, the *American Journal of Sociology*. Chicago went on to dominate American sociology until the Second World War. The term 'Chicago School' refers to the sociologists who worked in the department during this period and the type of sociology they produced. Much of their research used the city of Chicago itself as a laboratory. They produced studies of boy gangs, hobos, taxi dance halls, and an ecological theory of city growth (see Bulmer, 1984).

As in Europe, American sociologists studied social structure and change, but as America had not experienced 'Middle Ages', the changes that they studied were ongoing. The late nineteenth and early twentieth centuries were the years of mass immigration into the USA, the rapid expansion of cities, and the transformation of the economy from one dominated by farms and small businesses into one dominated by giant corporations. These were the changes that American sociologists studied, and their sociology was an instant 'hit', not just in spreading from coast to coast and attracting students, but also in making the news. There was huge interest in Robert and Helen Lynd's successive studies of 'Middletown' (actually Muncie in Indiana) (Lynd and Lynd, 1929, 1937). The first book was about how Middletown had expanded and had become a different place during the early twentieth century. The second book examined the impact of the recession in the 1930s. Lloyd Warner and colleagues' series of books on 'Yankee City' (actually Newburyport, a New England community) also made the news with its insights into how the town's status system had changed as old money had been joined by new money made in expanding manufacturing industries, and the formation of an industrial working class (Warner and Lunt, 1942). Samuel Stouffer and colleagues' series of books *The American Soldier* also captured the nation's attention (Stouffer et al., 1949). They explained how servicemen's experiences depended on exactly how these differed from their civilian lives. Talcott Parsons decided that American sociology needed to be topped by assimilating European social theory. In turn, Europe's sociologists decided to copy the Americans and start focusing on their own societies.

This is how a new (in Europe) sociology was born during the years that followed the Second World War. This was when Europe's economies were recovering and beginning what are now recalled as 'thirty glorious years' of steady economic growth, full employment, rising real wages, narrower economic inequalities and the consolidation of welfare states. Sociology studied these changes and how they were affecting different socio-demographic groups. This sociology was popular. It attracted students, and became a standard university offer. Books written by sociologists made the news. Their message was always that life was certainly better than before 1939, but that there were new problems and further improvement was needed, especially in the lower sections of the social class structure. This type of work cried out for a different kind of theory, complementary to the theories that had comprised European sociology up to 1939, and symbolic interactionism, a gift from America, was gratefully received.

Origins and uses of symbolic interactionism

George Herbert Mead (1863–1931)

George Herbert Mead worked at the University of Chicago, alongside sociologists, but did not describe himself as one. He positioned his work correctly, not in sociology, but at the juncture between psychology and philosophy, and he developed a theory of personality in which the self was treated as a product of social interaction. Mead believed that the ability to communicate using symbols – things that stand for something else, but principally language – sets humans apart from other animals (which was not an original observation). The most important symbols humans use are words, with which sentences can be composed, thoughts expressed and ideas formulated, following which people can act intentionally. It is generally believed that this sets humans apart from all other animals, whose behaviour is a mixture of instincts, modelling (copying) and conditioned reflexes. Language enables humans to imagine things that have never existed, and therefore to invent motor cars, computers and so on. We can also imagine how we would feel and act in situations that we have never encountered. It is intermittently argued that the sounds of certain other mammals (whales, dolphins and some apes) are languages. If so, this would have enormous implications for how humans treat and relate to these mammals. It would imply that other mammals can think and develop their own understandings of humans. However, no non-humans have the kind of history that humans have constructed from their ability to think, to develop and then act upon new ideas.

Mead's original contribution was to argue that the self, meaning self-consciousness, is a product of humans' ability to use language to talk to themselves, to take on the position of another person. Thus Mead claimed that we are able to see ourselves as we think others see us. Mead argued that we internalise the outlooks of significant others on whom we are dependent, initially in most cases our parents, but that subsequently other people become 'significant' and their outlooks are merged into what Mead called an internal generalised other. This 'me' is myself as I think others see me, which can reflect on what 'I' really think and do. Similarly, an 'I' can reflect on 'me' (how I think others see me). Without a socially created 'me', there could be no 'I' – myself as I think I really am (Mead, 1934). Thus the self is treated as a social product – a product of social interaction. This interaction is with symbols, usually language.

Herbert Blumer (1908–1987)

Herbert Blumer (1969) built on these ideas. He wanted to revamp sociology. He was harshly critical of abstract theories such as Talcott Parsons's functional model of social systems. Blumer was also against reducing social life to drab statistics. He wanted sociology to be a down-to-earth subject about life as experienced by ordinary people. So did Norbert Elias (see Chapter 6), but this was not the kind of sociology that Elias himself wrote. Rather, it was the kind of sociology that the Chicago School was producing. Blumer was offering a theoretical foundation which was received enthusiastically.

Blumer endorsed Mead's observation that interaction between people is usually symbolic. These interactions are unlike the mechanical cause–effect relationships between physical objects. Thus Blumer followed Max Weber (Chapter 5), albeit from a different start-point, in insisting that social science explanations could not take exactly the same form as in the natural sciences. People code meanings they wish to convey into symbols, usually words. A receiver then decodes the message and may respond accordingly, and symbolically. Clearly, there is immense scope for misunderstanding. In jointly addressing any problem or situation, actors must somehow agree, and if necessary 'negotiate' over, 'what is actually the case'. These negotiations may have to include what each 'I' has done, thinks and feels.

Many European sociologists were unimpressed. Symbolic interactionists were failing to address 'big' issues about historical change and the macro-structure of societies. However, symbolic interactionists do not accept that they are merely filling in details and leaving the analysis of whole societies to others. Their contention is that society *is* symbolic interaction, and that all larger patterns and relationships are maintained or changed only through interactions.

There are almost as many definitions of what a society 'is' – its metaphorical 'stuff' – as there are social theorists. They disagree not only on the main drivers of historical change, and how the parts of a society are inter-connected, but also on exactly 'what' the connections are between. Emile Durkheim's 'stuff' were social facts that imposed themselves on individuals with a moral force. Talcott Parsons's societies were a type of system – a social system – grounded in a cultural system and powered by the voluntaristic actions of socialised actors. For Karl Marx (and orthodox Marxists since then) a society was composed of social relationships, and all other relationships were built upon or around relationships of production. Max Weber's societies were composed of 'social action', meaningful behaviour. Norbert Elias's societies were moving figurations. For Jürgen Habermas a society is built from modes of thought, speech and related behaviour. Further definitions of the 'stuff' about which social theorists construct their theories appear in later chapters. In the 1960s symbolic interactionism added to the litany.

New sociologies

Erving Goffman, whose work was introduced earlier, led by example in promoting symbolic interactionist research. The problem for his followers was grasping exactly what Goffman was doing. Was he simply an unusually perceptive observer of the social 'stage', an original thinker who saw things differently or that others had missed, and who could write convincingly? Goffman made dramaturgical sociology look easy. It was certainly very different to classical European sociology. It was Goffman more than anyone else who was responsible for symbolic interactionism's enthusiastic embrace by many sociologists in the 1960s and 1970s, though as noted above, there always were and still are critics who feel that focusing on minutiae misses the big picture. Another more positive view was (but no longer is) that symbolic interactionist research could develop the 'theories of the middle range' that Robert Merton (1949) hoped would fill the gap between Europe's grand social theories and the kind of detailed studies of social life at which American sociology excelled. Symbolic interactionists certainly hoped to avoid the pitfalls of abstract theory on the one side, and fact collecting for its own sake on the other, that C. Wright Mills (1959) had lambasted in his blockbuster book *The Sociological Imagination*. This apart, most sociologists knew that they were unlikely to emulate the achievements of Marx, Durkheim and Weber. They might also lack the resources, and maybe the technical expertise, to undertake large-scale quantitative investigations. Goffman-style symbolic interactionism looked like a type of sociology within the capabilities of any postgraduate student.

One of the research methods favoured by symbolic interactionists is unstructured interviewing, in which investigators explore the minds of their subjects, trying all the time not to 'lead' them. Investigators try to discover how their subjects interpret their situations, what meanings they are trying to convey through their actions, and how they appraise the outcomes. Another favoured research method is participant observation, whereby a researcher gains access (with consent or unobtrusively) to real-life situations, and to the everyday thoughts and actions of the participants. Symbolic interactionist research is commonly 'ethnographic', which means studying people in their normal habitats, and scanning the whole of their lives.

The impact of symbolic interactionism in sociology in the 1960s and 1970s was dramatic. The relevant research offered new and immediate insights into long-standing issues. The impact was so dramatic that it led to the announcement of a stream of 'new' sociologies. Deviance was shown to be a label that some groups applied to certain acts, though other groups might not regard the relevant acts as wrong. Drug use was a favourite example. It was thereby shown that publicly labelling offenders as deviants had predictable consequences, including secondary deviance. Those labelled were likely to be excluded from law-abiding social networks, pushed into the company of other 'deviants' (those so labelled), thus not merely reinforcing, but amplifying the likelihood of further deviance. Here was a more plausible explanation of repeat offending than certain individuals being born evil or depraved beyond repair by early socialisation (Becker, 1963). Working-class children's failure in school was shown (or argued) to arise not from intrinsic cultural or inborn deficits, but rather (or also) from teachers interpreting the children's presenting cultures as deprived, then lowering their expectations of and demands on the children (Keddie, 1973).

Phenomenology and ethnomethodology

There has never been any doubt that two parties can view the same situation in different ways, but by making this into a central feature of social life, symbolic interactionism forced social researchers, as well as theorists such as the Frankfurt School and Jürgen Habermas (see Chapter 7), to engage with phenomenology. Alfred Schütz (1972) argued that the objectivity claimed by scientists is merely an example of a 'natural attitude', treating inter-subjective agreement as objective truth. In other words, the theories about 'things out there' of chemists, biologists and sociologists have exactly the same status as everyone else's common sense. Whether sociology can escape from this downgrading, and the implications if no escape is possible, remain matters for debate: there is no agreement. Critical theorists decided that they needed to be self-critical, querying their own assumptions. Others claim that a 'double hermeneutic' is required. This means taking into account the content of the investigator's mind, and also the minds of the investigator's subjects. Pierre Bourdieu (see Chapter 10) claimed to be achieving this.

Ethnomethodologists took a different course. They asked what special research methods were required to explore what Alfred Schütz called natural attitudes (everyday common sense). These methods were called ethnomethodology by the American sociologist Harold Garfinkel (1917–2011). A basic premise is that there is no point in simply asking people how they perceive a situation. Natural attitudes are taken for granted. They do not need to be vocalised, and may well be wholly or partly subconscious (Garfinkel, 1967). Ethnomethodological research appears weird to most observers. Experimenters may deliberately disrupt normal expectations, like behaving as if they were lodgers when in their own homes. The intention is to uncover assumptions about how co-resident family members will behave. Subjects may be asked repeatedly to explain their answers following an initial question such as 'Why are you at university?' Eventually people cannot explain: they become frustrated and annoyed. They insist that the questioner must surely understand what they mean. This is the point at which, it is claimed, the natural attitude has been revealed. One research method that has spread from ethnomethodology into general sociology is conversation analysis. The issue for ethnomethodologists is how orderly conversations are possible. What rules are being followed? How do participants agree to 'take turns', indicate that a turn is ending or that it has gone on for long enough? How are conversations drawn to a conclusion? How do the conversationalists know and agree that their conversation has ended? Recordings of natural conversations are analysed to identify implicit rules that are being followed. This kind of research may appear offbeat, but ethnomethodologists insist that they are uncovering the bedrock on which all social life rests.

For now we can observe that most symbolic interactionist research neither engages with phenomenology nor uses ethnomethodology. The complete symbolic interactionist research agenda is lengthy. Full explanation requires an investigator to ask:

- how a subject believes he is seen by others;
- how he sees himself;
- how he believes others interpret his actions;
- how he intends his actions to be interpreted;
- what the actions mean to the subject.

Then, of the other interacting party, a corresponding set of questions needs to be asked. Then a time dimension needs to be added. How does their interaction change the subject and the other?

Most symbolic interactionist research throws a spotlight on only some of these processes. This is why it has been possible for the volume of this type of sociological research to expand so hugely. The new sociologies of the 1960s and 1970s typically asked, and only asked, for example, how their subjects were affected by being labelled as deviant or academically less able. Alternatively, investigators explored resistance to being labelled by others. Sometimes researchers explored negotiations over 'What is actually the case?'

Applications in sport and leisure

This type of sociology is easily applied in sport and leisure studies. Researchers can explore the meanings different groups attach to leisure in general, and to specific leisure activities in which they do and do not take part. They can also explore how these meanings are negotiated with other participants, and with wider networks of significant others. In these ways it has been possible for small-scale studies to yield big findings:

- Sheryl Clark (2012) has investigated how interactions among teenage girls, teachers and coaches lead to some girls being regarded as, and feeling that they are, 'good at sport', while others are dissuaded from developing sporting feminine identities. Her research explains how, while at primary school, many girls enjoy and therefore play sports. Then in secondary school, and especially if they approach sports clubs, they learn how important it is to be good at sport. Others are liable to be defined as non-sporting. Here, we have an explanation of the attrition from participant sport that starts in the early teens. The explanation would never become apparent by simply looking at Durkheimian 'social facts' on participation rates.
- Karl Horning and his colleagues (1995) studied a small sample of German employees who had voluntarily opted to reduce their hours of work considerably and accept corresponding reductions in remuneration. This study demonstrates the benefits of becoming time-rich: none of those who were interviewed intended to turn back. The study also highlights some social costs – basically being regarded as odd and uncommitted to one's occupation and work organisation – that will inhibit other employees from downshifting. At the same time, the research also describes how the benefits of downshifting they were experiencing enabled the subjects to resist this labelling. They quietly celebrated their own good fortune.
- Studies of negotiations within families have clarified how men are usually able to gain their partners' acquiescence and privilege their own leisure time and interests (for example, Barrell et al., 1989).
- Symbolic interactionist research can generate theories and concepts. An excellent example in leisure research is Robert Stebbins's detailed investigations among enthusiasts in a variety of leisure activities which have led to the now well-known distinctions between serious, project-based and casual leisure (Stebbins, 1992, 2001, 2005).

The sheer lucidity of successful symbolic interactionist studies can create the impression that this kind of research is easily executed: that almost anyone can do it. This impression is false. It is not easy to operationalise symbolic interactionism. The research is always labour-intensive. It is not usually easy to induce people to talk about the meanings of their own and other people's actions. Asking people what they mean by leisure or sport will not yield exciting answers. Lay people (as opposed to leisure scholars) do not need or practise relevant vocabularies and discourses. People can participate in activities without discussing with one another, for example, why they are playing a particular sport and exactly what they derive from participating. Arts audiences may engage in such discussions. There are critical literatures which tell them what they should appreciate. Watching television does not have an equivalent. Sport players often arrive at a facility, change, play, shower, dress then depart: there are no illuminating conversations for a participant observer to overhear.

However, the main difficulty in conducting symbolic interactionist research lies in selecting a group, activity or situation, preferably a combination of all three, that will illuminate stability or change in a larger social pattern or set of relationships, like why many girls who enjoy sport when at primary school drop out while in secondary education (as above in Clark, 2012). The danger confronting all small-scale studies is that the significance of the findings may not extend beyond the group, activity or situation that is researched.

Symbolic interactionism is arguably the theory that is most easily used by sport and leisure scholars, and there are senses in which it is the most useful theory. The study of leisure needs to start from a recognition that people make choices, and therefore that their subjectivities – how they regard and feel about different activities, places and people, and how they believe significant others regard the same activities, people and places – have to be at the core of explanations of their behaviour. That said, symbolic interactionism is unlikely to make the dramatic interventions in sport and leisure that have been achieved elsewhere (mostly when this theory was first launched). These interventions depended on there being competing interpretations of events and behaviour, and which view prevailed making a difference to the winners and losers. This applied and still applies to how school teachers identify academic potential. It applies to whether the recreational use of 'soft' drugs is harmless pleasure or a threat to public health and order. People have different views on the attractions and benefits of particular sports and other uses of leisure. Why do some fanatics devote so much time and money to pigeon racing? Why do others spend their time and money exploring potholes, and in other cases climbing rock faces? In these instances people who are not attracted can simply spend their own time and money according to their own inclinations. Girls who are labelled 'not sporty' can do music or fashion. Most of us have enthusiasms that leave others cold and perplexed, but in leisure we can all go our separate ways. It is not zero-sum. One enthusiasm does not have to prevail at the expense of others. Hence the scarcity of exciting breakthroughs. This is despite sport and leisure offering plentiful scope for ethnomethodological exploration. Why do some people punish their bodies in gyms? Why do anglers sit day-long waiting for a fish to bite? The minorities who participate are self-selected enthusiasts who share their experiences with the like-minded. They do not need to explain to each other, or to themselves, exactly why they are committed to these activities. The attractions do not need explanation: they are simply experienced. Ethnomethodological exploration will clarify, but who will be interested?

There are exceptional leisure practices where the meanings are contested and which become public issues. Drug use is one example. Prostitution is another. Is the woman always a victim? Should her male clients be criminalised? Leisure researchers could use symbolic interactionism to address these battles for everyday common sense, but in practice the issues have been captured by deviance, gender and sex researchers. Whether opting for a short-hours job in order to be time-rich indicates low employment commitment is an issue that has been appropriated by employment and work–life balance scholars rather than leisure researchers. Maybe lack of awareness of the social theories they might use helps to explain these missed opportunities.

Nevertheless, there is far greater scope for symbolic interactionist research among the providers rather than the users of sport and other leisure services, especially in the voluntary and public sectors. Commercial businesses have to prioritise profitability. This is not negotiable. Voluntary associations and public agencies, state departments and the policy communities that proffer advice and information must decide, for example, whether sport is primarily for fun, health promotion or national prestige. Is state support for museums, heritage sites and high culture meant to enrich the lives of all citizens, to boost inward tourism, or is it simply subsidising the allegedly superior tastes of elites? Published documents do not normally reveal the 'negotiations', if any, behind the production of sport and leisure policies. Sites of decision-making are not normally thrown open to researchers except, as is often the situation, when they are among the interested parties who argue about 'what is actually the case', trying to fix a 'natural attitude' which can then be presented to the wider world as objective truth, agreed by the relevant experts. An ethnomethodologist would stand back or apart, and observe the 'negotiations', construction and, over time, challenges and modifications to the 'natural attitude'.

Conclusions

Symbolic interactionism was both a response to and a catalyst for sociologists embracing detailed studies of life within their own modern societies. This created a need for theories of the micro. We should note that symbolic interactionist theory spread globally from America, where by the 1960s sociologists already had over fifty years of experience studying urban neighbourhoods and status hierarchies, teenage gangs, occupational and ethnic communities. Herbert Blumer gave most credit for the groundwork to George Herbert Mead, but as we have seen, there had been earlier Americans working at the interfaces between philosophy, psychology and sociology, practising what would later be called social psychology. Charles Horton Cooley (1864–1929) did not describe himself as a sociologist, but he is now claimed as a founder of American sociology, best remembered for the phrase 'the looking glass self' (Cooley, 1909). William Isaac Thomas (1863–1947) goes down in history for his 1927 dictum 'If men define situations as real, they are real in their consequences' (Thomas, 1927). Symbolic interactionism had many American parents. Herbert Blumer gathered their ideas together in a way that gave studies of the micro a firm theoretical base. This was no longer what Auguste Comte had called social physics, later referred to as social statistics or, more dismissively, as head-counting or number-crunching. Nor was it just filling in details of a macro-picture sketched by the classical European theories. Phenomenology and ethnomethodology insist that the micro is the bedrock on which larger social systems rest. Symbolic interactionism certainly offered a more plausible account of the socialised human being than Durkheim's social facts which somehow imposed themselves onto individuals and into their minds. Symbolic interactionism made Max Weber's attempts to incorporate the subjective into causal explanations look clumsy.

As noted earlier, most of the relevant research is strictly quasi-symbolic interactionist. It implements only part of the agenda, and completely brackets out any consideration of phenomenology and ethnomethodology. Even so, symbolic interactionism opened the door to theoretically significant work that could be small-scale and accomplished with minimal funding. Also, it did not require the level of scholarship of Max Weber. When Barney Glaser and Anselm Strauss (1968) made the case for 'grounded theory', it became almost a virtue to conduct research with a mind that was uncontaminated by acquaintance with earlier work. A downside has been opening the floodgates to research projects whose additions to knowledge have been confined to the specific groups, activities and situations that have been investigated.

That said, symbolic interactionism has been especially influential in widening the research agenda in the sociology of sport and leisure. The classic theories raise questions about Big Sport (all of it) and Big Leisure. Are sport and the rest of leisure subject to an ongoing division of labour, the encroachment of capitalism and/or rationalisation? Symbolic interactionism enables researchers to address questions about particular sports, gardening, ocean cruising, local choirs and even audiences' relationships with media characters – fascinating issues that students and researchers are likely to be interested in, and even enthusiastic about.

Have there been disappointments? Up to now it has not proved possible to build upwards from micro-studies to meet the classical grand theories. Symbolic interaction may be a foundation of social life, but micro-interactions take place within macro-contexts that most actors play no part in making or remaking. Symbolic interactionism has changed the profile of sociology, but it has joined rather than replaced theories about the course of history, which has created modern contexts for the micro.

chapter 9

Michel Foucault (1926–1984)

Introduction

Enjoyment, intrinsic satisfaction, pleasure, freedom and choice are terms that appear in most definitions of leisure. The problem is that much of leisure is the exact opposite. Running and cycling for mile after mile is not fun. 'Fun run' is a misnomer. A competitive race or match may be enjoyable, but not all the prior hours spent training. Achieving and maintaining peak condition is painful. It is the same with dancing, singing and playing a musical instrument. Discipline has to rule. We use the freedom, the scope for choice, that characterises leisure to subject ourselves to horrendous regimes of practice and preparation. Rather than being self-determined, we submit our 'play' to the dictates of coaches, trainers and teachers. We need to submit in order to succeed. These are hardly odd aberrations or distortions: they are common features of leisure in the modern age. Free time is not to be wasted. True, the exceptionally talented can earn immense wealth and global fame, but they are far outnumbered by equally dedicated amateurs. Why do we punish ourselves? Michel Foucault has an explanation.

Foucault is a classical social theorist in that his work is in the genre of Comte, Marx, Durkheim, Weber, Elias and Habermas, addressing change in Europe since the Middle Ages, but Foucault's reading of history is very different. The titles of his main books are as good as any introduction to Foucault. His books are not about factories, politics, law or religion. Foucault wrote about clinics, prisons, asylums and sex: *Madness and Civilization: A History of Insanity in the Age of Reason* (1961/1988), *The Birth of the Clinic* (1963/1973), *Discipline and Punish: The Birth of the Prison* (1975/1977), *The History of Sexuality, Volume I: An Introduction* (1976/1980),

The History of Sexuality, Volume II: The Use of Pleasure (1984a/1985) and *The History of Sexuality, Volume III: The Care of the Self* (1984b/1986).

Foucault's other main books are about his methods – his 'archaeology' and 'genealogy', digging beneath the surface and searching back in time for the meaning of things: *The Order of Things* (1966/1973) and *The Archaeology of Knowledge* (1969/1972).

Foucault searched back in time, but not in the manner of a historian. As a student he studied philosophy and psychology, but subsequently regarded himself as a philosopher. Historians and philosophers were among his fiercest critics, but Foucault commanded their own and wider attention because he always had a different, provocative and interesting point of view.

It took ten years or more for Foucault's first books to be translated and published in the English language. At the start of his teaching career students did not find Foucault a particularly exciting lecturer. However, by the 1970s he could pack lecture halls throughout Europe and North America, and his books were appearing in English within two years of the initial French editions. Foucault was becoming increasingly influential, and has become even more so since his death in 1984. He would probably win the greatest number of nominations from present-day arts, humanities and social science scholars for their most influential thinkers since the mid-twentieth century. Most first nominations would no doubt go to someone from a scholar's own discipline, but Foucault would most likely win sufficient second and third votes to top the final league. He did not write about sport and leisure, but his ideas have obvious applications, and have been, and are continuing to be, applied throughout these fields. The keywords that signal Foucault's influence, even in the absence of his name, are the body, discourse and governance.

Background and career

Michel Foucault was born and brought up in Poitiers, in provincial France. His father was a local surgeon, and his mother was from a medical family. Their hope was probably that Michel (who was known as Paul as a child) would follow the family profession, but Michel (his own choice from his two given names) seems never to have been attracted. He described his father as stern, a bully. Michel spent two years at a strict Jesuit *lycée* which he described later as an ordeal. He did not complete upper secondary education (at a *lycée* in Paris) until 1946, at the age of 20. This was not due to academic difficulties, but to uncertainty about the subject in which he would specialise. He chose philosophy, a subject which continues to have a wider appeal in France than in Anglophone countries. Philosophy can be studied in upper secondary education in France. It is regarded as a particularly demanding subject, suitable only for the academically talented. At university Foucault studied philosophy and psychology, and from 1951 to 1955, as a postgraduate, he taught psychology and for a period worked as an unofficial intern in a psychiatric hospital. He was interested in medicine, but not in joining the profession.

While an undergraduate, Foucault made several suicide attempts (or they may have been para-suicides). He frequently self-harmed. A psychologist who examined Foucault attributed this to his patient's difficulties in coming to terms with his homosexuality. This was plausible, because between 1940 and 1944, when Foucault was aged 14–18, France was occupied by Nazi Germany, and the Nazis grouped homosexuals alongside Jews, Gypsies and mental defectives. However, Foucault seems always to have accepted his nature. He claimed in later life that he had spent his adolescent years chasing beautiful boys, helping with their assignments in order to gain their attention and approval. Fellow students recalled Foucault as socially awkward and distant. He was 'out' long before gay scenes became accepted parts of modern life. Homosexuality remained taboo in France until Foucault's closing years. His behaviour was not illegal in any of the countries where he lived (it would have been criminal in Britain until 1967), but neither was it socially acceptable.

Foucault was always a ferocious worker and writer. There were additional books to those listed above, plus numerous articles in periodicals and newspapers. Foucault would have been a persistent blogger if he had lived in the twenty-first century. He used his personal experience as evidence, arguing that there were circumstances in which suicide could be a rational choice. He used drugs before this was normalised in student cultures, and had experience of sado-masochist scenes. He explained in writing how all could be sources of pleasure. Foucault maintained a long-term love relationship, but this was never exclusive; he was always a promiscuous homosexual.

By the mid-1950s both Foucault's ideas and lifestyle were subject to mixed receptions in Paris, but he always had champions in academic life and in French government and politics. During 1955–1960, while still working on his doctorate, Foucault held a series of posts in Sweden, Poland and Germany as, in effect, a French academic and cultural ambassador. Post-1945 France could rightly regard itself as the major power in continental Europe. French had been *the* international language before 1939, though by then it was being challenged by English, the language of the British Empire and the USA. Throughout and beyond the 1950s France hoped that its language and culture would remain the European mainstream. In support of this ambition, the country funded posts at universities in other countries which could be occupied by a series of visiting French scholars, and Foucault was among these. Afterwards, from 1960 onward, Foucault was Paris-based, except during 1966–1968, when he took a post in Tunis in order to accompany his long-term lover.

Foucault became a well-known figure in Paris not just through the attention his literary output attracted plus his participation in gay scenes, but also on account of his political activity. He always aligned with 'the left'. For two years in the early 1950s he was a member of the French communist party, but left due to doctrinal disputes. Foucault never aligned for long with any formal movement. Disputes with Marxists sometimes led to him being labelled right-wing, but this was never justified. He was a persistent campaigner for penal reform and against racial discrimination, and throughout his career he was frequently on the streets of Paris supporting student demonstrators. He was arrested more than once, but was never charged, prosecuted or sentenced.

Foucault died of AIDS in 1984. It is believed that he contracted the condition while on a lecture tour in the USA. He was among the earliest cases when little was known about the causes of the condition and when there were no effective treatments. Foucault's family did not disclose the cause of his death, but friends made this public within two years. In the early 1980s public attitudes to homosexuality were still very different than they had become by the twenty-first century. In 1988 the UK government included 'Clause 28' within a local government Act which prohibited the 'promotion' of homosexuality in all maintained schools. This clause was repealed in 2003. Civil partnerships became available in England in 2005, and same-sex marriages in 2014. Needless to say, this cultural shift, of which Foucault experienced only the earliest stages, has not damaged his posthumous reputation.

As we proceed, it will become impossible to resist the impression that Foucault's scholarly career was driven, at least in part, by questions arising from his own experience as a homosexual. How and why had his sexual orientation been defined as an illness that needed to be treated and cured? Why were heterosexuals fearful of contamination? Why had homosexuality become a taboo, unmentionable subject? Why deny that there are multiple routes to sexual pleasure? How and why had medics been authorised to prescribe cures which included aversion therapies, chemical and other invasive treatments?

Epistemes and discourses

We need to bear in mind that Foucault studied philosophy and psychology (but not sociology) at both undergraduate and postgraduate levels, and began his teaching career lecturing in psychology. The psychologist in Foucault came to conclusions about how humans learn to think. He argued that we learn to use language by learning discourses which are ways of thinking, forming and expressing opinions and ideas about a topic. Discourses thereby shape the worlds in which we live. They tell us who we are and who other people are. We need to use discourses in order to make ourselves understood and to be accepted as competent actors in our societies.

The role of language in enabling humans to think and develop self-consciousness was not a new idea. We have seen in Chapter 8 that it was present in the work of George Herbert Mead, whose ideas were being incorporated into symbolic interactionism during the early stages of Foucault's academic career. What is novel in Foucault, apart from the terminology, is his emphasis on the role of discourses. Language enables humans to think, but discourses simultaneously impose limits on what can be thought, expressed and understood by others. It is the discourses we have acquired that allow us to think that sport might benefit our health and strengthen a nation's prestige and identity. Nowadays we can imagine that sport can be a profitable business. We no longer discuss gambling or bear-baiting as sports. We no longer think of sport as a way in which to worship a God. The discourses we have learnt channel all our thinking.

Now the philosopher in Foucault comes to the fore. He claimed that discourses are embedded in epistemes. These are underlying structures that govern what is an acceptable discourse, and ways in which truths can be distinguished from falsehoods. Epistemes cannot be heard or observed. They need to be 'dug out' from beneath the surface. In the 1950s and 1960s Foucault was part of a structuralist movement in French intellectual life which was influential in linguistics, literary criticism and social anthropology. French structuralism was entirely different from the structural functionalism associated with Talcott Parsons (see Chapter 3). The central claim of French structuralists was that what could be heard and observed needed to be 'deconstructed' then explained in terms of underlying structures which had to be inferred because they could not be directly observed. For Marxists the underlying structures were relationships of production. For others they were rules of grammar and ways of thinking which were believed to be genetically imprinted in the human brain. Hence the similarities between the grammars of all known languages, and the recurrence of certain ideas and beliefs, fables and myths in all societies. Hence also the ease with which young children are able to learn then instantly begin using their first languages. Foucault was later to dissociate himself from structuralism. He wished to emphasise what was distinctive in his own work. Foucault's underlying structures were epistemes. Foucault the philosopher was a relativist. He believed that truth could be established only within an episteme. Several competing epistemes could co-exist among a population, and contradictory discourses could arise within any episteme. There could be dominant and subordinate epistemes and discourses, or

Michel Foucault

there could be head-on confrontations. The dominant episteme varied by time and place, but truth claims could be settled only within an episteme. In modern scientific discourses truths can be established by experiment and observation. In theocratic societies the touchstones were holy texts interpreted by priests, and divine revelation. They reached the conclusion in different ways, but Schütz (the phenomenologist), Habermas and Foucault are in agreement that there can be no absolute truths.

Foucault was always a voracious reader. He felt able to plunge history into his mix, and we find Foucault viewing history through a philosopher's lens, claiming to have identified a major epistemic break between Europe's Middle Ages and modern times. In sociology (which Foucault had not studied) this claim had already become the orthodox view. Marx saw the movement from feudalism to capitalism as one of the revolutionary moments in history. Weber contrasted traditional thought, action and authority with modern rationality. Elias associated the end of the Middle Ages with the beginning of the civilising process. Neither Foucault nor any of the other theorists regarded the break, the great historical divide, as having occurred abruptly. Foucault's modern episteme and its discourses were seen as becoming increasingly influential from the sixteenth century onwards, then dominant during the nineteenth and twentieth centuries. All Foucault's books present evidence of the epistemic break between Europe in the Middle Ages and modern Europe.

What is distinctive about Foucault among other social theorists of the modern age? First, there is the fundamental foundation role accorded to epistemes and discourses, and the associated claim that knowledge and power constitute (one might alternatively say legitimate or consolidate) one another. Foucault's power is amorphous. It is present everywhere. It is also relational in separating those who must decide from those who must obey. Those with the power to do so determine what counts as true knowledge, which confirms the authority of those with power. Governance is (partly) through discourses. This is inescapable. We can reject one discourse only by adopting another. Symbolic interactionists have stressed the open-ended possibilities: whatever can be imagined can become reality. There are endless possible ways of defining situations, resolving a conflict and agreeing a solution to a problem. For Foucault, all 'negotiations' are governed and the possible outcomes are limited by the discourses we learn and must use if we are to act competently as members of our societies.

Second, there is the importance Foucault attaches to discourses that concede to scientific experts the power to declare what is normal not only in the natural world, but also in human conduct. Experts are also authorised to decide how abnormal persons should be disciplined into normality. As explained below, rather than a wholly emancipating force, science is seen by Foucault as spreading increasingly insidious control over people's lives. Here, although unaware of this, Foucault is agreeing with sociology's critical theorists (see Chapter 7). This is the obverse side to how science and medicine have conferred benefits on humanity, and Foucault did acknowledge the benefits.

Third, there is Foucault's choice of institutions, professions and discourses which are taken to represent modernity – prisons, psychiatric medicine and sexuality.

Overall, Foucault presents a gloomy view of the modern era. Weber was also gloomy about the spread of rationality and bureaucracy trapping citizens in an iron cage, and Weber could not identify an escape. Habermas (see Chapter 7) believed that the Enlightenment project could be rescued by the formation and enlargement of new public spheres. There is also an optimistic side to Foucault. Discourses can be exposed and challenged. Unlike the Marxist left, Foucault did not believe that progress must await an oppressed class seizing control of the means of production. The radical left must simply challenge ruling discourses. Symbolic interactionists have treated reality, what is actually the case, as needing constant negotiation. Foucault sought more than this. He was not seeking an epistemic break, but wanted to challenge the discourses which allow what is normal and acceptable to be defined narrowly. People might be constrained, but liberation is possible.

The disciplinary, carceral, administered society

Foucault's history books are long and rambling. The author flits like a gadfly, plucking evidence from the entire span of known history, from ancient Greece and Rome, early Christianity, and the early to late Middle Ages in Europe. There is far less depth and less context than in Max Weber's comparative studies of religions, or in Norbert Elias's research into the development of courtly society in German states from early modern times. In Foucault's defence, he is explicitly using his philosophical tool-kit, mainly his concepts of epistemes and discourses, to sift the evidence. In any case, historians offer far less on sexual conduct and the pre-modern equivalents of madness and insanity than about government, military affairs, religions, and even family life and village and urban settlements.

Foucault's history of modern medicine, *The Birth of the Clinic*, is a pivotal book because medical doctors, and specifically medical psychiatrists, feature prominently in the books on madness and sexuality. However, it is commonplace to treat medicine and law (which features in the book on prisons) as exemplary modern professions, and on these topics Foucault has ample material from historians. Historians may criticise Foucault's treatment of their topics and eras, but overall Foucault builds a formidable case: that modern societies have become more disciplined than any earlier civilisations. Rather than progressive emancipation, according to Foucault progress has meant more regulation. Modern societies are said to have increasingly required people to self-regulate and discipline their minds and bodies as instructed by qualified scientific experts.

The Birth of the Clinic is Foucault's most straightforward and least controversial book. The basic story is well known. This is about how medical doctors separated from medieval apothecaries, alchemists, barbers, faith healers and astrologists to become the experts on the diagnosis of ailments and prescriptions for their treatment. Doctors did this by using scientific methods of systematic observation, keeping records, and discovering which treatments worked best with different symptoms. Adding findings from biology, chemistry and physiology during subsequent centuries improved doctors' results and reinforced their authority. Crucially, doctors formed associations which trained and tested novices, conferred qualifications and thereby distinguished competent practitioners from quacks. In this way they created a model for other aspirant professions to follow. Medicine illustrates Foucault's thesis of power and knowledge constituting each other. Their knowledge is the basis of doctors' power, which includes the authority to define true knowledge. The twist in the tail of Foucault's story is how the prestige of medicine enabled doctors to capture psychiatry. This was, and often remains, despite the profession's lack of treatments that work. They diagnose, classify and treat mental and sexual abnormalities. More than this, they now offer authoritative advice on healthy families, healthy cities, healthy leisure and how to maximise well-being.

Madness and Civilization, a history of madness, was the first of Foucault's books, the outcome of his earliest research. The book is long, but its core message is straightforward. It is that madness as a mental illness did not exist, or at any rate did not exist as an ailment that needed treatment or could be treated, until the label was applied by medical psychiatry. There had always been people who acted and spoke in odd, incomprehensible ways. Sometimes they were regarded as articulating the voice of God, were venerated in churches and visited by pilgrims. Sometimes they were feared as possessed by evil spirits that needed to be exorcised, or the person had to be exiled (like lepers and others with communicable and incurable diseases), or killed promptly. Some served as sources of amusement. Others were simply tolerated in the families and communities where they lived. Then medical psychiatry began to classify different types of insanity. By the late nineteenth and twentieth centuries various cures were being tried: delivering electric shocks, administering drugs, and drilling into the brain. Otherwise the standard treatment was removal to a place of safety, an asylum. Psychiatrists believed that they were acting in the patients' best interests and that their treatments were more humane than anything that had been available previously.

part ii: the successors

During the 1960s Foucault became part of an anti-psychiatry movement. Its claims were as follows:

- The supposedly mad are often just different, or are adjusted to mad environments, which might be their families or the wider society.
- Diagnosis as insane can be a way of removing from society persons with unorthodox and inconvenient points of view, or who are an embarrassment to their families. Nazi Germany and the Soviet Union routinely had the regimes' critics diagnosed as mad.
- The symptoms displayed by patients in asylums are often consequences of long-term incarceration in total institutions, which makes inmates totally dependent, apathetic and childlike.

Foucault's three volumes on sexuality contain similar evidence and offer a similar message to 'madness'. They illustrate the numerous means of sexual pleasure that were known and practised by pagans in ancient Greece and Rome. Then we learn about how early and medieval Christianity defined lust as sinful, and insisted that the sole permissible use of (preferably joyless) sex was procreation within marriage. The regulation of sexual behaviour was undertaken by church authorities. Homosexuality was known throughout history. It had sometimes been disapproved of and discouraged. Sometimes it was regarded as inevitable or preferable to resort to prostitutes when men were separated from their families for long periods, as on military campaigns, or when they had no contact with or access to women, as in some monasteries. Or emotional bonds between men could be regarded as the noblest form of love.

The most startling observation in the three volumes is that there were no homosexuals until they were discovered or invented during the nineteenth century. Previously there were individuals who committed homosexual acts and maintained long-term same-sex relationships, but this behaviour was not seen as incompatible with heterosexual activity. The identification of 'the homosexual' occurred alongside the classification of other sexual deviants as part of a nineteenth-century scientific mania for classifying people. Psychiatrists identified persons afflicted by different mental illnesses and applied labels to them, other scientists classified humanity into different races, and psychologists placed geniuses and imbeciles at opposite ends of a spectrum of intelligence. Medics offered treatments and cures for sexual deviance. Exercise and cold showers were recommended as cures for masturbation. Homosexuals needed to exercise self-control, or accept restraint and punishment. Alongside persons with other communicable illnesses, homosexuals had to be prevented from spreading their vice. They could be offered various treatments – physical or chemical castration, or aversion therapies. It was said to be all in their own interests.

Here, Foucault presents an example of medicine treating problems of its own making.

Discipline and Punish is arguably Foucault's most important book, because it is not only about prisons and it dispenses with medical psychiatry as the villain. *The Birth of the Clinic* may be the pivotal book, illustrating the rise of the scientific expert and how power and knowledge constitute each other. *Discipline and Punish* is more illuminating on Foucault's view of the overall character of modern societies.

Discipline and Punish begins with how the use of prisons changed in Western Europe as countries modernised. In the Middle Ages prisons had been used to hold people awaiting trial, maybe to be tortured to extract confessions, and captives during warfare were sometimes imprisoned pending payment of a ransom, as happened to Richard I (the Lionheart). Or convicted offenders were sent to prison to await punishment, which could mean execution, maiming or flogging. During the eighteenth and nineteenth centuries the use of imprisonment as a punishment became more common. The length of sentences could be calibrated to the severity of offences. During this change, public floggings and executions slowly disappeared as forms of public entertainment. Imprisonment as a punishment was regarded as more humane, more civilised than what it replaced. During the modern era prison populations expanded not solely because imprisonment was being used as a punishment, but also because more laws were passed, so there was more traffic through courts, the number of lawyers increased and police forces were enlarged. There were more rules for citizens to observe and which could be broken.

Foucault was impressed by the widespread adoption of the panopticon prison design of the English utilitarian philosopher Jeremy Bentham (1748–1832). The panopticon design allowed a large prison population to be supervised by a small number of staff. It had tiers of cells arranged along 'spokes' which radiated from a central observation point. Foucault noted that it was impossible for a single officer to constantly observe every cell. But each occupant could never be sure that he (prisoners were usually male) was not under observation. Therefore, to avoid further punishment prisoners needed to regulate their own behaviour just in case they were being observed. This illustrates what Foucault called 'governance'. In medieval times rules had been imposed and enforced coercively by a sovereign – not necessarily *the* sovereign, the monarch, but more likely by a local magnate who, for all practical purposes, did not have to answer to any superior authority. Subjects were coerced, made fearful, by public executions, maiming and flogging. It was different in modern societies: people needed to self-regulate. There was far less coercion and far more self-discipline.

Foucault invites us to treat prisons as an extreme example, but nevertheless representative of modern societies. Factory-floor and open-plan office workers are subject to constant supervision. They can never be sure that they are not being watched. Nineteenth-century school rooms had teachers on pedestals from where they could observe large classes within which younger pupils could be taught by older monitors. Foucault's argument is that it has become so difficult to escape the risk of surveillance that people must self-regulate. Hence his description of modern societies as disciplinary or carceral (administered) societies. Rather than liberated, people are said to have become more docile, more obedient, subject to less visible but more insidious control than in any earlier era. We are said to be required to self-discipline our minds and bodies as a condition for being able to live normal lives in a modern society.

Assessment

Foucault's influence has spread widely because there are so many topics and ideas on which to build: medicine, especially psychiatric medicine, mental illness, sexuality, prisons, discourses and surveillance. It is impossible to pigeon-hole Foucault's work. He studied philosophy. This was always his job title. Yet his main work is not philosophy unless the label is appropriate for someone whose work cannot otherwise be placed, or philosophy is treated as an intellectual licence to roam freely. Foucault died at a relatively young age. He could not have regarded his work as complete. There are numerous loose ends that might have been welded together had he lived longer.

Much of Foucault's work must be described as history. He delved into crevices where historians rarely enter, namely sexuality and madness. He also tackled topics on which there is considerable historical scholarship: medicine, the law and penal policy. Wherever he searched, Foucault always emerged with a different, provocative point of view. There is Foucault the psychologist who understood how the acquisition of language enables individuals to think, then insisted that thought is governed by discourses. Yet what really characterises Foucault and sets him apart is his hostility – which goes beyond normal scholarly criticism – to certain features of modern life: how individuals can be labelled 'mad' then locked away, the treatment of persons with his own sexual orientation, imprisonment for long periods, which Foucault considered the opposite of humane, and the branch of the medical profession that was implicated in all this. Foucault was a tireless campaigner for groups who were unable to speak for themselves or whose views were dismissed as irrational babble. Foucault is a critic of modernity whose ideas demand attention, but can he be ranked highly as a social theorist? Prisons and asylums are surely not representative modern institutions. They are simply part of, and illustrate some features of, the modern age.

Foucault is a troublesome figure in modern social theory. He must clearly be rated as a major social theorist because his ideas have become so influential, but Foucault's own points of reference were not the work of contemporary or past social theorists. Rather, they were located in history, psychology and philosophy. Despite this, he can be seen as continuing Max Weber's desire to find an escape from 'the iron cage of bureaucracy', transposed by the Frankfurt School into the dominance of instrumental rationality, from which Habermas believes that escape is possible through the enlargement of old and the development of new public spheres. Other social theorists have been broadly in agreement with Foucault in highlighting how the modern age is rational, life is governed by instrumental reasoning, and by Elias's 'civilising process' that requires people to self-regulate and monitor their own behaviour.

Foucault died with much more work to do on the modern era. The loose ends in Foucault's work include his stress on the importance of discourses in the governance of how people think, and in enabling power and knowledge to constitute each other. Foucault's discourses set limits, yet he also recognises that there can be competing discourses and that all discourses can be challenged. Foucault could argue that we can challenge one discourse only by adopting another, yet it is clearly possible for people to have wholly original thoughts. Foucault himself is an example. His governance operates through discourses and also through surveillance. These may reinforce one another or they might operate separately, and in the panopticon it is not knowledge, expert or otherwise, that constitutes power: it is control of the means of surveillance. There are alternative Foucaults who can be used within the fields in which he himself worked, and more widely.

Applications in sport and leisure

Foucault did not write about sport and leisure, and given all the loose ends and the limited segments of modern life he investigated, his ideas can neither be tested and possibly rejected against, nor be expected to account for, the whole of sport, let alone the whole of leisure. Even so, his influence has spread into these fields because his views are easily mapped onto some features of and trends in modern sport and leisure.

Since the birth of modern clinics, asylums and prisons, bodies of expert knowledge and professions have multiplied. Social workers prescribe good parenting. There is authoritative advice on how poor households should ameliorate fuel and food poverty. Individuals are deemed irresponsible and culpable if they fail to follow expert advice. We may regard ourselves as sexually liberated, but in practice we are regaled as never before with expert advice and instructions on proper heterosexual, gay, lesbian and bisexual behaviour.

Governments have always been able to ban, tax and subsidise, depending on which uses of leisure they have wanted to encourage, discourage and prohibit. At certain times in pre-modern England the game of football was banned in order to encourage more useful recreations such as archery. Gambling and some sports considered cruel to animals have been banned or tightly regulated in many countries. In the USA the production and sale of alcohol products was prohibited during 1920–1933. Currently smoking bans are spreading all over the world. However, Foucaultian power is exercised primarily through discourses and surveillance. The outcome is subtle and insidious *governance*.

The clearest current example of discursive power in leisure is probably the health and fitness movement. This is where, within sport and leisure research, we are most likely to encounter Foucault (see Maguire, 2008; Markula-Denison and Pringle, 2006). The relevant discourses make the production of healthy bodies – fit for both work and leisure – into a personal responsibility. People are told by experts that they must avoid tobacco and recreational drugs, use alcohol sensibly if at all, eat healthily and take regular exercise. Experts prescribe the amounts and types of exercise that are required to sustain health-related fitness. Sports associations and commercial health and fitness enterprises are invited to join campaigns to boost levels of physical activity, especially within less active target groups. In gyms these discourses are amplified through symbolic interaction (Crossley, 2005). Nowadays the study of sport and leisure is often located among the health sciences. Its scholars become experts on healthy living and how this is best promoted. Yet as Foucault points out, discourses can be challenged. They can also be simply ignored. Most people do not join gyms or otherwise take as much exercise as the experts recommend. Most people are not eating healthily. In any case, experts disagree. Different fitness gyms and trainers prescribe different regimes. Some experts stress the extent to which health status is determined genetically. Accept this particular discourse, and people may eat, drink and play purely for pleasure, and let their genes do their pre-ordained work. Critics have asked whether Norbert Elias's 'civilising process' is still ongoing given today's permissiveness and wider limits of tolerance in sexual conduct, for example. Similar questions can be addressed about Foucault's experts. Since the 1960s all authorities – heads of universities, economists and medics – have been routinely challenged.

There are other parts of Foucault that could be, have not yet been, but need to be incorporated within sport and leisure studies. Jeremy Bentham's panopticon prison design now looks primitive compared with how surveillance has spread since Foucault's death in 1984. He died before the spread of closed-circuit television (CCTV). Whenever we exit our homes today we can expect to be under surveillance. Even if no one is watching the relevant monitor at the time, we cannot be sure that we are not being observed, and our conduct is most likely being recorded and may later be viewed and presented as evidence. This has become a normal part of daily life when we visit a shopping precinct (indoor or outdoor), use public transport, attend a sport event, and drive our cars along a highway or enter a car park. Even football grounds have become places where it is now an offence to be offensive (Waiton, 2012), where we must take care not to utter anything that might be construed as sexist, racist or homophobic, where even standing has become an offence, and where we are probably being caught on camera. The Big Brother in George Orwell's *1984* is increasingly fact rather than fiction. We are learning to live with the routine harvesting of electronic data: all our visits to websites, all purchases using 'plastic', emails and telephone messages by voice and text. Content that arouses the suspicion of authorities may lead to our computers being seized and the hard drives inspected. We are told that all this is in our own interests, necessary to keep us safe from terrorists and to apprehend criminals. The Foucaultian point is that we have no choice other than to submit if we wish to operate in our present-day societies.

A question for sport and leisure research is whether the assumption that we are under surveillance makes us feel more secure, able to drive and park our cars confident that we will not encounter reckless drivers or have our vehicles burgled or stolen, and able to jog or walk the streets safely. Are we able to relax, confident that we can enjoy ourselves without risk? Or are we constantly more inhibited, cautious about our speed while driving, whether our conduct on nights out might be construed as over-exuberant, and whether our tweets or Web searches could place us under suspicion as a result of displaying interest in some sexual peccadillo or terrorist activity?

Conclusions

Foucault did not claim to be a social theorist. He was part philosopher, part psychologist, part historian, but no part sociologist. He did not write about sport and leisure, and there is no Foucaultian general theory of society, comparable to Marxism or Parsons's systems theory, from which we can construct a sport or leisure theory. Foucault's offer to sport and leisure studies is modest when we discount expressing what we already knew in a different way (his work on epistemes and discourses) and seeing sinister implications in the familiar (surveillance). It is partly the context provided by Foucault's extra-curricular life that injects the excitement and raises expectations of an intellectual pay-off.

Foucault poses some new questions, or insists that we think again on issues that were already considered settled. He does this firstly by highlighting the role of discourses. Leisure options are governed by the availability of time and money, to which we must add the opportunities of which people are aware, plus their awareness of the benefits and risks that are involved. Leisure researchers already knew that people can only choose between activities of which they are aware. Hence the immense resources devoted to advertising and publicising. Foucault insists that all the discourses associated with different leisure activities be interrogated more rigorously. Researchers are routinely sceptical about the discourses offered by commercial purveyors of leisure goods and services. Foucault would insist that this scepticism be extended to the discourses of public agencies, and equally to the discourses of sports and other leisure researchers who claim scientific status for their knowledge, and claim the authority to define true knowledge. Does playing sport really enhance physical health when the risks of sports injuries and regular wear and tear on the body are taken into account? Do frequent sport players really make fewer demands on health services than the less active population? We are implicitly invited by Foucault to identify how discourses define the kinds of people for whom particular leisure activities are most suitable. Social inequalities in participation might sometimes be problems of the providers' own making. Modern sports were invented specifically for young males to play.

Sport and leisure researchers need to take surveillance seriously. Foucault was alert to the implications even though he died before the spread of CCTV and the creation of a parallel virtual reality. How, if at all, does behaviour in public places change when people are aware that they are or could be under surveillance? This question seems especially pertinent to behaviour online, which is where leisure time is increasingly spent. Data is harvested for the benefit of advertisers and sites that earn advertising revenue. The harvesting is from the sites we visit and the purchases that we make. Perhaps surprisingly, this does not appear to deter visitors and purchasers. We can grow accustomed to surveillance. Are there any limits? What about when people know that anything posted on Facebook or Twitter might be read by an employer and could deny them a job offer, a promotion or even result in dismissal? How many people fear falling under suspicion as a dangerous sexual deviant or an enemy of the state? Will more and more people become Internet hoodies? Will face-to-face relationships and direct voice communication regain their privileged positions in nurturing and maintaining trust relationships? These are among the many returns from Foucault which sport and leisure scholars can incorporate into their enquiries.

chapter 10

Pierre Bourdieu (1930–2002)

Introduction

We have all heard tales of business deals instigated on golf courses or cemented while in the clubhouse enjoying the nineteenth hole. So will it be useful to join a golf club? Will an application be accepted? Many parents are sensitive to the longer-term significance when choosing schools for their children, sports for them to play and clubs to join where they will avoid contact with the 'wrong types'. Those running sports (think of equestrian events) and arts (think of opera and ballet) where players and audiences are heavily skewed upwards in social and economic terms invariably insist that they want to be accessible to all classes, both sexes, all races, religions and ethnic groups. These proclamations typically accompany bids for state support. Then nothing changes. Participants insist that they are there purely for love of the sport or art. Are any business deals that are forged, job offers that are made and received, and dangerous liaisons that are avoided simply fortuitous outcomes? Or are leisure choices strategic acts of social positioning? Pierre Bourdieu is the social theorist with answers. His theory purports to explain what is going on, how it all works, and for whom leisure choices are most likely to lead to happy outcomes.

However, Bourdieu features in this book not because of his obvious relevance for sport and leisure scholars. He has been the most influential figure in global sociology since the mid-twentieth century. His achievement has been, in effect, to create an entirely new sociology. In this sense, Bourdieu is the only sociologist who can be acclaimed as a successor to Talcott Parsons. In the mid-twentieth century Parsons synthesised existing theories, added many of his own ideas, and thereby created a comprehensive framework for the practice of sociology. When Parsons and functionalism became unfashionable, sociology lacked an integrating theoretical scheme. Bourdieu has stepped into this gap. He has done this by inventing new concepts, or defining familiar concepts in new ways. The main Bourdieu concepts are habitus, field and capital. All are now widely used throughout global sociology. These are the Bourdieu keywords. Wherever they appear, they most likely signal Bourdieu's influence.

Bourdieu's main books about society deal with education and 'taste' – mainly tastes in the arts, but also sports – so he is one of the few major theorists (Elias is the other) who have tackled sport and leisure. Bourdieu's books on education include studies of academic life (Bourdieu, 1965, 1984, 1989) in which he deals with the location of sociology itself. So his work includes a sociology of sociology, and a sociology of the wider academic field within which sociology is located. This enables Bourdieu to claim that his sociology is reflexive and achieves a 'double objectification', meaning that his conclusions are objectively valid. The first 'objectification' is to locate its subjects' explanations in their social contexts, including their prior experience and socialisation. The second step-back does the same for the sociological observer (Bourdieu himself). The outcome is said to be superior and accounts to those of both unreflexive actors and unreflexive sociologists. Bourdieu also wrote about the current state of the world (Bourdieu, 1993), gender relations (Bourdieu, 1998) and his own methods of enquiry (Bourdieu, 1980). There is a complete Bourdieu sociology for others to practise, if they wish. Needless to say, this invitation has not been accepted by all sociologists.

Background and career

Bourdieu was the son of a civil servant, and grew up in provincial France. Like Foucault, he studied philosophy at university, but unlike Foucault, he then taught in a *lycée*, then did national service in Algeria. This was during the Algerian war for independence in the 1950s. Bourdieu remained in the country after completing his military service, and taught at the University of Algiers from 1958 to 1960. This led to a book on Algeria (Bourdieu, 1963) which contained sympathetic vignettes of the lives of both native Algerians and French settlers. Bourdieu was making a transition from philosophy to sociology via work that is best described as social anthropology.

From the mid-1960s Bourdieu was based in Paris. He was part of the 'events of '68', and his work around that time could be described as neo-Marxist. He was interested in social differences in cultural tastes, in how advantages were transmitted from parents to children, largely via education despite nominally equal opportunities, and the role of cultural tastes in the relevant processes. The influence of Durkheim, Weber and many others has been detected in Bourdieu's work. He is impossible to pigeon-hole. Bourdieu himself always insisted on the originality of his sociology, and also on its completeness.

Very early in his career Bourdieu began to attract a circle of followers, and his growing reputation eventually led to his occupying the most prestigious sociology professorship in France. His main books, apart from those in which he explains his methods and reviews his own life and work, are about education (Bourdieu, 1965, 1984, 1989; Bourdieu and Passeron, 1970) and cultural tastes (Bourdieu, 1979; Bourdieu and Darbel, 1969). Throughout nearly all his work Bourdieu displayed an interest in the significance of judgements of taste and cultural consumption, so he can be cited as an example of the study of leisure leading to insights of general, and generally acclaimed, sociological importance. Norbert Elias used sport and other forms of leisure as sources of examples of his historical master trend, the civilising process. In Bourdieu's sociology cultural tastes and related forms of behaviour have an elevated significance. They become part of what it means to belong to a particular class, age or ethnic group, and to be a man or a woman.

Throughout his career the enduring influence of Bourdieu's fieldwork experience in Algeria remained evident, matched only by his (participant) observation in academic life in France. There is plenty of data in Bourdieu's books. He was not a 'pure' theorist. However, the data are always introduced to illustrate and support Bourdieu's theoretical positions rather than to rigorously test them. Bourdieu consistently claimed that although his evidence was entirely from France, and mostly from the 1960s and 1970s, his arguments could be generalised. This is one of Bourdieu's claims that has been disputed. However, even if his empirical evidence has proved time- and place-specific, Bourdieu's concepts have travelled well.

Keywords

Habitus

Bourdieu did not invent the (French) word *habitus*, but he is responsible for the term's incorporation into English and other global languages. A habitus, in Bourdieu's sociology, is the dwelling in which an individual lives, but the dwelling is not external to the person; it is constructed within the individual's mind. The habitus is said to be acquired through social experience, initially in the family in most cases. The habitus may subsequently develop, but necessarily from foundations laid earlier on. A habitus is said to contain dispositions, ways of classifying, thinking, feeling and acting. It is largely beyond consciousness, and thereby enables people to create performances in speech and behaviour as matters of routine without any conscious calculation. It operates in a similar manner to Michel Foucault's discourses in enabling people to think, speak and act. In so far as members of a social class, sex or ethnic group acquire similar habituses, we may speak of the habitus of a class, ethnic group and so on. However, the habitus and the routine performances it produces are always the properties of an individual person. In Bourdieu's sociology it is habitus that locks 'agency' into explanations.

We should note that Bourdieu's concept of habitus (like Foucault's discourses) is not telling us anything of which we were otherwise completely unaware. We (in global sociology) were already aware of all the relevant processes and phenomena – socialisation, personality, attitudes, the internalisation of culture, the actor's definition of a situation, and orientations to action. The term 'habitus' rolls all these into a single package. The outcome is a concept which appears to have massive descriptive and explanatory power, but this achievement comes at a cost and involves a fundamental deception. A habitus cannot be observed. It can only be inferred from its alleged outcomes (speech and behaviour). The habitus is then said to explain the speech and behaviour from which it has been inferred. Such explanations are circular. The power of the concept withers as soon as its uses in causal explanations are unpacked. If we unpack habitus, its elements can be measured separately and the strength of links can be established between socialisation practices, personality traits and attitudes, and actors' behaviour in given situations. When we separate the elements, the links with outcomes – in educational achievement and leisure behaviour – turn out to be disappointingly weak or non-existent. However, in practice the elements work in combination. Their combination generates the power which is expressed in the concept of habitus.

Field

A field, in Bourdieu's sociology, can be a network, an arena, any relatively autonomous social microcosm where there is a structured system of social positions and rules that govern behaviour in the field. A sport is a field. A sport club is a smaller field. The field of (all) sport is a larger field. A sociology department is a field. The entire discipline is a larger field. These are what we otherwise call social institutions, organisations, associations, groups, movements and communities. The term 'field' blurs the differences and merges these formations. It highlights common features. In Bourdieu's sociology we enter any field with a given habitus, with the result that we immediately feel 'at home' or ill at ease, that we do not fit in. This depends on whether we are predisposed to grasp the 'rules of play' in the field in question. Once we have entered a field, it is said that we do not simply play pre-scripted roles, though we must do this – we must observe the rules. Field injects 'structure' into explanations in Bourdieu's sociology.

However, actors also exhibit agency. After entering a field they can deploy resources they have brought with them, which Bourdieu calls 'capitals' (see below), and actors may thereby seek to add to their resources/capitals, and in doing so advance their positions within the field. It is presented as much the same whether the field is a coffee house in North Africa or a sociology department in France.

Capital

A form of capital, in Bourdieu's sociology, is any resource which, like economic capital, possesses exchange value and can be added to or lost. The most important forms of capital Bourdieu recognises are social capital, cultural capital and economic capital. An individual's stock of each can vary in quantity and in its value per unit. 'Social capital' refers to trusted social relationships: people you know and from whom you can seek assistance when operating in any field, which may be a university department or a labour market. It is an advantage to have connections with individuals who occupy influential positions. Cultural capital includes tastes such as in art, music and literature. It also includes knowledge which may or may not be certificated (through possession of a university degree, for example). Reputation, and most certainly celebrity status, are forms of cultural capital. Their value will vary according to the field in which they are used. Some resources may have intrinsic value (they are enjoyed for their own sake). This will depend on the dispositions (habituses) of the actors. However, forms of capital may also derive value from their proximity to one another. The value of cultural tastes depends partly on the economic and social capital of those who possess the tastes in question. 'Who you know' varies in value according to their economic and social capital. Bourdieu's social actors always try to maximise their resources by deploying their existing capitals so as to advance their positions and increase their stocks of all forms of capital within the fields in which they operate. Bourdieu insists that his sociology does not reduce everything to economics and import 'economic man' into his own discipline. His actors are multi-valent: they deploy and seek resources other than money. However, Bourdieu's social actors bear a canny resemblance to the 'utility maximisers' of classical economics.

Bourdieu's view is that cultural preferences are not objectively higher and lower than one another. Which and whose culture is 'high', according to Bourdieu, is a culturally arbitrary judgement. No one's aesthetics are intrinsically superior. Here, Bourdieu's position is uncontroversial within sociology. His arguments, which date from the 1960s (Bourdieu and Darbel, 1969), are directed at the arts establishment, the self-styled cultural elites who persuade themselves (and hopefully others, but not

Bourdieu) that their tastes are objectively superior to those who derive enjoyment wholly from popular genres. That said, Bourdieu argues that there is an important sense in which 'high' culture is objectively different. This lies in the existence of elites, experts in their fields, who can pronounce authoritatively on the merits of works of art, musical compositions and performances, and so on. The existence of rules and authoritative judges makes this kind of culture 'legitimate' and clearly different from art forms where the sole arbiter of value is 'Do I like it?' This socially constructed legitimacy enables people with the tastes in question to establish and maintain 'distinction' (Bourdieu, 1979). Bourdieu claims that the relevant tastes, the love of art, have to be learnt. One needs to be taught the rules, to be schooled in the relevant arts, which helps to preserve the distinction between the 'cultured' and the 'uncultured' public. Norbert Elias's comparable distinction is between the civilised and the uncivilised.

Bourdieu has social capital working in a different way than Robert Putnam (2000), an American political scientist. Putnam's social capital (usually measured by memberships of voluntary associations) is the property of an entire society or community therein. When social capital is high there are collective benefits – less crime, higher educational attainments and healthier citizens – though Putnam distinguishes between bonding and bridging social capital, with the former strengthening solidarity within and the latter forming links between social groups. Bourdieu's social capital (like all his other capitals) belongs to individuals and members of their social networks. It does not benefit all, but just insiders at the expense of outsiders. Bourdieu's capitals combine to distinguish different classes, and to make each class distinctive.

Applications by Bourdieu

As noted above, Bourdieu's books do not just present, but apply his concepts to data, and his reputation rests on the outcomes, which are impressive. They demonstrate his sociology's ability to persuade us to see the familiar differently, and to highlight the significance of features of social life that might ordinarily receive cursory attention at best.

Sociology of sociology

Bourdieu's sociology of sociology, and his observations on (French) academic fields in general (Bourdieu, 1965, 1984), are amusing and ring true for academic readers of his books: even the details travel remarkably well. As always, Bourdieu is able to assemble impressive amounts of data to back his arguments. These are that:

- There are hierarchies of academic institutions and disciplines, with medicine, law and philosophy at the top. Science and engineering rank last. The arts and humanities stand mid-way.
- Individuals' academic careers rise (or fail to rise) not so much on the basis of the quantity of their work, but on the cultural capital they are able to deploy. It is said to be especially important to be able to restrict oneself to academic language (Bourdieu, 1965). Using plain French (or English) is a handicap. Bourdieu himself was renowned for his long, tortuous sentences.
- Within sociology there are sub-fields which have especially high status and within which promotion comes most easily. Theory trumps number-crunching. Among leisure fields, the arts (high culture) clearly beat sport and everything else.

Social stratification

Social classes, in Bourdieu's work, are initially the occupational aggregates that are found in all the standard social class schemes. However, this is built on by Bourdieu so that a social class becomes the occupational group plus all the types of capital to which it corresponds – income and wealth (economic capital), the typical class positions of people known (social capital), and cultural tastes. Max Weber's 'status' is unpacked into Bourdieu's various types of capital. Bourdieu then shows that although there are correspondences, the associations between economic and cultural capital are far from perfect. Indeed, within France's top occupational class he shows that the relationship between economic capital (income) and (legitimate) cultural capital is actually inverse (Bourdieu, 1979). In other words, economic and cultural elites are not the same people, though they co-exist within the highest socio-economic class. Bourdieu then explains why the partial disconnect between the capitals is socially significant, not least in facilitating the transmission of class positions (what Bourdieu terms 'reproducing' these positions) from parents to children.

Class reproduction

There may appear to be some exaggeration in Bourdieu's account of how lower-class French children were being failed in the school system in the 1960s despite the system's claims of social impartiality and the opening of equal opportunities for all (Bourdieu and Passeron, 1970). At that time, according to Bourdieu, France's schools and their teachers expected academically able pupils to be conversant with the country's 'legitimate' culture. Entering school with this type of capital was therefore read (by teachers) as an indicator of academic ability. Lower-class children's different cultural capital was said to be assaulted by symbolic violence as soon as they entered the classroom. Higher-class children had already learnt from their families what to expect, what would be expected of them, and what they could expect to gain from their schooling. The habituses of lower-class children were different and, in the schoolroom, were judged deficient. The value of their own cultural capital was simply not recognised. Rather, it was disparaged. The outcome was the failure of lower-class children, manifestly due to their lack of ability (indicated by their lack of 'legitimate' cultural capital). Possession of legitimate cultural capital led to attainments in elementary education, then promotion to and attainments in types of upper secondary education (at academic *lycées*) which, along with the students' original cultural capital acquired from their families, facilitated admission to France's prestigious higher education institutions (the *grandes écoles*) which produced, in Bourdieu's term, a 'state nobility' (Bourdieu, 1989).

Anyone versed in English-language sociology of education already knew that class cultural differences at least helped to explain the persistent link between children's social class origins and their achievements in education. What was Bourdieu adding? He was proposing the crucial significance of 'legitimate' cultural capital – that is, knowledge of 'high' culture. This may or may not have been the case in French education in the 1960s. Bourdieu was unable to present evidence that it was their lack of this particular kind of culture rather than, for example, low educational and occupational aspirations and expectations that was causing lower-class children to under-achieve compared with children from higher-class backgrounds. However, he could show that in France at that time (the 1960s) it was this particular kind of taste that set France's upper socio-economic classes apart from the rest (Bourdieu and Darbel, 1969).

Maybe at other times and places different kinds of cultural capital have been crucial. This will not undermine Bourdieu's main point, which is that in societies where upper-middle-class parents are unable to directly pass their occupations to their children, they remain able to transmit a culture that advantages their children by being read in schools as an indicator of educability which, alongside the looseness of the fit between economic and cultural capital, creates an impression that lower-class children fail not because they are held back by socio-economic barriers, but through their lack of the academic aptitude and ability that are required if one is to succeed. In this way, the reproduction of inequalities, and the inequalities themselves, are legitimised, meaning that they are made to appear fair to all.

Pierre Bourdieu

Applications in sport, leisure and related fields

Sporting and other habituses

Bourdieu is exceptional in the extent to which his concepts have been taken up throughout sociology. They are not field-specific (to use one of Bourdieu's own terms). Bourdieu's ideas prove more obviously useful than those of any other major social theorist in investigating sport and other forms of leisure.

The concept of habitus proves particularly useful in understanding how individuals are attracted to and retained in particular leisure fields. Whether people build long-term careers in sport seems to depend on whether a sporting habitus is acquired during childhood. The relatively high partici-pation rates in Scandinavian countries look explicable only in these terms. The Scandinavians say that they were 'born this way' (Green et al., 2015). This is how they feel: active outdoor recreation is built into their human natures. As noted earlier, there is a circularity in using habitus as an explan-atory concept, but its strength lies in signalling dispositions that make individuals feel instantly 'at home' in a sporting field, and estranged from their inclinations if they are unable to play. Love of sport and many other forms of leisure appear to develop in much the same way as the love of art Bourdieu himself examined (Bourdieu and Darbel, 1969). A habitus formed during childhood, then relevant capitals (tastes and skills) acquired during childhood and youth are likely foundations for 'serious' long-term leisure careers (see Stebbins, 1992) in the relevant fields.

Needless to say, just as individuals will be most enthusiastic about par-ticular forms of art, so they will feel most 'at home' when playing specific sports. A general sporting habitus can become focused as players become immersed in the social bonds and culture of a particular sport. Loïc Wacquant (2004) offers a vivid ethnographic account of his boxing career in a Chicago gym: how a 'pugilistic habitus' was acquired then deployed in the 'sweet science'. He explains how it is possible for a fully immersed participant to feel at home in this 'show business with blood'.

The value of the habitus concept is certainly not confined to studies of sport and leisure. It is equally useful in explaining how some individuals feel instantly at home in particular educational settings, and in districts where they live and (in some, but not all cases) feel that they really belong (see Savage et al., 2004, 2005).

More capitals

Bourdieu distinguished economic, social, cultural and symbolic capital – the latter is any possession, skill or knowledge that is prestigious – and

Bourdieu appears to have regarded this list of capitals as exhaustive. However, subsequent investigators have identified additional forms of capital which can be deployed in specific fields, which can be added to, and which possess exchange value. Catherine Hakim (2011) has proposed an additional type of 'erotic capital' (sexual attractiveness). She argues that women have more erotic capital than men because the latter have the greater interest in having sex. Hence erotic capital is a resource which women mainly (but also men) can deploy in the labour market, in sport and careers in other cultural industries, in most other work situations, and very obviously in most everyday leisure settings.

Bob Stewart and colleagues (2013) have explained that although working out in gyms may not create social, cultural or symbolic capital, it does boost 'bodily capital' (bodies that function better and look better) and 'psychological capital' (self-esteem and psychological resilience). These forms of capital can have exchange value. It is known that people who are considered 'better-looking' progress further in their occupational careers than others with the same educational and class origins, ethnicity, gender and other predictors (Sala et al., 2013).

However, it is likely that many people play sport and engage in other leisure activities purely for the intrinsic enjoyment, and that positions (status) within sporting and other leisure fields are dependent overwhelmingly on field-specific capital (performance in and knowledge about the relevant sport, music or hobby) rather than any other kind of cultural capital, or social or economic capital. Knowledge of Pierre Bourdieu's work may be a valuable form of cultural capital in a sociology department or seminar, but totally useless in other fields.

Legitimate culture

Bourdieu claimed that legitimate tastes (better known as 'high culture') distinguished France's middle class and accounted for their children's advantages in education. Even if this was the case in France in the 1960s, does it apply elsewhere and in the twenty-first century?

Bourdieu's claim as regards educational advantages has been interrogated by Anna Zimdars and her colleagues (2009). They have investigated whether possession of Bourdieu's legitimate cultural capital is an asset, net of other indicators of social class, when applying for admission to the UK's prestigious Oxford University, where interviews are an important part of the selection process. These investigators found that in 2002 reading widely was an asset when applying for a science course, and extensive cultural knowledge was an asset when applying for an arts course. However, distinctively highbrow cultural participation and consumption did not help anyone.

Does a taste for high culture still distinguish advantaged classes? Recent evidence from Britain is partly supportive. The Great British Class Survey (Savage et al., 2013) achieved over 160,000 initial responses to an online questionnaire. Respondents provided information about their economic capital (income and wealth), social capital (whether they knew anyone from a list of occupations) and cultural tastes. The highest class cluster, which the investigators label an elite, was far more likely to express a taste for high culture than any of the other class clusters. However, the elite's cultural tastes were not exclusively highbrow.

Class and culture: the omnivore thesis

During the 1990s Bourdieu's ideas encountered the omnivore thesis. 'Omnivores' were first discovered, and the term was coined, by Richard Peterson (1992), an American sociologist who found that the American middle classes liked popular as well as classical music. This was at odds with Bourdieu's treatment of exclusively 'legitimate' (high-culture) tastes and disdain for anything lowbrow as distinguishing the middle classes. Subsequently middle-class omnivorousness has been discovered in tastes in art, reading matter, films and food as well as music, and omnivorous middle classes have been discovered throughout the Western world (see Eijck, 1999; Eijck and Rees, 1998; Gronow, 2009; López-Sintas and García-Álvarez, 2002; López-Sintas et al., 2008; Warde et al., 1999). Tony Bennett and his colleagues (2009), in their study of cultural consumption in Britain in the 2000s, found that the middle classes were the more likely to consume all kinds of culture, with just one big exception – television programmes.

Since 1992 the omnivore thesis has been tweaked in several ways:

- Sullivan and Katz-Gerro (2007) point out that the present-day middle classes are voracious (they consume a lot) as well as omnivorous in their cultural practices.
- Collective omnivorousness has been distinguished from individual omnivorousness. There are still some members of the middle class whose tastes are exclusively highbrow.
- Also, there are distinguishable taste clusters (sub-cultures) within the generally omnivorous middle classes: everyone does not like every musical or theatrical genre (Tampubolon, 2010).
- Tony Bennett and his colleagues (2009) have shown that the main cultural divide in present-day Britain is not between those with middle-class and those with different working-class tastes. Nor is it between an included mainstream and an excluded minority. The main divide is between an omnivorous middle class and the (more numerous) rest

whose cultural consumption is almost wholly via the media and who rarely if ever attend any type of concert, exhibition or theatrical performance.

- The evidence of Bennett and his colleagues also locates the dividing line between omnivores and the rest more precisely than in any previous research. It is not between all non-manuals and all manuals, or beneath all professionals and managers. The omnivores tend to be higher-level managers plus lower- and higher-level professionals – that is, the occupational groups which are now normally entered via higher education. Higher education appears influential in the formation of groups with distinctive cultural tastes and leisure practices.

- This research also found that, at the time of the study, this main cultural divide mapped closely onto party political preferences. The groups most likely to support the Conservative Party were the non-omnivorous non-manuals. Some middle-class omnivores were Labour Party supporters, but at the time of the survey they were more likely to express support for the Liberal Democrats or some other non-Conservative option (Roux et al., 2008).

A debate about whether omnivorousness is compatible with cultural tastes and practices acting as marks of distinction was resolved quickly in the 1990s. It was decided that omnivorousness itself could be the marker. The present-day middle classes are said to be distinguished by their wide range of cultural tastes and knowledge. Persons lacking the necessary breadth and depth of cultural capital can be marginalised, and will very likely exclude themselves, from middle-class networks (see Erikson, 1996; Peterson and Kern 1996).

There has been some debate about the extent, if any, to which the middle-class omnivore can be considered a 'new' late twentieth-century arrival. Was there really a time when the entire middle class was composed of highbrow univores? As is often the case, apart from Bourdieu's own research in France in the 1960s, we lack survey evidence from the early and mid-twentieth century which can be compared directly with recent evidence about middle-class cultural tastes and practices. However, in the Netherlands there appears to have been a definite historical shift towards middle-class omnivorousness (see Eijck and Knulst, 2005). The main explanations of change that have been offered (assuming that change really has occurred) are:

- the mass media, which have made exposure to popular culture unavoidable in all social classes;
- the volume of upward social mobility into the middle classes from the mid-twentieth century onwards, which created middle classes composed mainly of the upwardly mobile, who are assumed to have carried their lower-class tastes into their social classes of destination.

Eijck and Knulst (2005) have speculated that middle-class omnivorousness could be just a historical stage, and that eventually popular culture will be dominant in all social classes.

The ways in which middle-class tastes are distinctive may have changed since Bourdieu gathered his own evidence, but subsequent research has confirmed the existence of clear class cultural differences. That said, it has not been shown that these tastes act as forms of capital which enable parents to hand their own class positions to their children, or that cultural capital can be exchanged for other kinds of capital, including economic capital, despite the plausibility of this suggestion. These issues require further investigation.

Social capital

In contrast, there is firm evidence that social capital can assist in the inter-generational transmission of class positions and, in some cases, in accomplishing upward social mobility. Indeed, in so far as cultural capital has exchange value, this may well depend wholly on the social capital – the types of people one associates with – as an outcome of possessing particular cultural tastes. Among the British 1970 birth cohort, being a member of a sports club, church or community group at age 16 was associated with positive adult outcomes net of other predictors. In contrast, membership of a youth club at age 16 was associated with negative adult outcomes (Feinstein et al., 2006). What made the difference? The most plausible explanation is the social composition of the different groups. Leisure projects that attract mainly the disadvantaged may lead to additions to the participants' social capital, but this will have exchange value only within the disadvantaged's own social milieu. The disadvantages of those concerned may thereby be amplified (Nichols, 2004; Skogen and Wichstrøm, 1996). It appears that parents who wish to pass advantages to their children will be acting wisely if they encourage their children to steer clear of the 'wrong crowds'.

UK evidence indicates some interesting trends over time in the distribution of social capital, measured by memberships of voluntary associations. It has been found that there is now more concentration within the middle class than in the mid-twentieth century, due mainly to declining working-class memberships of trade unions and working men's (sic) clubs alongside the growth of (mainly public sector) white-collar trade unions (Li et al., 2002, 2003, 2005). This, alongside the evidence which shows that television viewing is the sole type of cultural consumption in which working-class exceeds middle-class participation, suggests that the middle class is becoming stronger as a socio-cultural formation while the working class is becoming a weaker socio-cultural entity.

Conclusions

Bourdieu's social theory is less complete than Talcott Parsons's. He is not a true successor. Bourdieu is silent on how and why historical change has occurred, and how and why contemporary societies differ from one another. Yet Bourdieu's influence is growing in the second decade following his death in 2002, whereas Parsons's influence had already been waning for many years when he died in 1979. Bourdieu's influence, evident in the widespread use of his keywords, continues to expand because a field can be in any part of any society. It can be in any of the arenas that have become the concerns of sociology's many specialisms. It can be any sport or leisure field. Whatever the field, actors can be seen to enter then deploy their resources. Habitus may have suspect explanatory power, but it highlights a tendency for individuals to settle in niches where they feel at home, which can be in any field.

Bourdieu's sociology renders behaviour meaningful at the level of the individual actor, but it is not purely micro-sociology. It can engage with macro-issues like society-wide class inequalities in educational attainment and the implications of society-wide social differences in cultural tastes.

Maybe Bourdieu places too much emphasis on reproduction. His actors do not enter fields then challenge and re-negotiate meanings and rules. Bourdieu's actors are not sufficiently reflexive to decide to behave contrary to their initial, habitus-ingrained dispositions. One begins to wonder why anything ever changes. Nevertheless, Bourdieu's sociology highlights important tendencies, which may be considered good enough. Up to now sociology does not have a theory, and it does not really need a single theory, that will account for everything. It is best to treat Bourdieu's work, like other macro-theories, as highlighting tendencies rather than trying to account for everything. Treated in this way, Bourdieu's tendencies look powerful.

One is that the initial habituses and capitals we acquire from our families vary in their exchange value and hence our ability to increase the value of all our capitals. Generally, in Bourdieu's view, the links between economic, social and cultural capital facilitate the inter-generational transmission of positions in the social hierarchy, while simultaneously the acquisition of valuable social and cultural capital may assist upward social mobility. However, we must note and stress and Bourdieu never intended to suggest otherwise, that a person cannot join and be accepted by, say, the middle class, simply by acquiring appropriate tastes, and maybe attending classical concerts and art exhibitions. Such a person would also need the right social capital (for introductions) and preferably to be at least in the process of entering a commensurate job. Otherwise the aspiring individual would be excluded or marginalised in the relevant field, and made to feel ill at ease. His or her application for golf club membership would most likely be rejected. Beverley Skeggs (1997, 2004) has drawn attention to how members of the working class who try to become respectable risk exposure and rejection, then ridicule for their pretensions. Meanwhile, members of the middle class can 'slum it' while remaining secure in their middle-class occupations and social networks. Yaish and Katz-Gerro (2012) have shown that in Israel cultural tastes are independent of current income, but participation (the ability to act on tastes) does depend on economic resources. Hence the tendency for social and cultural capital to work best for persons who already possess more or less commensurate economic capital.

Another of Bourdieu's claims is that leisure is largely, or at least partly, about exchange relationships, and that the meanings of particular tastes, interests and skills lie partly in their exchange value. Choices of leisure activities are to be seen as motivated not solely by a quest for personal enjoyment or well-being, nor are the outcomes to be measured solely in these terms. Rather, these choices are seen as acts of social positioning. The significance of playing sport, for example, will depend on which sport, where a person plays, and with whom, and people's sporting choices are expected to be influenced by these wider social implications. That said, we must recognise that much leisure behaviour will have nothing to do with social positioning, but will be simply about pleasure, relaxation and well-being, and enjoying the company of family and existing friends. The social and cultural capitals that are expanded during leisure usually have exchange value and can advance a person's position only within the relevant leisure field. Exactly which sport and leisure capitals have exchange value which can be used outside the relevant sport and leisure fields, and exactly who uses them in this way, are issues that still await investigation.

There is more that sport and leisure research can learn from Bourdieu about the exchange value of particular tastes and activities. The 'more' arises from Bourdieu's concept of field. Tastes acquire their significance from their positions in fields, and hence their proximity to actors from particular places, from particular classes, and of a particular gender, ethnicity, age and so on. We are invited to treat what are normally called variables or factors such as gender, social class and place not as independent and dependent, set in cause–effect relationships, but as defining one another. So a leisure activity gains much of its meaning from who does it. Conversely, particular uses of leisure become part of what it means to be a particular kind of man (or woman), middle-class, American, English, French and so on. This immediately renders absurd the idea that we might somehow remove constraints and make the same leisure activities equally accessible and useful to everyone. The appearance of open access is important not just when seeking state funding, but in obscuring non-meritocratic ways in which classes are consolidated socially and culturally, and how positions are transmitted and advantages perpetuated.

PART III
The present

chapter 11

The latest modern age

Introduction

Virtually all sociologists who have written about Western societies since the 1970s have offered or adopted, explicitly or implicitly, some type of theory about how these societies have changed, or are still changing, since a former industrial age. The new times have variously been described as post-Fordist, post-industrial, post-modern, post-welfare, globalised, neo-liberal, liquid, and an information or knowledge age. The terms used by the German sociologist Ulrich Beck (1944–2015) were 'latest modernity', 'modernity II' and 'reflexive modernity'. His work is highlighted here because the book that earned Beck global eminence, *Risk Society*, first published in Germany in 1985, emphasised different features of the new modernity, and different change drivers, than earlier accounts (Beck, 1985/1992). Beck changed how we think about the new era. His work uniquely links macro global trends in the economy and politics to the micro, the inter-personal, including, but not confined to, intimate love relationships.

Until his death in 2015 Beck was the leading social theorist about the latest stage in modernity. Needless to say, other sociologists have contributed to how we conceptualise and think about our latest modern age, especially the British sociologist Anthony Giddens (1938–), who has co-authored with Beck alongside making independent contributions (Giddens, 1990; Beck et al., 1994), and Zygmunt Bauman (1925–), originally a Polish sociologist, but settled in Britain since 1971 and, rather like Norbert Elias (see Chapter 6), enormously productive since formally retiring in 1991 (see, for example, Bauman, 1998, 2006, 2007, 2011). Beck's widespread influence, indeed eminence, do not mean that he was right. Beck has many critics within sociology. These and other contributors to debates about our latest modern era are introduced later in this chapter. However, Beck's work is a useful centre-piece around which to organise contributions to theories about the new times which are still history in progress.

All the European theorists in this book – Durkheim, Marx, Weber, Elias, Habermas, Foucault, Bourdieu and Beck – led lives which bore the imprint of the continent's tumultuous events of the nineteenth and first half of the twentieth century. In Beck's case the imprint came early and was brief. He was born in 1944 in Stolp, a town on the Baltic coast of Pomerania which was in Germany at the time, then in 1945 became part of Poland and was renamed Słupsk. Poland's eastern and western borders were both moved westward by the victorious Soviet Union in 1945. Until then Vilnius (now capital of Lithuania) and Lviv (now in Ukraine) were Polish cities. Many Poles from its former eastern territories were moved into the country's post-war new western territories. Germans from these territories moved westward. The Beck family was part of the twentieth century's largest act of ethnic cleansing (as it has subsequently been described). Millions of Germans were expelled from liberated countries in East and Central Europe. Thousands were victims of extra-judicial murder, sometimes merely because they spoke German. This was during a savage peace which followed the end of the war. Germans remember, but have realised since 1945 that they must remain silent, suppress any anger and never complain. Their twentieth-century history helps everyone to understand why, since 1945, Germans have been determined, no 'ifs' and no 'buts', to embed their country in a union with its European neighbours. In 1945 the Becks moved along the Baltic coast and settled in Hanover, which was a good choice in that it became part of the Federal Republic of (West) Germany rather than the (East) German Democratic Republic. Thereafter Ulrich Beck had a conventional education and academic career, based mainly in Munich. European theorists who follow Beck will lead the more conventional lives of the American theorists in this book – Parsons, Goffman, Blumer, and also Inglehart and Fukuyama, who feature in Chapter 12. The European exceptions will be those who began their lives in pre-1989 communist Europe.

Post-industrial society pre-Beck

The historical progress of advanced Western economies into a post-industrial era was forecast, and there were firm indications that the movement was well under way, long before Ulrich Beck's *Risk Society* appeared. The new post-industrial era took its name from changes in the economies of the relevant countries. The best-known and most widely cited account of these changes was Daniel Bell's *The Coming of Post-Industrial Society* (1974).

The drivers were economic growth and technological changes, which were said to be responsible for two shifts in employment. One of these shifts was from jobs in manufacturing into service sectors. New technologies, whose introduction was called mechanisation or automation at the time, were more easily applied in manufacturing (where machines replaced human workers) than in services such as health care and education, and also public administration, financial and business services, where machines did not replace staff, but enabled them to work more effectively and sometimes to do more (but ICT has subsequently changed this in most service occupations). Also, it appeared to be the case that, as populations became more prosperous, demand for more goods grew more slowly than demand for services, especially education and health care. The second shift was out of manual or blue-collar and into non-manual, white-collar jobs (office, management and professional occupations). This shift was occurring because, it appeared at the time, it was easier to mechanise lower-skilled than higher-skilled occupations. Also, overall the workforces in service sectors had higher proportions of employees in white-collar jobs than the workforces in manufacturing, agriculture and extractive industries. These trends, it was argued, demanded more highly educated and highly qualified workforces – claims which are still heard today. Knowledge was said to be superseding physical capital as the key factor of production. It was argued that economic growth required investment in education to become a top priority. By the 1970s the industrial working classes were already ceasing to be the mass of the people. Class structures were undergoing embourgeoisement. The economic base of working-class trade unions and political parties was shrinking, and as predicted many decades ago, the centre ground of politics in Western countries has indeed now shifted rightwards.

A more controversial pre-1980s claim was that there would be less paid work per head of population in post-industrial societies. Leisure scholars were heavily involved in either propounding or contesting this view. In the 1960s and 1970s the scholars who claimed that there would be less work were able to argue that leisure time would therefore account for a larger part of people's lives. This sounded credible at the time. From the nineteenth century up to the 1970s the demands of work had been rolled back. A normal working day had been shortened to seven or eight hours. A normal working week had been shortened from six to five days. A normal working year had been shortened with the introduction then enlargement of holiday entitlement. A normal working life had also been compressed as a result of children then young people spending more years in education, while state and private pensions enabled people to retire from paid work with many years of life ahead. It was expected that as societies became even more prosperous, people would continue to take a proportion (possibly a growing proportion) of the benefits in reduced hours of work. Another view was that, whatever their own preferences, humans would gradually be replaced by machines which were cheaper, more efficient and more reliable. Some forecasters envisaged people enjoying 'the time of their lives' for the first time in history (Best, 1978). Others feared that people would be stranded in a wilderness of boredom (Glasser, 1970). The former attractive possibility was seen to depend on greater emphasis on education for leisure rather than education for work, and heavier investment in public leisure services (Jenkins and Sherman, 1981). André Gorz (1982) argued that rather than the working class abolishing capitalism as Marx had predicted, it was capitalism that was abolishing the working class. Gorz's socialist solution was a citizens' wage which would reduce people's need to work, and therefore the volume of labour supply. We shall see below that none of these forecasts have proved spot-on. A point to note is that leisure scholars in this pre-Beck period, which was when leisure studies first became a collective enterprise, a distinct field for teaching and research, were heavily involved in debates on the likely character of the forthcoming modern age. They have subsequently lost, but can and should reclaim this position.

It was in the 1970s that commentators first began to draw attention to physical limits to economic growth: eventually the world's stocks of fossil fuels and other minerals would be exhausted (Heilbroner, 1976; Meadows et al., 1974). Most of those who accepted that growth could not continue indefinitely also agreed that action could be deferred. We also learnt that there were social limits to growth in the sense that beyond the level that economically advanced countries had already reached, 'more' did not mean more satisfied, contented and happier people. Fred Hirsch (1977) explained why. A positional element in personal consumption was growing in size. In other words, people became more satisfied as they acquired more income and possessions only if this meant that they had more than other people in their comparison groups. Hirsch likened what was happening as standards of living continued to rise to a crowd where everyone stands on tiptoe and no one sees further. All this has been confirmed by subsequent research and evidence (see Layard, 2003). Governments and an inter-disciplinary army of scholars are currently seeking alternative indicators of progress, but in elections it is still the economy that matters. Are you better off? Do you feel better off than at the time of the last election? These rather than 'Are you happier today?' are still the questions on which the outcomes of elections seem to hinge. However, there are people who opt out of high-salary, long-hours jobs in favour of more relaxed lifestyles. The numbers are complicated, and whether they amount to a trend, are still unknown.

Ulrich Beck

Risks

Beck's *Risk Society* (1985) offered a novel interpretation of how the economically advanced societies were changing. The book took its title from a new kind of risk: nuclear disaster and climate change were examples. It was not just the specific risks that were new, but their character. Science was the cause, and could offer no solutions. The risks were incalculable and uninsurable. No country or group could insulate itself. Beck argued that this new modern condition required us to become reflexive, more so than in the past, examining the changes we make and the risks we take, and to try to control and limit unintended effects (Beck, 1985, 1994).

Risk Society was written and published after the partial nuclear meltdown at Three Mile Island in the USA in 1979, and just before Chernobyl in Ukraine, where an explosion and fire at a nuclear plant in 1986 released large quantities of radioactive particles across an extensive area in Eastern Europe. Throughout the 1980s there was ongoing concern about the depletion of the ozone layer which had been observed since the late 1970s. There have been subsequent nuclear incidents, including Fukushima in Japan in 2011, where three out of six nuclear reactors were struck by a tsunami which had been triggered by a powerful earthquake. However, throughout the 2000s climate change has been the main concern.

Beck alone was not responsible for highlighting this and other 'green' issues, but he was among the first to recognise, as more and more commentators have done since the 1980s, that the big natural environment issue is not the danger of running out of fossil fuels, but the damage their extraction and use inflicts on humanity's habitat. Later Beck (2013a) cited the threatened global financial meltdown in 2008–2009 and the subsequent Eurozone crisis as examples of the risk society. Both crises were man-made, and according to Beck, neither was predicted (but on this he was wrong). However, he was on firmer ground in arguing that none of the relevant scientists (the economists) have been able to offer trusted solutions.

Globalisation

The global character of these new risks was identified as one aspect of globalisation, but Beck saw this as driven primarily by more open markets, including the global capital markets in which the 2008–2009 financial crisis was created. A result was the reduced ability of national governments to protect their citizens. In this way societies had become more fragile, less reliable places. Major employers could relocate from a region and leave an economic wasteland. An entire industry could be lost to international competition. Rather than developing countries catching up, Western workforces were having to compete against labour costs in the emerging market economies. Beck (2000) described the outcome as a progressive 'Brazilianisation' of employment – more low-paid, insecure jobs. Zygmunt Bauman (2006) describes these new times as a 'liquid modernity'. The solid, reliable fixtures of the industrial age have gone.

Individualisation

Risk Society made the concept of 'individualisation' mainstream in sociology. This was said to be the result of weaker families, and weaker neighbourhood and religious communities. In turn, this weakening was said to have been due originally to the creation of welfare states. Individuals had become less dependent on help from their families, which in turn had become less dependent on help from neighbours. However, an effect of globalisation was that more risks were borne by individuals when governments were unable to guarantee employment and secure adult lives for all.

Beck was aware that links between childhood social origins and adult destinations remained as strong as ever, but fewer families were able to buy a good education, and children from poor families could qualify for entry to prestigious schools. Welfare states were offering access to health care and decent housing as rights of citizenship. Young people were no longer dependent on their families in ways that had applied in the past. Few could rely or needed to rely on appointment to a family business or professional practice: most of these had become joint stock companies or state services. Employment was open to all the talents. Parents who wished to do so could still pass on advantages, but this had to be via a child's agency. The child needed to be taught to aim high and work hard. Thus biographies had become private projects, and responsibility for one's successes and failures was personalised. Friends and places to live, like employment careers, were no longer 'given', but had become personal choices. Changes could leave people feeling like strangers in the places where they had been born and reared, but people could select and move into neighbourhoods where they felt 'at home' (Savage et al., 2005).

Cosmopolitanism

In all his books Beck complained that sociology lacked the language, the concepts, needed to make sense of the changing world. Somewhat exaggerating, he claimed that 'class' and 'country' had become zombie concepts – still used, but stripped of explanatory power (Beck, 2013b). Young people, according to Beck, increasingly inhabit cosmopolitan spaces in colleges, cities and workplaces (Beck, 2012; Beck and Beck-Gernsheim, 2009). The term 'cosmopolitan' can be applied to people and/or places. Cosmopolitan people feel equally at home in any of the many countries where they study, work, visit or live (always temporarily). The cosmopolitan will necessarily carry a passport issued by a specific country, but will feel no greater attachment to that country than to many others. Ideal-typically, the cosmopolitan is a citizen of the world, a member of humanity rather than any nationality. A cosmopolitan place is where visitors from elsewhere are welcome and made to feel at home.

This was Beck's vision of a cosmopolitan Europe and a European Germany rather than a German Europe. Older nationalities were not expected to collapse into a European nation. The people of Europe would retain their national languages, cultures and identities while willingly sharing their homelands with other Europeans and maybe visitors and settlers from the wider world. Beck (2013a) presents us with an 'Erasmus generation', cosmopolitan in outlook and, according to Beck, certain to prefer 'more Europe' rather than a return to nationalism, national currencies and border controls. According to Beck, we live in a metamorphosing world, as in the nineteenth century, when sociology was born and the changes that were then in process were incomprehensible until concepts such as industrialisation, urbanism and bureaucracy were given their modern meanings. This requires reflexivity, and Beck himself, of course, claimed to be a reflexive thinker. He criticised German politicians who prioritised domestic votes and who fashioned top-down policies to address Europe's problems (Beck, 2013a). Beck himself claimed to be a bottom-up thinker, and believed that he spoke for Europe's people, especially the young people, who would be receptive to 'revolutionary ideas' such as his own which were for 'more Europe', funded by European taxation.

Intimate relations

Ulrich Beck and his wife, Elisabeth Beck-Gernsheim, explored the implications of the latest modernity for personal life. One outcome, they claimed, is 'the normal chaos of love' (Beck and Beck-Gernsheim, 1995; see also Giddens, 1993). People seek security and confirmation of their identities in intimate relationships which, like employment careers, have become personal choices. People seek 'pure relationships' where they are bound together not by external pressures, but simply by inter-personal attraction. Women are no longer bound in relationships by their need for economic security for themselves and their children. Men no longer need to marry for regular legitimate sex and a wife who will ensure that the husband's labour power is reproduced from day to day in a caring home. Personal attraction becomes the sole bond, and the maintenance of a relationship depends on the emotional and psychic benefits each partner experiences.

People seek and need intimacy, yet personal biographies in education and employment pull them apart as never before. There are more reconstituted families, and more people with successive batches of children from successive relationships. There has to be an assumption of temporariness. Nothing is for keeps. Travel for education, work and leisure has become increasingly common, and leads to more cases of 'distant love', living together apart as well as living apart together, which happens when partners become estranged while still sharing the same abode. Migration separates husbands from wives, children from grandparents, yet ICT enables them to remain in touch daily or even more frequently (Beck and Beck-Gernsheim, 2002, 2013). Welcome to the Becks' brave latest modern world.

Beyond Beck

Ulrich Beck has many critics (for example, Atkinson, 2007; Curran 2013a, 2013b; Mythen, 2004, 2005). The main and recurrent criticism is the dismissive way in which Beck treats social class. Former classes are said to dissolve in a whirlwind of individualised reflexivity. Actually, Beck's alleged sins are all of exaggeration (frequently true) and omission or failing to foreground trends that others consider important (which is probably inevitable). Beck's language certainly exaggerates the extent of change during the last fifty years. European countries metamorphosed into entirely different societies between the Middle Ages and early modern times. This took several centuries. Unlike tadpoles and frogs, present-day Western countries are still recognisable versions of their mid-twentieth-century selves. There is relatively little in Beck's books on either the economy or politics. Following *Risk Society* in 1985, economic change is not foregrounded except in *The Brave New World of Work* in 2000, where the main argument is about the Brazilianisation of labour markets. There is little on politics until the tirade against Germany's politicians and 'Merkeliavelli' in *German Europe* (Beck, 2013a).

Employment and social mobility

As regards Western economies, a feature of the post-1980s period which Beck does not foreground is that the former embourgeoisement of occupational structures has not continued. White-collar employment has been the front line for onslaught by ICT, which also enables much of this work to be offshored (see Urry, 2014). The most rapid employment growth in the twenty-first century has been in precarious, low-paid, non-standard-hours jobs (see Standing, 2011). The pre-Beck forecast of more leisure for all or mounting technological unemployment has proved wrong. Forecasts of jobless growth continued long after *Risk Society* was published (see, for example, Aronowitz and DiFazio, 1994; Dunkerley, 1996; Forrester, 1999), but the scenario has been averted in most of Europe and North America by the creation of more low-paid jobs (zero-paid in the case of some internships) and jobs with short-hour contracts (zero-hours in some cases). The main trend in inter-generational social mobility is that more is now downwards and less is upwards (Bukodi et al., 2015).

Time pressure

However, while more short-hours jobs have been created, on average people with full-time jobs are working for as many hours as previously. The former long-term historical decline ended some time in the 1970s or 1980s, depending on the country. There has been no increase in the typical full-time employee's hours spent at paid work, but total paid working time per household among adults of working age has risen as a result of the growing number of multi-earner families (more married women in employment). Perhaps surprisingly, domestic technology has not reduced total time spent on housework and child care. The experts are not agreed on why there has been no decline despite new technologies in the home and at work enabling more to be done in less time. Some blame demanding employers and a culture of 'presenteeism' created by fear of job loss or forfeiture of promotion prospects, combined with the 'addictive power of consumption' (Schor, 1991). Others say that the explanation is basically cultural in a different sense; a need to be busy, busyness as a sign of status, idleness as an indication that a person is useless (Gershuny, 2005). We use domestic technologies to raise standards of home and personal care, and parents spend more time with young children. We collect friends on social media. This may not make us more satisfied with our lives, but we still want to do more and have more.

We are rarely contacted outside normal working hours by our bosses. Communications from and to families and friends during official work time are far more common intrusions by email and cellphone. Maybe, but we can still feel that we need to check constantly for work-related emails and texts (Bittman et al., 2009). More people complain of time pressure. The perceived pace of life is accelerating (see Wajcman, 2015). We appear to pile pressure on ourselves. The seriously rich, those best able to do so, appear to shun retirement. Lives of affluent leisure are currently being enjoyed by some members of the baby-boomer cohorts who have been able to retire from well-paid management and professional jobs on final salary pensions. These pensions will not be available for persons currently in mid-working life or younger. Young people today whose main careers lie in the future keep incredibly busy, combining study, part-time jobs and the need to keep in touch with friends (often multiple times each day using ICT), and then they must spend some time with their families. All this is lost, faded into the background, in Beck's version of late modernity.

Wider economic inequalities

There is little in Beck's books about how economic inequalities have widened within countries while narrowing between the BRICS and the old West. It is difficult to reconcile widening inequalities in wealth and income with Beck's claim that class has become a zombie concept. Beck (2013b) insists that class has become 'too soft' a concept to retain explanatory value. This view may be justified in respect of working classes that have diminished in size, lost their distinctive ways of life and ceased to be the base of efficacious political movements. Whether either the capitalist class (now often self-described as 'business') or the new upper middle classes of highly paid professionals and managers have become zombies is much more debatable.

Places

'Country' is another of Beck's zombie concepts. This is another exaggeration. Smaller European states have never been genuinely sovereign. The USA has never been more sovereign, and likewise the more influential BRICS countries – Brazil, Russia, India, China and South Africa – plus the mineral-rich Middle East states. Place of birth and the passport you carry continue to make a huge difference. Beck's new modern world is populated by cosmopolitans who reflexively construct biographies as they move between countries for education, work and leisure, whose main problem is maintaining close, intimate relationships. In practice, even most young Europeans are not part of Beck's Erasmus generation. The majority never attend university. It is only the masses in rich countries, and just the rich in others, who travel for leisure. The hyper-mobility of some depends on the immobility of others – the nannies, office, restaurant and hotel staff (see Elliott and Urry, 2010). Well-qualified young people from the EU's post-2004 member states move westward to work in low-skilled, low-paid jobs because back home the salaries in jobs commensurate with their qualifications are even lower. Migrants who enter the EU from outside its borders to live and work often do so in the twilight. They are the original excluded group referred to by Jacques Delors during his 1985–1994 presidency of the European Commission. They are marginal in the labour market and have no political or welfare rights.

New technologies

There are further features of the latest modern age which, if not entirely absent, have a lower profile in Beck's work than they may merit. Some regard ICT as the defining feature of the era, as indicated by terms such as knowledge economy and information age. These new technologies are said (by Castells, 1996, for example) to have dissolved the boundaries of organisations and countries (for flows of information, but not human bodies). New technologies have certainly reduced the significance of distance and made communication between all parts of the world virtually instant. This is called time–space compression. It has been ongoing throughout the modern era, but ICT has been a new giant stride. The walls of businesses, including banks and also governments, have become porous.

New networks are created, then dissolve and are replaced. When at leisure, we can play computer games. These have existed since the 1970s, but have become more complex and challenging: there are now mass-participation online games. We can contribute to collective projects such as Wikipedia. We can post blogs (currently most likely on Twitter). We can chat on social media sites (currently most likely Facebook, but for how long?).

Most jobs have changed in some way by incorporating ICT. Almost everything that used to be done in an office can now be done on the move using a laptop, smartphone or tablet, but note that this part of everything does not include face-to-face communication, which even heads of businesses in the ICT industries consider essential to establish and maintain trust relationships (Wajcman, 2015).

Does ICT change everything, or is it just froth around familiar work, family and leisure routines? It may be too soon to say. In the USA, which had the world's highest penetration, in 2000 less than 10 per cent of households had broadband. There was no Twitter, no Facebook and no online shopping. Before the end of the nineteenth century the basic technologies of radio and moving pictures were invented and were being used, but it was not until the 1920s that radio broadcasting to domestic audiences commenced and picture palaces were under construction to play the 'full-length' movies Hollywood was then producing. The information age's equivalents may still lie in the future.

Political change

As noted above, Beck has little to say about politics, except that in 1985 in *Risk Society* globalisation was disempowering national governments, then in *German Europe* in 2013 Germany's politicians were berated for blocking the progress of the 'European project'.

If national governments have surrendered power to the EU and the European Central Bank, and to the International Monetary Fund and the World Trade Organization, this has been their choice. The widespread adoption of neo-liberal policies, leaving as much as possible to markets, reducing government spending and squeezing welfare budgets, has been another domestic political choice and a feature of the latest modern age.

Meanwhile, voter turnout at elections has been declining, as have the shares of votes going to what have hitherto been major political parties and are still the parties most likely to form governments. The bonds between 'the people' and 'democratic' governments have become weaker. However, despite hints of new ICT-aided ways of practising politics (Castells, 2012; Castells et al., 2012), together with new 'third way' (Giddens, 1998) and 'green' alternatives, the emergent parties that have mounted the strongest challenges to established parties of government in Europe have been advocating an older politics either of the left (Syriza in Greece and Podemos in Spain, for example) or nationalism (such as the Front National in France).

Demography

Beck says little about demographic change. Young people are spending longer in education. Nearly all countries now have ageing populations. Employment careers account for a diminishing proportion of lifetime.

However, despite the exaggerations and omissions or diminutions, Ulrich Beck is still our major theorist of the changes that have occurred since the late twentieth century. This is because he offers not just a list of changes, but a set of concepts – mainly risk, globalisation, individualisation and reflexivity – with which to explore how the changes are inter-related. The construction of the latest modern age itself, as well as its theories, is still work in progress. In the meantime, all scholars who study the present have no alternative but to engage.

Applications in sport and leisure

Our present age is a topic on which sport and leisure scholars must be more than users: they can participate in constructing theory. It is a mistake to ask only 'How is leisure affected by . . . ?' because trends in leisure are helping to construct the latest modern age. Some features of this age are already incorporated within sport and leisure scholars' work. This is inevitably the case because late modern trends are reshaping the demand for and the supply of the leisure goods and services that sport and leisure scholars study, and which their students will be employed in producing. The leisure industries are catering for extended youth and young adult life stages, and simultaneously for expanding numbers of seniors. Everyone involved in leisure provision experiences the widening inequality between the well-off and the rest. Sport and leisure scholars know that public spending on leisure is being squeezed. More provision is commercial. More spending is by private consumers. It is still unclear whether the voluntary sector will fill gaps left or be weakened by the withdrawal of state support (see Roberts, 2015b).

Time

'Acceleration' is another feature of the latest modern age that leisure scholars necessarily confront and address. People complain that life has speeded up. We increasingly complain about time pressure (see Wajcman, 2015). New technologies enable us to do things (work things and leisure things) more quickly. So we can save time and have more literally free time at our disposal. Work regimes, set by employers, oblige us to use the time saved by technology to do more. Are we choosing to clutter our leisure in a similar way? We do not have to do this, yet it might be in our interests to 'do more' if we can afford to do so. Sport and leisure researchers find consistently that 'doing more' is good for well-being (Iso-Ahola and Mannell, 2004). Literally spare time appears to be a burden. Our ability to play simple and more complex computer games while at home or on the move, to blog, to send and receive emails and text messages, may be mitigating boredom during otherwise idle time, as television has done since the 1950s. This may simultaneously be adding to the time pressure about which people complain. There are advocates of 'slow' – slow food, slow travel and so on (for example, Hohlbaum, 2009; Honore, 2004, 2008). Instead of taking more holidays we can choose to take longer and slower holidays. In practice, we are taking more and shorter holidays than formerly. So overall leisure appears to be contributing to acceleration rather than easing time pressure with other roots in work and family routines. Dating sites are too slow, so some singles engage in speed-dating. Yet overall we are spending more time than ever before watching television, often using 'catch-up' options. We also spend more time in front of computers (offline and online), plus laptops and smartphones. More time is spent stationary in traffic jams and on airplanes, where we are more likely to feel bored and frustrated rather than relaxed. Are ICT devices enabling us to relax, to mitigate boredom, to switch off, or are they adding to the cluttering of time and making life accelerate even more, putting our time and lives under unremitting pressure? When at leisure, we can decide when to read and answer electronic messages, which was impossible when everything was face-to-face or using a landline telephone. We may also feel compelled to check constantly just in case we are missing something or someone who cannot wait. We may be subject to more surveillance at work and in public spaces via CCTV, but their latest gadgets enable teenagers and adults to exercise more control and enjoy greater privacy in their relationships with friends.

Ecology

Other features of the latest modern age have yet to be incorporated satisfactorily into Beck's or any other theory. This is where sport and leisure scholars need to step in. We (all of us) have known since the 1970s that eventually the earth's fossil fuels and other minerals will be exhausted, and that our ways of producing and consuming are changing the natural environment on which human survival depends. Yet the rate of growth in energy consumption during leisure exceeds the rate of growth in energy consumption overall (Aall et al., 2011). Leisure may be where we could most easily cut back, but it is not where we first do so. We remain in love with our motor cars and air travel. Even during recessions, high-energy-using forms of leisure continue to grow. Following a brief one-year blip after the 2008–2009 financial crash, global tourism resumed its long-term upward trajectory. In richer countries, spending on old and new media, and on sports goods and services, continued to rise. People are not opting for more local, less energy-hungry uses of leisure (Roberts, 2014, 2015a). It appears that the populations in richer countries decide to maintain energy consumption during their leisure even while cutting back on 'essentials', including food and heating their homes. Leisure cutbacks tend to be in low-energy-consuming activities such as visits to local pubs and restaurants, and spending less during each outing. Leisure is close to the heart of the problem and must be at the heart of any solution to the ecological challenges reflexive citizens face in the latest modern age.

Liquid modernity

The claim that the societies in which we live have become more liquid, more fragile than formerly, needs to be interrogated systematically against, rather than just illustrated with, possibly atypical leisure evidence. The reverse could apply – leisure life could have retained its former solidity. Tony Blackshaw is one leisure scholar who has tackled the leisure implications of the loss of older solidities and reliabilities not just theoretically, but on the basis of successive studies in West Yorkshire, where he is based. Blackshaw argues that the effects of general trends in work, family life and uses of leisure vary according to cohort. He has shown (Blackshaw, 2003) how some adult working-class males use leisure to cling to masculine identities that have become redundant in the labour market and also in family life. During their nights out together these men assure one another that their preferred world is still real, that basically nothing has changed. However, Blackshaw has also illustrated how others regret the loss of old solidities. His losers are the cohort he calls the 'inbetweeners', who spent childhoods in a solid modernity, then experienced the disintegration of the world in which they had felt comfortable (Blackshaw, 2013). Yet Blackshaw also presents our current 'liquid modernity' as creating the scope for people (the post-inbetweeners) to use leisure to build and express preferred identities:

> It is my contention that in the liquid modern world we live in, which is founded first and foremost on freedom, leisure moves steadily into its position as the principal driving force underpinning the human goal of satisfying our hunger for meaning and our thirst for giving our lives a purpose.
>
> (Blackshaw, 2010, p. 120)

Workplaces and neighbourhoods may be changing their characters more rapidly than in the past, and the 'menu' of leisure activities and inactivities on offer may also be subject to more rapid change than ever before. There are forever more places and ways in which we are tempted to spend our holidays. There are more kinds of music we can access. There are more sports we can watch on more sports-dedicated television channels. We are able to channel-surf, to watch more – and more different – sports, and we are able to travel to more places as tourists, but we can also use our wider scope for choice to retain familiar routines: to listen to what has always been our favourite music, to follow the sports teams to which we became attached during childhood, and to use the same trusted tour organiser who will offer a similar holiday experience to what we experienced last year and the year before that. These are likely leisure benefits of 'liquidity'.

However, Finn Bowring (2015) has explained that more and more choice, more 'freedom from' old restrictions, must result in Durkheim's anomie (see Chapter 2). 'Freedom from' and 'freedom to' (to have access to decent housing, employment and a range of leisure opportunities, for example) can only be guaranteed by states, and for individuals genuine freedom is said to require participation in public affairs, but this is not one of the many possible uses of leisure time that has been increasing.

Individualisation

This is the final issue for leisure scholars to confront. More geographical mobility and more variety in work schedules – and hence more desynchronisation of time rhythms within families, among neighbours, and among students in upper secondary and higher education – make it more difficult than in the past for the same groups to meet for leisure at the same times every week, throughout a year, and from year to year. This leads to the development of individualised leisure careers, and is a likely explanation for the switch from large team sports to individual exercise and other forms of non-competitive energetic leisure such as swimming, surfing and skiing that can be practised at individuals' discretion or when pairs or foursomes happen to be available. Competitive amateur team sports can survive only by using whoever from larger pools of players happens to be available for a given fixture. However, there are other possible explanations of these trends: less investment in and higher user charges for public playing fields and other sport facilities, and better-off sections of the population able to afford gym subscriptions and to travel and purchase the equipment to surf, scuba-dive, climb and ski.

Individualisation does not imply solitariness. It is rather a case of the composition of every individual's network of friends and acquaintances changing constantly. Overall, there may be less stability in leisure-time companions, but this is not incompatible with the maintenance of long-term, indeed lifelong, friendship and family bonds, especially with ICT enabling people to keep in touch frequently, even daily, and to remain feeling close irrespective of distance and varied time schedules. Leisure may in some ways illustrate and even amplify individualisation, but it may simultaneously be where people are able to reconcile fluid sociality with maintaining especially valued relationships.

Conclusions

There can be no genuine conclusions here because as yet we have nothing that resembles a completed theory that identifies the change drivers and the overall character of the latest modern age. We are unsure whether this age is already here or still in formation. Today it is easier to look back at the earlier transformation associated with industrialisation, urbanisation, the formation of nation states and the spread of democracy. Yet even with historical distance there are competing theories, each of which may be more helpful in identifying still ongoing trends and tendencies than attempts to grasp what is new. Forecasts are repeatedly confounded. The expansion of 'knowledge jobs' has ended. The leisure society in which everyone was to enjoy more work-free time and to have more money to spend in this time has failed to materialise. A new kind of technological unemployment has not spread remorselessly. Economic growth has not been stalled by the exhaustion of natural resources. As scarcity drives up prices, more reserves are discovered and become exploitable. Risks associated with nuclear power, the ozone layer and climate change are being managed, or we are learning to live with and accept the risks as normal.

One feature of the latest modern age which now commands attention is the stagnation of living standards at the bottom and in the middle in the old West, while the wealth of dollar billionaires continues to expand. Finance businesses, not traditional banks, but those whose business is simply making money, and the lawyers, accountants and others who service these finance businesses, are able to pay annual salaries to some staff that exceed the lifetime earnings of the typical employees who live and work in the same cities. These are salaries, not profits. The dot.com economy is where a few successful start-ups can quickly turn their owners into dollar billionaires without needing to create large organisations with huge payrolls.

Another feature of the latest modern age that is currently under the spotlight is 'acceleration', the time crunch, sometimes referred to as work–life balance. Acceleration is definitely happening in workplaces. New technologies enable people to do more and work faster, and employers ensure that this is how the technologies are used. They have done this throughout the history of capitalism, in which 'time is money', a commodity which can be put to productive use. The significance of ICT when people are at leisure still remains unclear, though the quantity of time spent online has grown remarkably: from zero in 1990 to an average of 20 hours a week by UK adults and 27 hours among 16–24-year-olds in 2014 (Ofcom, 2015).

There are many avenues through which sport and leisure scholars can engage and contribute to debates about the character of this modern age, and the driving forces that are propelling us into and through it. Sport and leisure scholars have under-used the theories about the original and the latest modern ages that are available, and are still under-performing in contributing to the development of these theories. These are challenges to which incoming cohorts of scholars must respond.

chapter 12

Modernisation theory

Introduction

Ronald Inglehart (1934–) is an American sociologist, based at the University of Michigan. In the 1960s and 1970s he conducted research in economically advanced Western countries and found that cohorts who had grown up since the Second World War had different values than their parents. The latter had experienced the war and the 'hungry 30s', and attached high priority to economic security – jobs and keeping clear of poverty. The post-war cohorts took these for granted. They wanted more. Their values were originally described as post-scarcity or post-materialist (Inglehart, 1977, 1997).

After 1981 Inglehart's research was broadened and extended into the World Values Surveys of which he became the director. The seventh wave of these surveys is being conducted during 2016–2018 in almost a hundred countries. These surveys have detected two global value shifts, both occurring mainly through generational replacement:

- The first is from traditional to secular/rational values. Traditional values emphasise the importance of religion, parent–child ties and deference to authority. People who embrace these values tend to reject divorce, abortion, euthanasia and suicide, and display high levels of national pride and nationalist outlooks. Secular/rational values imply exactly the opposite. This shift tends to begin when countries start to grow economically, classically through developing manufacturing industries.
- The second shift is from survival values to self-expression values. Survival values emphasise the importance of economic and physical

security. Self-expression values place high priority on environmental protection, tolerance of foreigners, gays and lesbians, gender equality, and demands for participation in decision-making in economic and political life. This shift is associated with the expansion of higher education and the formation of new middle classes. These groups, the highly educated who are employed in middle-class jobs, mainly in major cities, tend to lead in the adoption of these values.

Economic growth (industrialisation) appears to be the initial change driver. Subsequently, secular/rational and self-expression values become the change drivers supporting demands for democracy and freedom for individuals to express their identities and pursue lifestyles of their choice (Dalton and Welzel, 2014; Welzel, 2013; Welzel et al., 2003).

We shall see below that this account of current global changes, now embraced in what is called modernisation theory, is just the latest in a succession of social theories which have claimed that all societies are following the same evolutionary or developmental path. Like previous versions, present-day modernisation theory is contested. It is used here as a convenient entry point to debates about global trends in the twenty-first century. Like theories about the latest modern age (see Chapter 11), this is a theory that sport and leisure scholars can not only use, but can contribute to its acceptance and development or rejection.

Modernisation theory

The earliest versions of modernisation theory (its current post-1980s title) were the classical sociological theories of evolution (the term used at the time) that were presented in this book's early chapters: the theories of Comte, Marx, Durkheim and their contemporaries. They treated all societies as progressing along the same evolutionary path, with Western countries at the head.

The evolutionary parts of these theories became suspect during the early twentieth century. It became apparent that it was impossible to situate African tribal societies, the Australian Aborigines, the New Zealand Maoris, China, India and the Middle East states as ahead or behind one another on the same evolutionary road. Also, at that time Western countries were dividing into those that were communist, fascist and democratic.

Then, after the Second World War, modernisation theory (though still not under that title) was revived. The fascist regimes disappeared from Europe with the defeat of the Axis countries, then in the 1970s from Spain and Portugal, and also Greece, which had temporarily departed from democracy in the 1960s. During this same period some sociologists claimed that capitalist and communist countries were destined to converge, driven by a common logic of industrialism. Socialism and capitalism were treated as alternative routes to a common destination rather than different end-states (Bell, 1960; Kerr et al., 1960). This was during the decades when Western countries were strengthening their welfare states, governments were playing lead roles in macro-economic management, and when communist authorities were discussing how market mechanisms might be inserted into their centrally planned 'command' economies. Development studies (as they were called) contributed to the revival of 'all on the same track' thinking. Poorer countries were treated as striving to catch up with those that were more developed. Later, in the 1990s, the Human Development Index (which combines data on economic output, mortality rates and education, with some versions adding gender equality and democracy) was developed and promoted under United Nations auspices, thereby contributing to the view of a world composed of countries which are all progressing in the same direction.

No one ever assumed that all countries would eventually reach the same level of development. World systems theory (see Wallerstein, 1979), a niche specialism within sociology, treats the world as *the* social system; countries are sub-systems. Empires and religions spanning many countries have a history that stretches back into antiquity, but in the modern era inter-country links and flows have become more numerous and deeper. During the modernisation of the West many other countries became colonies, and then, according to one view, were systematically under-developed (see Frank, 1969). Neo-colonial relationships may have persisted in post-colonial times with 'comprador classes' in dependent countries mediating between exploiters and exploited (see Kamruzzaman, 2014). However, a twenty-first-century view is that these older international relationships have been transformed by the formation of a global capitalist class (see Robinson and Harris, 2000; Sklair, 2001). Individual owners of capital are necessarily based in specific countries, but their capital can circulate globally. This does not mean that all countries are becoming equal. Some contain 'global cities' which act as nodes in global financial circuits (Sassen, 1991). Their citizens derive some benefit – shares in surplus value, to use a Marxist expression – from their proximity to financial centres. These transformations have allegedly set all countries on the same historical track, but some will remain more powerful and prosperous than others.

We are racing ahead historically, and need to step back. Before the end of the twentieth century the 'all following the same path' thesis had encountered new problems. Rather than converging, during the 1970s and 1980s the communist and capitalist countries appeared to diverge. The communist countries had retained centrally planned economies and remained one-party states, while the West's economies were becoming less planned and more neo-liberal. Meanwhile, Japan and Singapore, the first of the 'Asian tiger economies', seemed to be pioneering distinctively Asian versions of capitalism, a market economy and democratic politics. Then by the 1990s some sociologists were highlighting divergences among Western countries: namely, between different European types of welfare capitalism (Esping-Andersen, 1990), and also between Europe and America (Martinelli, 2007).

However, in 1989 the single-track global modernisation side of the argument received a tremendous boost when communism began to collapse, first in Central and Eastern Europe and then throughout Eurasia. Supporters of change in these countries began to describe their reforms as 'modernisation', the countries having been retarded by communism. Hence the current title – modernisation theory. By the 1980s the West was entering post-industrial times, and neo-liberalism was the ascendant economic doctrine. The prescription for countries that were abandoning communism was 'big bang' shock therapy. Economic assistance from the West was conditional on the application of this thinking. This was the context in which Francis Fukuyama, an American political scientist, declared that 'the end of history' was in sight, with the market economy, capitalism and democracy destined to triumph all over the world (Fukuyama, 1992). However, before long another American political scientist, Samuel Huntington, was counter-predicting a new 'clash of civilisations' as the end of the Cold War allowed earlier lines of conflict to resurface, especially between the Christian West and Islam (Huntington, 1996). This forecast preceded 9/11 in 2001, but gained huge credibility thereafter.

Meanwhile, as we have seen, the World Values Surveys have been offering hefty support for the single global trajectory thesis, but with several important additions and qualifications. In addition to the global value shifts described earlier, these surveys have shown that some (though not all) less-developed countries are catching up economically and in the adoption of modern values. Many have been closing the gap with the West. An outcome was net increases in happiness in 45 out of the 52 countries that participated in both the 1981 and 2007 World Values Surveys. In Western countries happiness had already peaked. Western workforces may complain about Brazilianisation and a 'race to the bottom', but judged globally, neo-liberal free trade policies have lifted millions more clear of poverty. That said, some countries have remained economically stagnant, so the top–bottom gap has widened. Also, the surveys have confirmed that there can be late-development effects: the latest countries to modernise can, in certain respects, leap to the head of the global procession. They can start to industrialise using the latest technologies and management practices, carrying none of the 'baggage' that first-wave industrial countries have accumulated (see Dore, 1973, 1976). Thus late-developing countries, at least their modernised sectors, can rapidly become hyper-modern, and may offer the old West a glimpse of its own likely future.

Simultaneously, the 'all on the same modernising track' thesis has been subjected to important qualifications by evidence from the World Values Surveys. The surveys have shown that traditional cultures and national histories continue to leave powerful imprints: whether a country experienced a communist era, whether the main religion has been and remains Islam, whether the country has a long history of Protestantism, and the Indo-Chinese countries' distinctive Oriental cultures continue to make a difference. Moreover, these differences do not appear to be disappearing or even diminishing through generational replacement. Also, wide differences have been created within many late-modernising countries. In these countries the ways of life of many, often most of the people, remain basically traditional. These sections of the countries' populations are not being pulled along any modernising path, and it seems unlikely that it will ever be possible to absorb the entire global population into the modern economic sectors where modern leisure and broader modern ways of life are possible.

A problem for modernisation theory's advocates is how much of the 'all on the same track' proposition survives once all these qualifications have been admitted. This problem is encountered when applying the theory (treating it as a hypothesis or set of hypotheses) to sport and leisure in late-developing countries. A theory that can admit endless qualifications becomes irrefutable, in which case it needs to be replaced or reconfigured radically. This is a task on which sport and leisure scholars are well placed to contribute. The opposite of the 'all on the same track' view is that we are witnessing the formation of multiple modernities. Which side of this argument is supported by the existing sport and leisure evidence?

Applications in sport and leisure: Asian cases

Globalisation is not the issue. It is helping to drive change and construct the latest modern era in all countries, but current modernisation theory implies that indigenous forces alone will set all countries on the same track once they have begun to develop economically. Globalisation itself – increased flows between countries of goods, services, information and people – will not necessarily make societies more alike. It is just as likely to accentuate differences.

In any case, global flows of leisure products are not new. The modern sports that were invented in the late nineteenth century spread so rapidly that in 1896 it was possible to hold the first modern Olympic Games. Music and film have been marketed globally since the 1920s. Top sport events have been televised globally for several decades. Flows of all kinds have increased, and nowadays every country's radio and television broadcasts can be made available live to global audiences. McDonald's restaurants are everywhere, as are many other chains and branded goods. There are international markets for the services of talented sports stars, musicians and actors, though international flows of sport players still tend to be along paths created when European nations built overseas empires (McGovern, 2002), and despite the increased flows, the most popular music, actors, and sports teams and players in every country are usually locals. The most popular television programmes are invariably locally sourced. Global products are given different meanings in different places. Wearing Western fashions and listening to Western popular music in Eastern Europe and the Soviet Union in the 1980s indicated support for change: in the West there were no such connotations. So every country creates its own mixtures, including hybrids, from the global and the local. This process is known as 'glocalisation'.

Homogenisation is neither happening nor a test of the latest version of ('all on the same track') modernisation theory. We are looking for declines in the influence of religion and other traditions: not their disappearance, but that when retained, this should be through choice rather than just because they are traditions that have to be respected. We are looking for evidence that children do not feel obliged to follow parents' examples or advice in their leisure practices. We are looking for tolerance of diversity, which should be more evident in leisure than anywhere else. We should expect increased variety in leisure choices within countries while collectively citizens' choices may continue to exhibit distinct national and regional characteristics.

Here, we focus on sport and leisure evidence from Asian countries. This choice is partly based on the availability of evidence, but it is mainly theoretically guided. Some Asian countries such as China and Japan were never colonised by European powers. Those that were colonies did not become settler societies (like the USA and Australia, for example). The limited penetration of Christianity indicates the Asian countries' insulation from Western cultures. Some Asian countries have been changing rapidly in recent decades. During the late twentieth and early twenty-first centuries some of these countries have been among the world's fastest-growing economies. By the late twentieth century Japan had become a major economic power, and India and China are now following. These countries are of special interest because if alternatives to Western modernity, including Western leisure, are appearing anywhere, this should be happening in the Asian countries. Countries that became colonies of European powers, especially those where settlers became majorities of the populations, would be expected to develop into similar modern societies to their European parents. Islamic countries would be as good as Asian societies as test cases of whether there are alternatives to the Western version of modernity, except that those countries that have experienced rapid economic growth in recent decades have done so by exploiting mineral resources rather than industrialisation. Africa is a continent where spectacular economic development is still awaited. One can argue that more research and more time are required in order to make reliable judgements in respect of Asian countries, but in the mean time these are modernisation theory's strongest test cases.

Leisure in Asia: different and better?

Throughout Asia there is some resistance not just to the spread of Western leisure into these countries, but also, among researchers, to the global adoption of the Western leisure concept. Yoshitaka Iwasaki and his colleagues (2007) have pointed out that the traditional languages of East and South Asia did not contain a word whose meaning corresponds with the English-language 'leisure'. All the languages have now incorporated 'leisure', which has acquired specific local meanings within Hindi, Mandarin and so on. For example, in South Korea the everyday meaning of 'leisure' does not include time spent watching television (KyungHee Kim, 2011). Initially these languages associated 'leisure' with the West. Leisure was something that Western people had and exported (as tourists) beyond their own (Western) countries. Most people in Asia knew that they did not have that kind of leisure. Within their own countries leisure was a (mainly tourist) industry with which their own engagement, if any, was most likely to be as employees.

Some Indian and Chinese scholars claim that their alternatives to Western leisure are not only different, but better, and are now challenging Euro-American hegemony in sport and leisure studies (see, for example, Dodd and Sharma, 2012). They claim that Western leisure is materialist and consumerist, dedicated to having more, doing more and spending more. Oriental scholars draw upon Hindu and Buddhist sages, Lao Tse and Confucius to advocate a conception of leisure as a state of mind or being (Li, 2009). Their ideal is balance within the self, between the self and others, and between society and nature. Some (for example, Ma Huidi and Er, 2009) wish to attach the English-language word 'leisure' to this ideal. The following quotations are not from ancient texts or religious mystics, but from scholars who are all members of or associated with the International Sociological Association's Research Committee on Leisure:

The prime motivation of today's [Western] societies is the acquisition of material goods. This has a chimera like quality that does not lead to fulfillment or satisfaction but rather takes the form of greed . . . . Leisure is a state of 'being' as against one of 'having' or 'doing' . . . . It is necessary to know that leisure is a discovery of the Self by a bold and critical enquiry into the self.

(Sharma, 2006)

Leisure is the spiritual home of all human beings in which we can contemplate on both the starry sky above and the moral rules that are inside us . . . . Leisure is as essential to our life as are sunshine, air, and water. Without leisure, no life can continue. Leisure helps us to balance the body with the mind, the material with the spiritual life, physical with mental abilities, and material enjoyment with spiritual refreshment.

(International Sociological Association Research Committee on Leisure, 2009)

If modern leisurism fails to realize its ideal according to ontological analysis, then modern day materialism would surely triumph, and the prospect of mankind would be pitch black. The aim of modern leisurism [Fan Zeng's term for the study of leisure] is to keep human desire in proper relation with Nature's provision by following the 'thing-in-itself' of the universe . . . . Leisure as we understand it is salvation for the human soul.

(Fan Zeng, 2010, p. 33)

Western scholars should not be surprised by this resistance to the Western leisure concept and the globalisation of their Western leisure practices. At the time when over half the populations of European countries still lived in villages without any modern amenities, the modern leisure concept would have been considered inapplicable to most Europeans' ways of life. At that time there was much opposition to the destruction of traditional ways of life in Europe. The words 'sport' and 'leisure' were given their modern meanings in Western countries only when the countries modernised. Asian critics of modern Western leisure echo a series of Western scholars such as Sebastian de Grazia (1962) who have condemned contemporary leisure as a corruption of earlier purer versions.

Oriental scholars and Western researchers concur that traditional Asian cultures continue to exert a powerful influence (see Jianyu Wang and Stringer, 2000). So do traditional Western cultures, but in ways that pass unobserved until modernising societies with different traditions are encountered, and nowadays in the West and Asia the local voices that defend traditions are opposed by other local, and in Asia typically younger, voices that regard the traditions as a constraint. Lucetta Tsai (2006), for example, complains about the Confucian insistence that women in Taiwan must continue to be frugal, passive and subservient, with the result that their leisure often consists of nothing except sleeping, watching television and learning English. There is evidence from all over Asia of young people in the cities, especially the well-educated young people who have obtained middle-class jobs, adopting Western mindsets. The World Values Surveys in Shanghai have found that the city's young people put self-development ahead of contributing to society. They are individualistic, intent on building their own lives (Jiaming Sun and Xun Wang, 2010). College-educated Indian youth insist that they are forward-thinking rather than traditional (or 'backward'), though most continue to respect their parents and try to accommodate the latter's wishes. For example, the young people are likely to negotiate arranged marriages with their own chosen partners (see Wessel, 2011). This leisure evidence is exactly what modernisation theory predicts. Meanwhile, other evidence from Asia points in the contrary direction.

Work and leisure

Koreans claim to have the world's longest work schedules (KyungHee Kim, 2011; Moonkyum Kim, 2010). The Japanese are close behind (Harada, 1994; Horne, 1998). Employees are expected to demonstrate their dedication by not exhausting all their official holiday entitlement, and never leaving work until after, or arriving later than, their official finish and start times. Tiredness and taking public naps are marks of status in Japan, signalling that a person is working properly (Steger, 1996). Leslie Chang (2008) studied young Chinese women who had migrated from villages to work in Doonguan, a sprawling industrial city in the south of China. The girls normally worked at least ten hours a day, six days a week. After work they would crowd into evening classes to learn English or, even more popular, how to be successful. They were earning more than US$50 a month. Their aim was always to become managers or to run their own businesses, but in practice most were likely to return to their villages to marry. In the mean time, their status back home was boosted if they sent money and returned periodically with gifts.

The conventional explanation for long working hours and low pay in Asia is that the countries are still in the early stages of industrialisation, and that levels of pay will rise and working hours will decline as the economies become as productive as in more advanced Western countries. It is true that long hours and low pay were the lot of European and North American workforces when these countries were beginning to industrialise.

However, the situations in new industrial countries in the early twenty-first century are not basically the same as in the West over a hundred years ago. Businesses in the new industrial economies can install the latest technologies, they can sell their output at global market prices, and the workforces are much better educated than their nineteenth-century Western counterparts. Employers in India, China and South Korea can keep pay low and expect long hours of work because all these countries have huge surpluses of labour and weak (if any) trade unions.

Long hours of work can be required by Asia's employers, but the traditional cultures, especially those influenced by Confucianism, are also responsible. In China, Korea and Japan time has never belonged to an individual, but always to a group – a family, a village or a firm. There has been no 'free time' for people to use at their discretion, purely for pleasure (North, 2010). Having spare time can lead to anxiety. This indicates that work is not being done (Li, 2009). If not working in a paid job, a person can be doing domestic chores or learning, thereby making the individual more useful in the future. Respect for seniors means that employees are reluctant to leave before or to arrive at work later than their 'boss' – the employer, department manager or team leader (Tan Soo Kee, 2008). It is an employee's duty to be available if required. There is a difference in these countries between being 'at work' and actually 'doing work'. Firms are notoriously wasteful with their employees' time (Harada, 1994).

Ma Huidi's research in Beijing has identified groups whose leisure, using a Western definition, appears close to zero. She reports how the retired in Beijing rarely attend any of the events or programmes the city organises for its seniors, and that their daily lives typically evolve around the care of grandchildren, with other waking hours spent watching television, walking in the neighbourhood and chatting with neighbours (Ma Huidi et al., 2010). Another of Ma Huidi's studies has examined the lives of Beijing's migrant farmers. 'Migrant farmer' is an official status in China. The citizens' official residences are in their home villages, but they have temporary permission to live and work in the city. This temporary status can be passed from parents to children (see Kwong, 2011), and the migrant farmers are a long-term reserve workforce, ineligible for permanent jobs, who make livelihoods from markets and as day labourers while living in 'pigeon-hole' shacks beneath and between proper buildings. These migrant farmer families are certainly not workless. Quite the reverse: their lives are work-dominated. They are always either working or looking for work. Their pure leisure time is near zero. They feel that they always need to be working, earning money. Any spells of idleness are a source of worry (Ma Huidi and NingZequn, 2010).

Female migrant Indonesian family care-givers in Taiwan also lead work-dominated lives. They typically live and work away from their own families (which remain in Indonesia) while the migrants spend three-year spells away from home during which their work is typically to provide in-home care for ageing host family members in middle-class Taiwanese households. The care-givers work for long hours, and often feel lonely and tired (Yi-Chung Hsu and Yu-Cheng Hsu, 2012).

One can appreciate why researchers who study such lives, and the subjects themselves, should reject the Western leisure concept, possibly but not necessarily in favour of the traditional value of people 'being' in harmony with themselves, and with their social and physical environments, be these environments rural or urban. Look in one place, at one group, and Asia looks 'different', but look elsewhere and one can encounter the hyper-modern.

The new middle classes

Unn Målfrid Rolandsen (2011) estimates that in China's cities (discounting the rural population, which is currently becoming a minority) just 11 per cent of households can be considered middle-class in terms of occupations and incomes. Yet surveys find up to 60 per cent of city residents describing themselves as middle-class. The middle class is clearly China's new class of aspiration, certainly for young people. The situation is similar in India. Estimates of the size of present-day India's middle class range from 100 million to 400 million (Donner, 2011). Both are large figures: the lowest (100 million) exceeds the size of the largest European countries, yet amounts to less than 10 per cent of India's total population. Throughout present-day Asia middle-classness is an increasingly popular claim or aspiration, and while there is no agreed definition or, therefore, agreement on size, there is a consensus that the middle classes are both growing and heterogeneous.

The new middle classes are highly visible to visitors and locals in all cities in present-day Asia. When in public places, the middle classes are typically spending money on Western leisure goods and services. They were responsible for the explosion in leisure spending that by the 1990s had opened golf ranges, karaoke bars, fitness clubs, theme parks and resorts throughout Japan (Harada, 1994). During the 1990s South Korea recorded spectacular growth rates in leisure spending, mostly on the acquisition of international (Western, but locally manufactured) products (Moonkyum Kim, 2010; Sokho Choe and Hyejung Cheon, 2010). Koreans will spend on leisure goods – sports and other leisure gear, cameras, books, video games and DVDs – even when they know that they will not have the time to use, read or view the products (KyungHee Kim, 2011). College education and white-collar employment are generally seen as basic requirements for being middle-class, but they need to be accompanied by a middle-class lifestyle to clinch the claim, and everywhere the relevant lifestyle is identified by its consumerism.

Levels of income and consumer spending are still much lower in India and China than in some other Asian states (Japan and South Korea, for example), and China's commercial sector is still tightly controlled by the authorities. The middle class's spending habits were relatively modest in Quanzhou, the coastal city in south-east China featured in Rolandsen (2011). Young people congregated in Internet cafes. Middle-class adults had Internet access at home. The adults' typical weekend leisure consisted of shopping, walking in a nearby mountain area, an afternoon in a tea room or bookshop/cafe, and maybe an evening in a booked room at a karaoke parlour. Leisure in Quanzhou was closely supervised by the city authorities, but public facilities (museums and galleries) were rarely visited except by inward (foreign) tourists. Local middle-class leisure was catered for by commerce and organised informally. The authorities wanted to encourage 'healthy' leisure which would develop the people culturally and make them more valuable for their society. Commerce was seen as a threat, liable to spread unhealthy practices, and even chaos (which everyone feared). Yet the growth of commercial leisure was also welcomed as a sign of modernisation and economic strength. Thus liberalisation was interspersed with clampdowns on Internet cafes and karaoke parlours, especially those favoured by the city's young people.

Governments in all the East Asian countries know that they need to stimulate domestic consumption in order to keep their economies growing. Hence the five-day 40-hour work week laws introduced in South Korea during the 2000s (KyungHee Kim, 2011). In the first-wave industrial Western countries hours of work were rolled back before the Second World War, prior to the subsequent take-off in consumer spending. In Asia it appears that increased leisure spending is leading, and that leisure time will grow more slowly, if at all.

Wang Qiyan (2007) has compared leisure time and its uses in Japan and China. He notes that each country has its own traditional leisure practices, but at present the main differences between the countries appear to be due to Japan being the more advanced economically. Thus the Japanese have more free time, and higher participation rates in most forms of leisure. This suggests that Asian countries are following a standard modernisation trajectory, but with distinctive Asian features within which country and regional specifics are embedded.

One need only glimpse into the cultural mosaic that is present-day India to appreciate that there are many varieties of middle-class leisure. Everywhere class-appropriate behaviour varies by age and sex. Everywhere there are further differences between the older and new middle classes. In China the latter are very different from communism's intelligentsia and nomenklatura. In India the new middle class is different from the colonial middle class that was composed of civil servants and professionals who serviced the governing classes (see Breckenridge, 1995; Ganguly-Scrase and Scrase, 2008; Jaffrelot and Veer, 2008; Liechty, 2003; Lukose, 2009; Varma, 1998). Consumerism is always the distinctive new feature, but it is always embedded in continuities with the past, which in India vary by region, ethnicity and caste.

Discussion

Some leisure differences among the Asian countries are explicable in terms of their relative levels of economic development, as is also the case with differences among the countries of Europe (Gronow and Southerton, 2011; López, 2011). These differences are fully consistent with modernisation theory. This theory can also accommodate differences due to the retention of traditional national and regional pastimes and forms of recreation. Traditional forms of exercise remain popular throughout Asia (see Kwai-Sang Yau and Packer, 2002; Li-Ming Chiang et al., 2009), and there is no reason why these should be sidelined in favour of Western sports, though the West's commercial fitness clubs have spread rapidly throughout Asia (for those who can afford the fees). That said, it seems likely that Asian leisure will remain distinctive in several ways, some of which may be due to late development while others are likely to prove Asia-specific:

1 Western-type time structures and uses of leisure are spreading among the urban middle classes, who are, and are most likely to remain, minorities within the populations of most Asian countries. Singapore may be the sole exception. First-wave industrial countries were able to involve their entire workforces in modernised employment. Communism did likewise by prioritising full employment, which outside the cities involved creating enough jobs on collective farms and in the factories that were scattered throughout rural regions. This system provided jobs even when workforces were far from fully occupied. The reforms in what are now ex-communist countries have invariably led to shutdowns and labour shakeouts. Establishments have become more efficient. Labour has become available for re-absorption elsewhere, but has often been left under-employed outside the formal economic sectors. The new industrial countries in Asia, and also throughout Latin America and Africa, attract waves of migrants into their cities, where many find employment only in these cities' so-called informal sectors. If people cannot be offered modern types of employment, they will never be able to access modern leisure.

2 Asians with jobs in the formal economy are likely to continue to work long hours. The growth of the countries' modern economies has taken off in the historical era when hours of work in the West were ending their former long-term decline. Money is likely to remain the majority preference in Asia whenever choices can be made. Spare time has never been intrinsically valued, and there is no reason why this should change.

3 It is likely, though this still has to be confirmed in time-use studies, that workers in Asia's cities already spend, and will continue to spend, less time at home than workers in the West who have identical work schedules. In Confucian cultures the home has been and remains a place where authority is exercised by senior males, and others are expected to comply (Freysinger and Chen, 1993). This aside, Asia's cities are densely populated. Most people, all except the very wealthy, live in small apartments. They do not have dens, workshops, studies, playrooms or gardens to which they can retreat, and where young people can entertain friends. This could be one reason why Asians do not hurry to leave work. Traditional cooking in Asia is time-consuming, and preparing meals at home can be more expensive than eating out in cheap pavement cafes. Otherwise, simply walking and possibly window shopping appear to be staple, low cost, out-of-home uses of leisure time throughout urban East Asia.

4 Asians are likely to make less use of public leisure services than citizens in Europe and North America because they are less available to them. Leisure policies in Asia are subordinate to economic policies (Yongkoo Noh, 2010). Governments have treated leisure as an industry rather than a branch of the social services. The countries modernised at the time when tourism was becoming one of the world's biggest industries, and publicly funded investment has often been channelled into tourist infrastructure – hotels, resorts and other attractions. The countries seek to host big events which may require hundreds of households to be displaced to create space for new facilities. Western countries modernised and developed their public leisure services before leisure became so commercial. Locals in Macao (China) complain of being squeezed out by tourists and their facilities, mainly expensive hotels and casinos (Vong Tze Ngai, 2005).

5 The voluntary sectors in the new industrial countries are also likely to remain under-developed compared with their Western counterparts. This will be partly on account of the absence of religious reformations which in the West created the space that voluntary associations were able to fill (DeLisle, 2004). It is common elsewhere for government permission to be required before citizens can organise voluntarily. In any case, it seems unlikely that the number and variety of voluntary leisure associations that were founded decades ago in the West could

be developed *de novo* alongside twenty-first-century commercial alternatives. As Robert Putnam has noted, the recent trend has been for North Americans to go 'bowling alone' – that is, in informal groups – rather than playing in teams that compete in leagues (Putnam, 2000).

Conclusions

Modernisation theory can be used as political polemic, but it can also be used to organise comparative evidence on sport, leisure (and other) practices. It focuses attention on directions of change as an alternative to profiling sport, leisure and other practices in different countries, then grouping the countries according to their differences and similarities.

Some convergences in sport and leisure are inevitable outcomes of globalisation. Throughout the world people are able to watch the same films, listen to the same music and watch the same televised sport events. They are all exposed to consumer advertising of the same internationally marketed branded products. The Internet is global, and all over the world (some) people are using smartphones. The global flows are still mainly from the West to the rest, so some opposition within the rest to the intrusion of Western cultures and practices is to be expected.

The most impressive evidence in support of modernisation theory is from the World Values Surveys, whose data cover what people say rather than what they actually do. The sport and leisure evidence is about doing, and we can assess whether the trends are in line with the value shifts that modernisation theory highlights. This chapter has offered evidence solely from Asia, which would be insufficient to prove a global trend, but one 'black swan' is sufficient to refute claims that a trend is worldwide, and Asia is a big 'swan'.

The sport and leisure evidence from Asia is consistent with the weakening of traditions, the influence of religion, and deference towards parents and other traditional authorities. These trends are strongest among young people who have joined their countries' new middle classes. They are likely to resent or seek to 'negotiate' the application of any remaining traditional constraints. It is unclear whether these young people are less nationalistic than their parents. Also, if security and survival values can be equated with materialism, they are being joined rather than replaced by self-expression values. Young people who can afford to do so display an immense appetite for consumer goods and services. Even so, the selves they seek to express retain features of traditional cultures. In India diversities in middle-class lifestyles appear to reflect mainly long-established gender norms and regional and caste cultures. The leisure evidence does not indicate that young middle-class adults are adopting consumer practices that are consistent with environmental protection, or that they support the gender and sexual equalities that have become *de rigeur* in the West. Nor is there evidence for stronger demands for more say in decision-making at work or in politics. At present there are no signs of Western-type democracy spreading globally alongside economic development. China, all the Central Asia republics and Russia remain big exceptions.

A trend that is apparent but is not highlighted in reports from the World Values Surveys is how late modernisation is dividing countries internally into progressing and lagging sectors. The latter are presumed to be progressing, but more slowly. This presumption may be incorrect. The new middle classes are highly consumerist. Their leisure tends to be spent privately or in informal networks that use commercial rather than public or voluntary sector facilities. These new middle classes are minorities everywhere. There are many more citizens in villages and in cities who are surviving (occasionally thriving) in the informal economies. Traditional ways of life are undermined by the intrusion of mass media which widen young people's horizons and raise their aspirations. Local crafts and shops are replaced by branded products and accessible chain stores. This may be the future of the old West: affluent middle classes and the seriously wealthy at the top, and new lower classes created as industrial working-class jobs disappear and working-class ways of life, organisations and politics dissolve.

If all countries are travelling towards a common destination, this is its most likely character, but for now, surely, we are in an age of multiple modernities. Sport and leisure everywhere take their meanings from local contexts in which regional and national histories and cultures leave powerful impressions.

chapter 13

Conclusions

Types of theory

There can be no conclusion in the form of declaring one theory the winner or attempting to create a synthesis of all the theories. In the mid-twentieth century Talcott Parsons created a synthesis of European social theories (but did not include Marx). Despite its merits (see Chapter 3), Parsons's synthesis was criticised heavily for its complexity and abstract character. Today there are even more theories to take into account. So there is no climatic synthesis to end this book.

There can be no single winner among the theories because there are two distinct types of social theory. Some theories are 'analytical'. They provide concepts that (according to the theorists) can be applied in studying any society, in any place, at any time. Talcott Parsons, Pierre Bourdieu and the symbolic interactionists are theorists of this type. Other theories are about historical change. The classical and successor theories are specifically about changes in Europe since the Middle Ages. The theories that are currently under construction are about ongoing changes in the twenty-first century. Parsons endorsed Durkheim's view that the division of labour had been the master trend in history, but his reputation as a major theorist rests on his analytical theories of systems, mainly his theory of the social system.

It is futile to seek one winner within each group of theories. Each of the analytical theories highlights specific social processes and formations that should be found somewhere within any society. The strengths of one of the analytical theories do not discredit the others. The processes and formations that are highlighted may, but will not necessarily, be present in any specific sport or other leisure activity. The activity may or may not be performing what Talcott Parsons called latency functions. It may or may not involve the social positioning and exchange of 'capitals' that Pierre Bourdieu highlights. Symbolic interaction can be found everywhere. This is one theory that really does work universally.

The classical and successor theories are about historical change. The theories of Durkheim, Marx, Weber, Elias, Foucault and Habermas were all produced in Europe, by Europeans. They are theories about how the changes that began when the Middle Ages were ending led to industrialisation, urbanisation and demands for democracy from the eighteenth century onwards. These theories were produced in Europe and are about changes in Europe, but post-Parsons they were adopted in and applied to the settler colonies (mainly North America and Australasia) which experienced similar occidental processes of urbanisation, industrialisation and democratisation. However, the theories do not map so easily onto societies that did not have Middle Ages, hence their relatively tepid embrace. Theories about the latest modern age are about trends since the late twentieth century in these same societies which have become post-industrial, absorbed ICT, instigated globalisation, and adopted and then spread neo-liberal political economies globally. The eventual outcomes of these changes are not as yet visible, so the theories must be regarded as still under construction.

The main advocates of modernisation theory have been Americans. The USA became the main global power during the twentieth century – economically, militarily and politically. The West, led by the USA, won the Cold War. Modernisation theory was produced in its aftermath. It envisages the rest following the West. As Chapter 12 explained, this was not a new late twentieth-century idea, but it gained renewed plausibility when communism ended. However, it now looks unlikely that the twenty-first century will become *the* American century. We are witnessing the rise of the BRICS. The West today may need to look to the rest to glimpse features of its own future. Modernisation theory is best treated as a set of propositions with which to debate. European theorists are inevitably sensitive to persistent differences within their own continent, and at present tend to agree that we are currently in an age of multiple modernities. Some member states of the present-day European Union spent periods under communism, which continues to leave an imprint. Some member states were once Ottoman domains, and tend to have different attitudes towards refugees from Middle East wars than the more sympathetic member states in northern Europe.

All the theories in this book have occidental authors. They are theories about occidental countries and their modern histories. Theories about the present are still occident-centred. The rest of the world is still 'the other'. This does not mean that the theories are wrong. They are products of centuries during which the West really did dominate or lead the rest. The twenty-first century may prove different, and its major theorists may be from 'the rest'. They may tell a different story in which the centuries of colonialism and Western hegemony were a brief episode in a longer world history that led to the rise of the BRICS and the ascendance of some combination of Arabic, African, Latin, Islamic, Confucian and Hindu cultures. The theories in this book are inevitably products of their own age. To repeat, this does not mean that they are wrong, but the age of which they speak will probably look different when viewed from the end of the twenty-first century and beyond.

The social theories that are currently most used in studies of sport and leisure (and elsewhere) are predictably those that have been produced most recently: Foucault, Bourdieu, Beck and other theories about the latest modern age. Modernisation theory is less used because comparative studies of sport and leisure are relatively rare, and when conducted, the investigators are more likely to stress the unique features of the countries on which they focus rather than similarities and differences *vis-à-vis* global trends. We should note that all the latest theories incorporate some ideas from earlier classical and successor theories, and the classics themselves continue to be frequent points of reference for present-day scholars. Norbert Elias's insistence that sociology should not be divorced from history may be considered vindicated by even the oldest theories continuing to be regarded as relevant to understanding the present. Personally, I find the classical and successor theories more illuminating about the present day than the theories that focus on changes since the 1970s, but others will disagree.

This and that, either/or and convergences

Some of the history theories are compatible. It is possible to agree with 'this one' and 'that one'. There is no need to choose. Most of the history theories identify changes in human thought as the driver of history. The exceptions are Durkheim (and Parsons), for whom it was the division of labour, and Marx, for whom it was changes in modes of production. Weber saw the modern era as distinguished and driven forward by rational minds. For the original members of the Frankfurt School and Habermas it has been the ascendance of instrumental reasoning. For Elias it was the need for individuals to exercise greater self-control and submit to the civilising process. For Foucault it was governance by expert discourses plus surveillance which required individuals to be self-disciplined. One can regard all these characterisations as highlighting different features of the same modern thinking.

In other cases it is either/or. Among thought theorists there is disagreement on the extent to which, and the circumstances in which, humans' ability to think enables them to redirect history. The original critical theorists of the Frankfurt School and their heir, Jürgen Habermas, can be regarded as optimists. In this they have followed Georg Hegel and Auguste Comte. Habermas proposes old and new public spheres, which may be leisure spheres, as sites from which societies can be reimagined then rebuilt. Symbolic interactionists join the optimistic thought theorists in placing no limits on humans' ability to renegotiate reality. Weber and Foucault are relatively gloomy thought theorists. Weber could see no escape from the 'iron cage of bureaucracy' and disenchantment. Paraphrasing George Ritzer, rationality was breeding oppressive irrationalities. Ritzer has followed Weber in encouraging resistance, but seeing no end to the ongoing 'McDonaldization' of contemporary societies. Foucault likewise practised and advocated resistance, but saw no end to governance by expert discourses and surveillance obliging people to exercise self-discipline.

If Foucault had lived longer, he would have become aware of the achievements of feminist and anti-racist movements, and tolerance for wider varieties of sexual orientations and conduct. Here is one point of implicit contemporary convergence. Max Weber believed that for ideas to make a difference there needed to be an affinity with material conditions, and it was this affinity that allowed Calvinism to be the spark that ignited the development of capitalism. Although Marx and subsequent Marxists have all been materialists 'at the end of the day' and 'in the final analysis', Marx himself clearly believed that the proletariat needed a theory, specifically the theory he was offering, in order to become a revolutionary force. However, even then conditions had to be right: there needed to be a blatant contradiction between what the forces of production were capable of delivering (freedom from want for all) and what the prevailing relationships of production would deliver. Marx expected this blatant contradiction to arise in one of the most developed capitalist countries, probably Britain. In the event, the first Marxist party to gain control of a government was the Bolsheviks in Russia, a backward country that had been further devastated by war. The version of socialism that was built in the Soviet Union has become a long-term millstone for the worldwide 'left'. Despite this, Marxist thought continues to foster confidence that at some point in the future its blatant internal contradictions will lead to the downfall of capitalism. The point of convergence is that post-Weber, all scholars have accepted that ideas can make a difference and therefore must always be taken into account, but whether ideas do make a difference to the course of history, and if so, the character of this difference, always depends on the surrounding conditions. These also need to be taken into account.

There has been another implicit convergence. In the mid-twentieth century a major battle in sociology was between supporters of consensus theorists (Durkheim and Parsons) and supporters of the conflict theorists (Marx and Weber). This battle has been dormant for years, basically because the conflict side won. It is now accepted that modern societies contain groups with different interests, and that changes are usually instigated by specific groups. Durkheim and Parsons both explained what they believed to be the main historical trend (the division of labour) as a response to the need for societies to become stronger and better-balanced. Even if the conflict theorists won the argument, they can concede that societies can remain stable for long periods, which implies that Parsons's functions are being performed, including the latency function, in which sport and other leisure practices can play a part. Also, changes are sometimes introduced, and may be introduced consensually, because a society has become unbalanced in some way. The new regulations for financial institutions that were introduced following the 2008–2009 banking crisis are examples.

Finally, Durkheim's social facts merit a revisit, if only so that we can move beyond Durkheim. Sport, leisure and all other social researchers need to distinguish between recurrent patterns, trends and events. Levels of participation in and attendance at spectator sports are examples of recurrent patterns, classic Durkheimian social facts. These levels may move upwards or downwards over a period of time, as opposed to fluctuating from year to year. In the former instance we have a trend. Sport events that are repeated throughout a season, then the following season, are a pattern. Megas are usually pure events. They happen, after which (unless there really is a legacy) things return to the previous normality. The riots that occurred in several major English cities in 1981, and which were repeated in 2011, were events. Investigators have a legitimate interest in all three phenomena. In each instance they need to decide whether they are trying to explain a recurrent pattern, a trend, or an event or series of events.

All the theories could be right in their different ways and to greater or lesser extents, and they share another common feature. The theorists were all men, as most social theorists still are. This reflects the character of the historical periods in which the theories were produced. In the nineteenth and early twentieth centuries public life was for men – politics, business, and intellectual life as well. The classical theorists did not address sex – what we would now call gender – divisions. The exception was Karl Marx's collaborator, Friedrich Engels. Otherwise the classic theorists shared the assumption of their era that sex differences were natural and inevitable. The successor theorists, writing in the second half of the twentieth century, did engage with gender, but apart from the symbolic interactionists they continued to set politics and the economy at the centre of their theories, and both politics and the economy remained male-led throughout the relevant decades. However, throughout the last fifty years a wave of feminist critique has targeted 'malestream' social thought. There has also been a trend towards genderlessness in employment, politics and academic life. These changes are reflected in theories about the present. Maybe the twenty-first century will be women's century. Maybe the history of the modern era will be rewritten to foreground women's lives, but this will not change history. Changes from the beginning of the modern era were, and in the present day are still, being driven in the economy and politics. Religion was also an important source of change in the early modern era. Until the late twentieth century the drivers were mostly men and the major enduring theories about these changes were the work of men. In this sense, the theories are products of their time, which does not make them wrong any more than it guarantees their validity.

Social theory in sport and leisure

Sport and leisure scholars should not be searching for the right theory or even the best theory. Sport and leisure are too varied for any single coherent theory to fit the lot. Sport can be a UEFA Champions League football fixture, a casual game of pool in a bar or a solitary jog. Leisure can be a round-the-world holiday or an evening watching television. In any case, as we have seen, there are few either/or choices among the theories.

Post-Weber, it has been accepted that the social sciences cannot offer the same kind of explanations as the natural sciences. The study of society has to be a *social* science. In the natural sciences, lower-level laws are explained by a smaller number of higher-level laws. The entire body of knowledge is a theory. The ultimate aim is the theory of everything. Societies are different, because people are different from inanimate matter and all other mammals. Humans have languages which enable them to think. We can have unpredicted ideas. Yet, as Weber demonstrated, it is still possible for social science to deliver causal explanations. Sport and leisure scholars have access to a rich stock of social theories which enable them to identify particular sport and leisure trends and patterns that are part of wider trends and patterns. When this is indeed the case, the sport and leisure instances are best explained as part of the wider patterns and trends.

'If this is indeed the case' is an important qualifying phrase because most sport and leisure practices have not been part of many of the trends associated with modernisation or the modern practices that have been outcomes. Talcott Parsons, Norbert Elias and Jürgen Habermas are the only theorists in this book who noted explicitly that people need 'time out', space for latency to operate, in Parsons's language, to act in impulsive, emotional, uncivilised ways, in Elias's terms, or in Habermas's terms, to indulge in communicative speech and action for its own sake among social equals. We can escape from Foucault's expert discourses and avoid or ignore surveillance. We can become non-rational, non-instrumental during our leisure. We can see how Durkheim's division of labour has created a wide range of new modern sports and other leisure activities, plus specialist public agencies, voluntary associations and businesses that offer numerous things to do and places to go. Simultaneously, people continue to spend much of their leisure time with families and relatives, neighbours, school and college friends and workmates rather than with leisure-specific companions. Talcott Parsons is the only theorist who can explain why leisure is so ubiquitous. Marxism has found sport and leisure difficult to handle because until the late twentieth century so much remained outside the capitalist marketplace. Most sport and much of the rest of leisure were served by public agencies and voluntary associations, and free time was and is still spent informally in people's own homes, on the streets or in other public spaces among families and friends. It is only since the late twentieth century that capitalism has begun to take over swaths of participant and spectator sport and has become dominant in broadcasting in Europe. Sport and leisure are among the parts of society where Marxism looks anything but outdated. Quite the reverse: it has much to say about sport and leisure in the twenty-first century – more than in the nineteenth and most of the twentieth centuries.

During his own lifetime Marx's big achievement was to set the economy rather than government and politics or human thought at the centre of explanations. Weber agreed, despite having a different explanation of the rise of capitalism. Marx stressed how societies are composed of classes with different interests. Again Weber agreed, while insisting that stratification throughout history and in modern societies was more complex than Marx had suggested. These originally Marxist positions have been accepted so widely that they have ceased to be regarded as distinctively Marxist. They remind us that the economy is the first place to look for explanations of changes in sport and leisure. In the twenty-first century this means interrogating the implications for sport and leisure of the financialisation and globalisation of capitalism, and wider economic inequalities within most countries alongside narrower inequalities between countries.

This does not mean ignoring what other social theories have to offer. All sports and all other uses of leisure are social inventions. Sociology is the home of a rich stock of theories that sport and leisure scholars can use – far richer than the total offered by psychology, economics, geography, politics and other social sciences.

Sport and leisure scholars do not need and are ill-advised to try to create their own topic-specific theories. They thereby dig themselves into ghettoes where they speak only to one another. There are ready-made social theories which will amplify and connect sport and leisure voices to wider debates about how modern societies have developed and how they are currently changing. Up to now the study of sport and leisure has not been the source of any theories whose use has spread outwards. In this respect, sport and leisure are like all sociology's specialisms. Sport and leisure scholars are best advised to scan, take and use their selections from the stock of theories that has been built since the nineteenth century. This will best serve the study of sport and leisure: there is no need to build theories anew.

Bibliography

Aall, C., Klepp, I.G., Engeset, A.B., Skuland, S.E. and Stoa, E. (2011), 'Leisure and sustainable development in Norway: part of the solution and the problem', *Leisure Studies*, 30, 453–476.

Adorno, T. and Horkheimer, M. (1977), 'The culture industry: enlightenment as mass deception', in Curran, J., Gurevitch, M. and Woollacott, J., eds, *Mass Communication and Society*, Edward Arnold, London, pp. 347–383.

Alexander, J., ed. (1985), *Neo-Functionalism*, Sage, London.

Aronowitz, S. and DiFazio, W. (1994), *The Jobless Future: Sci-Tech and the Dogma of Work*, University of Minnesota Press, Minneapolis, MN.

Atkinson, W. (2007), 'Beck, individualization and the death of class: a critique', *British Journal of Sociology*, 58, 349–366.

Bancroft, A. (2012), 'Drinking without fun: female students' accounts of pre-drinking and club drinking', *Sociological Research Online*, 17, 4, 7.

Barrell, G., Chamberlain, A., Evans, J., Holt, T. and Mackean, J. (1989), 'Ideology and commitment in family life: the case of runners', *Leisure Studies*, 8, 249–262.

Baudrillard, J. (1988), *Selected Writings*, Policy Press, Cambridge.

Baudrillard, J. (1998), *The Consumer Society*, Sage, London.

Bauman, Z. (1998), *Work, Consumerism and the New Poor*, Open University Press, Buckingham.

Bauman, Z. (2006), *Liquid Times: Living in an Age of Uncertainty*, Polity Press, Cambridge.

Bauman, Z. (2007), *Consuming Life*, Polity Press, Cambridge.

Bauman, Z. (2011), *Collateral Damage: Social Inequalities in a Global Age*, Polity Press, Cambridge.

Beachain, D.O. and Polese, A. (2010), '"Rocking the vote": new forms of youth organisations in Eastern Europe and the former Soviet Union', *Journal of Youth Studies*, 13, 615–630.

Beck, U. (1985/1992), *Risk Society: Towards a New Modernity*, Sage, London.

Beck, U. (1994), *Reflexive Modernization: Politics, Tradition and Aesthetics in the Modern Social Order*, Polity Press, Cambridge.

Beck, U. (2000), *The Brave New World of Work*, Cambridge University Press, Cambridge.

Beck, U. (2012), 'Redefining the sociological project: the cosmopolitan challenge', *Sociology*, 46, 7–12.

Beck, U. (2013a), *German Europe*, Polity Press, Cambridge.

Beck, U. (2013b), 'What "class" is too soft a category to capture the explosiveness of social inequality at the beginning of the twenty-first century', *British Journal of Sociology*, 64, 63–74.

Beck, U. and Beck-Gernsheim, E. (1995), *The Normal Chaos of Love*, Polity Press, Cambridge.

Beck, U. and Beck-Gernsheim, E. (2002), *Individualization: Institutionalized Individualism and Its Social and Political Consequences*, Sage, London.

Beck, U. and Beck-Gernsheim, E. (2009), 'Global generations and the trap of methodological nationalism for a cosmopolitan turn in the sociology of youth and generation', *European Sociological Review*, 25, 25–36.

Beck, U. and Beck-Gernsheim, E. (2013), *Distant Love: Personal Life in the Global Age*, Polity Press, Cambridge.

Beck, U., Giddens, A. and Lash, S. (1994), *Reflexive Modernization: Politics, Tradition and Aesthetics in the Modern Social Order*, Polity Press, Cambridge.

Becker, H.S. (1963), *Outsiders: Studies in the Sociology of Deviance*, Free Press, Glencoe, IL.

Bell, D. (1960), *The End of Ideology*, Free Press, New York.

Bell, D. (1974), *The Coming of Post-Industrial Society*, Basic Books, New York.

Bennett, T., Savage, M., Silva, E., Warde, A., Gayo-Cal, M. and Wright, D. (2009), *Culture, Class, Distinction*, Routledge, London.

Best, F. (1978), 'The time of our lives', *Society and Leisure*, 1, 95–114.

Bittman, M., Brown, J.E. and Wajcman, J. (2009), 'The mobile phone, perpetual contact and time pressure', *Work, Employment and Society*, 23, 673–691.

Blackshaw, T. (2003), *Leisure Life: Myth, Masculinity and Modernity*, Routledge, London.

Blackshaw, T. (2010), *Leisure*, Routledge, Abingdon.

Blackshaw, T. (2013), *Working Class Life in Northern England, 1945–2010: The Pre-History and Afterlife of the Inbetweener Generation*, Palgrave Macmillan, Basingstoke.

Blau, P.M. (1964), *Exchange and Power in Social Life*, Wiley, New York.

Blumer, H. (1969), *Symbolic Interactionism: A Perspective on Method*, Prentice Hall, Englewood Cliffs, NJ.

Bourdieu, P. (1963/1979), *Algeria 1960*, Cambridge University Press, Cambridge.

Bourdieu, P. (1965/1994), *Academic Discourse: Linguistic Misunderstanding and Professorial Power*, Polity Press, Cambridge.

Bourdieu, P. (1979/1984), *Distinction: A Social Critique of the Judgement of Taste*, Routledge, London.

Bourdieu, P. (1980/1990), *The Logic of Practice*, Polity Press, Cambridge.

Bourdieu, P. (1984/1988), *Homo Academicus*, Polity Press, Cambridge.

Bourdieu, P. (1989/1996), *The State Nobility: Elite Schools in the Field of Power*, Polity Press, Cambridge.

Bourdieu, P. (1993/1999), *The Weight of the World*, Polity Press, Cambridge.

Bourdieu, P. (1998/2001), *Masculine Domination*, Polity Press, Cambridge.

Bourdieu, P. and Darbel, A. (1969/1991), *The Love of Art*, Polity Press, Cambridge.

Bourdieu, P. and Passeron, J.-C. (1970/1977), *Reproduction in Education, Society and Culture*, Sage, London.

Bowring, F. (2015), 'Negative and positive freedom: lessons from, and to, sociology', *Sociology*, 49, 156–171.

Breckenridge, C., ed. (1995), *Consuming Modernity: Public Culture in South Asia*, University of Minnesota Press, Minneapolis, MN.

Bukodi, E., Goldthorpe, J.H., Waller, L. and Kuha, J. (2015), 'The mobility problem in Britain: new findings from the analysis of birth cohort data', *British Journal of Sociology*, 66, 1, 93–117.

Bulmer, M. (1984), *The Chicago School of Sociology*, University of Chicago Press, Chicago, IL.

Burawoy, M. (2005), 'For public sociology', *American Sociological Review*, 70, 4–28.

Carrington, B. and McDonald, I., eds (2009), *Marxism, Cultural Studies and Sport*, Routledge, London.

Castells, M. (1977), *The Urban Question: A Marxist Approach*, Edward Arnold, London.

Castells, M. (1996), *The Rise of the Network Society*, Blackwell, Oxford.

Castells, M. (2012), *Networks of Outrage and Hope: Social Movements in the Internet Age*, Polity Press, Cambridge.

Castells, M., Caraca, J. and Cardoso, G. (2012), 'The cultures of the economic crisis: an introduction', in Castells, M., Caraca, J. and Cardoso, G., eds, *Aftermath: The Cultures of the Economic Crisis*, Oxford University Press, Oxford, pp. 1–14.

Chang, L.T. (2008), *Factory Girls: From Village to City in a Changing China*, Spiegel and Grau, New York.

Clark, S. (2012), 'Being "good at sport": talent, ability and young women's sporting participation', *Sociology*, 46, 1, 178–1, 193.

Clarke, J. and Critcher, C. (1985), *The Devil Makes Work*, Macmillan, London.

Collin, M. (2007), *The Time of the Rebels: Youth Resistance Movements and 21st Century Revolutions*, Serpent's Tail, London.

Collins, T. (2013), *Sport in Capitalist Society: A Short History*, Routledge, London.

Connerton, B., ed. (1976), *Critical Sociology*, Penguin, Harmondsworth.

Cooley, C.H. (1909), *Social Organization*, Scribner, New York.

Crossley, N. (2005), *In the Gym: Motives, Meanings and Moral Careers*, Working Paper 6, CRESC Working Paper Series, University of Manchester, Manchester.

Csikszentmihalyi, M. (1990), *Flow: The Psychology of Optimal Experience*, Harper and Row, New York.

Curran, D. (2103a), 'Risk society and the distribution of bads: theorizing class in the risk society', *British Journal of Sociology*, 64, 44–62.

Curran, D. (2103b), 'What is a critical theory of the risk society? A reply to Beck', *British Journal of Sociology*, 64, 75–80.

Dalton, R. and Welzel, C., eds (2014), *The Civic Culture Transformed: From Allegiant to Assertive Citizens*, Cambridge University Press, New York.

Davis, K. and Moore, W.E. (1945), 'Some principles of stratification', *American Sociological Review*, 10, 242–249.

Delisle, L.J. (2004), 'Leisure and tolerance – a historical perspective', *World Leisure Journal*, 46, 2, 55–63.

Dilthey, W. (1976), *W. Dilthey, Selected Writings*, ed. Rickman, H.P., Cambridge University Press, Cambridge.

Djilas, M. (1957), *The New Class*, Thames and Hudson, London.

Dodd, J. and Sharma, V., eds (2012), *Leisure and Tourism: Cultural Paradigms*, Rawat Publications, Jaipur.

Donner, H., ed. (2011), *Being Middle Class in India*, Routledge, Abingdon.

Donner, H. and Neve, G. De (2011), 'Introduction', in Donner, H., ed., *Being Middle Class in India*, Routledge, Abingdon, pp. 1–22.

Dore, R. (1973), *British Factory–Japanese Factory*, Allen and Unwin, London.

Dore, R. (1976), *The Diploma Disease*, Allen and Unwin, London.

Dumazedier, J. (1967), *Towards a Society of Leisure*, Free Press, New York.

Dumazedier, J. (1974), *Sociology of Leisure*, Elsevier, Amsterdam.

Dunkerley, M. (1996), *The Jobless Economy?* Polity Press, Cambridge.

Dunning, E. and Rojek, C., eds (1992), *Sport and Leisure in the Civilizing Process: Critique and Counter-Critique*, University of Toronto Press, Toronto.

Dunning, E., Murphy, P. and Williams, J. (1988), *The Social Roots of Football Hooliganism*, Routledge, London.

Durkheim, E. (1893/1938), *The Division of Labour in Society*, Free Press, Glencoe, IL.

Durkheim, E. (1895/1938), *The Rules of Sociological Method*, Free Press, Glencoe, IL.

Durkheim, E. (1897/1970), *Suicide: A Study in Sociology*, Routledge, London.

Durkheim, E. (1912/1956), *The Elementary Forms of Religious Life*, Allen and Unwin, London.

Durkheim, E. (1922/1956), *Education and Sociology*, Free Press, Glencoe, IL.

Durkheim, E. (1925/1973), *Moral Education*, Free Press, New York.

Durkheim, E. (1928/1959), *Socialism and Saint-Simon*, Routledge and Kegan Paul, London.

Durkheim, E. (1957), *Professional Ethnics and Civic Morals*, Routledge and Kegan Paul, London.

Eijck, K. van (1999), 'Socialisation, education and lifestyle: how social mobility increases the cultural heterogeneity of status groups', *Poetics*, 26, 309–328.

Eijck, K. van and Knulst, W. (2005), 'No more need for snobbism: highbrow cultural participation in a cultural democracy', *European Sociological Review*, 21, 513–528.

Eijck, K. van and Rees, K. van (1998), 'The impact of social mobility on patterns of cultural consumption: individual omnivores and heterogeneous status groups', paper presented at *International Sociological Association Congress*, Montreal.

Elias, N. (1939/2000), *The Civilizing Process: Sociogenetic and Psychogenetic Investigations*, Blackwell, Oxford.

Elias, N. (2013), *Studies on the Germans*, ed. Mennell, S. and Dunning, E., University College Dublin Press, Dublin.

Elias, N. and Dunning, E. (1986), *Quest for Excitement: Sport and Leisure in the Civilizing Process*, Blackwell, Oxford.

Elias, N. and Scotson, J.L. (1965), *The Established and the Outsiders*, Frank Cass, London.

Elliott, A. and Urry, J. (2010), *Mobile Lives*, Routledge, Abingdon.

Engels, F. (1845/1969), *The Condition of the Working Class in England*, Granada, St Albans; Grafton, London.

Engels, F. (1902/2001), *The Origin of the Family, Private Property and the State*, University Press of the Pacific, Honolulu, HI.

Erikson, B.H. (1996), 'Culture, class and connections', *American Journal of Sociology*, 102, 217–251.

Esping-Andersen, G. (1990), *The Three Worlds of Welfare Capitalism*, Princeton University Press, Princeton, NJ.

Fan Zeng (2010), 'The philosophy of leisure', in Modi, I., Ma Huidi and NingZequn, eds, *Leisure and Civilization: Interdisciplinary and International Perspectives*, China Travel and Tourism Press, Beijing, pp. 30–34.

Feinstein, L., Bynner, J. and Duckworth, V. (2006), 'Young people's leisure contexts and their relationships to adult outcomes', *Journal of Youth Studies*, 9, 305–327.

Florida, R.L. (2002), *The Rise of the Creative Class: And How It's Transforming Work, Leisure, Community and Everyday Life*, Basic Books, New York.

Forrester, V. (1999), *The Economic Horror*, Polity Press, Cambridge.

Foucault, M. (1961/1988), *Madness and Civilization: A History of Insanity in the Age of Reason*, Tavistock, London.

Foucault, M. (1963/1973), *The Birth of the Clinic*, Tavistock, London.

Foucault, M. (1966/1973), *The Order of Things*, Vintage, New York.

Foucault, M. (1969/1972), *The Archaeology of Knowledge*, Tavistock, London.

Foucault, M. (1975/1977), *Discipline and Punish: The Birth of the Prison*, Tavistock, London.

Foucault, M. (1976/1980), *The History of Sexuality, Volume I: An Introduction*, Random House, New York.

Foucault, M. (1984a/1985), *The History of Sexuality, Volume II: The Use of Pleasure*, Penguin, Harmondsworth.

Foucault, M. (1984b/1986), *The History of Sexuality, Volume III: The Care of the Self*, Penguin, Harmondsworth.

Frank, A.G. (1969), *Capitalism and Underdevelopment in Latin America*, Monthly Review Press, New York.

Freud, S. (1930), *Civilization and Its Discontents*, Hogarth Press, London.

Freysinger, V.J. and Chen, T. (1993), 'Leisure and family in China: the impact of culture', *World Leisure and Recreation*, 35, 3, 22–24.

Fukuyama, F. (1992), *The End of History and the Last Man*, Penguin, London.

Fulbrook, M. (1991), *A Concise History of Germany*, Cambridge University Press, Cambridge.

Gabriel, N. and Mennell, S. (2011), 'Handing over the torch: intergenerational processes in figurational sociology', in Gabriel, N. and Mennell, S., eds, *Norbert Elias and Figurational Research: Processual Thinking in Sociology*, *Sociological Review*, 59, s1, Sociological Review Monograph Series, Wiley-Blackwell, Oxford, pp. 5–23.

Ganguly-Scrase, R. and Scrase, T. (2008), *Globalisation and the Middle Classes in India: The Social and Cultural Impact of Neoliberal Reforms*, Routledge, London.

Garfinkel, H. (1967), *Studies in Ethnomethodology*, Prentice Hall, Englewood Cliffs, NJ.

Gershuny, J. (2005), 'Busyness as the badge of honour for the new super-ordinate working class', *Social Research: An International Quarterly*, 72, 287–314.

Gerth, H.H. and Mills, C.W., eds (1946), *From Max Weber: Essays in Sociology*, Oxford University Press, New York.

Giddens, A. (1990), *The Consequences of Modernity*, Polity Press, Cambridge.

Giddens, A. (1993), *The Transformation of Intimacy: Love, Sexuality and Eroticism in Modern Societies*, Polity Press, Cambridge.

Giddens, A. (1998), *The Third Way: The Renewal of Social Democracy*, Polity Press, Cambridge.

Giorgi, L., Sassatelli, M. and Delanty, G., eds (2011), *Festivals and the Cultural Public Sphere*, Routledge, London.

Glaser, B. and Strauss, A. (1968), *The Discovery of Grounded Theory*, Weidenfeld and Nicolson, London.

Glasser, R. (1970), *Leisure: Penalty or Prize?* Macmillan, London.

Goffman, E. (1959), *The Presentation of Self in Everyday Life*, Doubleday Anchor, New York.

Goffman, E. (1961), *Asylums*, Penguin, Harmondsworth.

Goffman, E. (1964), *Stigma: Notes on the Management of Identity*, Penguin, Harmondsworth.

Goffman, E. (1974), *Frame Analysis*, Penguin, Harmondsworth.

Goodwin, J. and O'Connor, H. (2006), 'Norbert Elias and the lost Young Worker Project', *Journal of Youth Studies*, 9, 159–173.

Gorz, A. (1982), *Farewell to the Working Class: An Essay on Post-Industrial Socialism*, Pluto Press, London.

Gouldner, A.W. (1971), *The Coming Crisis of Western Sociology*, Heinemann, London.

Gramsci, A. (1971), *Selections from Prison Notebooks*, New Left Books, London.

Grazia, S. de (1962), *Of Time, Work, and Leisure*, Twentieth Century Fund, New York.

Green, K., Thurston, M., Vaage, O. and Roberts, K. (2015), '"We're on the right track, baby, we were born this way!": exploring sports participation in Norway', *Sport, Education and Society*, 20, 285–303.

Green, M. and Oakley, B. (2001), 'Elite sports development systems and playing to win: uniformity and diversity in international approaches', *Leisure Studies*, 20, 247–267.

Gronow, J. (2009), '"High-brow" culture as status: the devaluation of cultural capital in Europe or what happened to the good taste?', paper presented at *39th World Congress of the International Institute of Sociology*, Yerevan.

Gronow, J. and Southerton, D. (2011), 'Leisure and consumption in Europe', in Immerfall, S. and Therborn, G., eds, *Handbook of European Societies*, Springer, New York, pp. 355–384.

Gross, E. (1961), 'A functional approach to leisure analysis', *Social Problems*, 9, 2–8.

Gruneau, R. (1983/1999), *Class, Sports and Social Development*, University of Massachusetts Press, Amherst, MA.

Guillen, M.F., Garvia, R. and Santana, A. (2012), 'Embedded play: economic and social motivations for sharing lottery tickets', *European Sociological Review*, 28, 344–354.

Habermas, J. (1962/1989), *The Structural Transformation of the Public Sphere: An Inquiry into a Category of Bourgeois Society*, Polity Press, Oxford.

Habermas, J. (1976), *Legitimation Crisis*, Heinemann, London.

Habermas, J. (1984/1988), *The Theory of Communicative Action* (2 vols), Polity Press, Cambridge.

Hakim, C. (2011), *Honey Money*, Allen Lane, London.

Hall, S. and Jefferson, T., eds (1976), *Resistance Through Rituals*, Hutchinson, London.

Harada, M. (1994), 'Towards a renaissance of leisure in Japan', *Leisure Studies*, 13, 277–287.

Hargreaves, J. (1986), *Sport, Power and Culture*, Polity Press, Cambridge.

Haworth, J. and Hart, G., eds (2007), *Well-Being: Individual, Community and Social Perspectives*, Palgrave Macmillan, Basingstoke.

Haworth, J.T., Jarman, M. and Lee, S. (1997), 'Positive psychological states in the daily life of a sample of working women', *Journal of Applied Social Psychology*, 27, 345–370.

Heilbroner, R. (1976), *Business Civilization in Decline*, Norton, New York.

Held, D. (1980), *Introduction to Critical Theory*, Hutchinson, London.

Henderson, K.A. (2011), 'A continuum of leisure studies and professional specialties: what if no connections exist?', *World Leisure Journal*, 53, 76–90.

Hirsch, F. (1977), *The Social Limits to Growth*, Routledge, London.

Hohlbaum, C.L. (2009), *The Power of Slow*, St Martin's Press, London.

Homans, G.C. (1961), *Social Behaviour: Its Elementary Forms*, Harcourt Brace, New York.

Honore, C. (2004), *In Praise of Slow*, Orion, London.

Honore, C. (2008), *Under Pressure: Putting the Child Back in Childhood*, Orion, London.

Honwana, A. (2013), *Youth and Revolution in Tunisia*, Zed Books, London.

Horne, J. (1998), 'Understanding leisure time and leisure space in contemporary Japanese society', *Leisure Studies*, 17, 37–52.

Horning, K.H., Gerhard, A. and Michailow, M. (1995), *Time Pioneers: Flexible Working Time and New Lifestyles*, Polity Press, Cambridge.

Huntington, S.P. (1996), *The Clash of Civilizations and the Remaking of World Order*, Simon and Schuster, New York.

Inglehart, R. (1977), *The Silent Revolution*, Princeton University Press, Princeton, NJ.

Inglehart, R. (1997), *Modernization and Postmodernization*, Princeton University Press, Princeton, NJ.

International Sociological Association Research Committee on Leisure (2009), *Beijing Consensus on Leisure Civilization*, International Sociological Association Research Committee on Leisure, Beijing.

Iso-Ahola, S.E. and Mannell, R.C. (2004), 'Leisure and health', in Haworth, J.T. and Veal, A.J., eds, *Work and Leisure*, Routledge, London, pp. 184–199.

Jaffrelot, C. and Veer, P. van de, eds (2008), *Patterns of Middle Class Consumption in India and China*, Sage, Delhi.

Jenkins, C. and Sherman, B. (1981), *The Leisure Shock*, Methuen, London.

Jiaming Sun and Xun Wang (2010), 'Value differences between generations in China: a study in Shanghai', *Journal of Youth Studies*, 13, 65–81.

Jianyu Wang and Stringer, L.A. (2000), 'The impact of Taoism on Chinese leisure', *World Leisure Journal*, 42, 3, 33–41.

Jones, O. (2014), *The Establishment: And How They Get Away with It*, Allen Lane, London.

Kamruzzaman, P. (2014), *Poverty Reduction Strategy in Bangladesh*, Policy Press, Bristol.

Keddie, N., ed. (1973), *Tinker, Tailor . . . The Myth of Cultural Deprivation*, Penguin Harmondsworth.

Kerr, C., Dunlop, J.T., Harbison, F.H. and Myers, C.A. (1960), *Industrialism and Industrial Man: The Problems of Labor and Management in Economic Growth*, Harvard University Press, Cambridge, MA.

Konrad, G. and Szelenyi, I. (1979), *The Intellectuals on the Road to Class Power*, Harvester, Brighton.

Kwai-Sang Yau and Packer, T.L. (2002), 'Health and well-being through t'ai chi: perceptions of older adults in Hong Kong', *Leisure Studies*, 21, 163–178.

Kwong, J. (2011), 'Education and identity: the marginalisation of migrant youths in Beijing', *Journal of Youth Studies*, 14, 871–883.

KyungHee Kim (2011), *Work and Leisure and Leisure Policy in Korea*, PhD thesis, University of Liverpool, Liverpool.

Land, C. and Taylor, S. (2010), 'Surf's up: work, life, balance and brand in a New Age capitalist organization', *Sociology*, 44, 395–413.

Layard, R. (2003), *Happiness: Lessons from a New Science*, Allen Lane, London.

Lenin, V.I. (1939), *Imperialism: The Highest Stage of Capitalism*, International Publishers, New York.

Li, M.Z. (2009), 'Leisure and tourism in the changing China', *World Leisure Journal*, 51, 229–236.

Li, Y., Pickles, A. and Savage, M. (2005), 'Social capital and social trust in Britain', *European Sociological Review*, 21, 109–123.

Li, Y., Savage, M. and Pickles, A. (2003), 'Social capital and social exclusion in England and Wales (1972–1999)', *British Journal of Sociology*, 54, 497–526.

Li, Y., Savage, M. and Tampubolon, G. (2002), 'Dynamics of social capital: trends and turnover in associational membership in England and Wales, 1972–1999', *Sociological Research Online*, 7, 3.

Li-Ming Chiang, Cebula, E. and Lankford, S.V. (2009), 'Benefits of tai chi chuan for older adults: literature review', *World Leisure Journal*, 51, 184–196.

Liechty, M. (2003), *Suitably Modern: Making Middle Class Culture in a New Consumer Society*, Princeton University Press, Princeton, NJ.

Linder, S. (1970), *The Harried Leisure Class*, Columbia University Press, New York.

Lindsay, J. (2004), 'Gender and class in the lives of young hairdressers: from serious to spectacular', *Journal of Youth Studies*, 7, 259–277.

Liston, K. (2011), 'Sport and leisure', in Gabriel, N. and Mennell, S., eds, *Norbert Elias and Figurational Research: Processual Thinking in Sociology*, *Sociological Review*, 59, s1, Sociological Review Monograph Series, Wiley-Blackwell, Oxford, pp. 160–179.

López, M.D.M.-L. (2011), 'Consumption and modernization in the European Union', *European Sociological Review*, 27, 124–137.

López-Sintas, J. and García Álvarez, E. (2002), 'Omnivores show up again: the segmentation of cultural consumers in Spanish social space', *European Sociological Review*, 18, 353–368.

López-Sintas, J., Garcia-Alvarez, M.E. and Filimon, N. (2008), 'Scale and periodicities of recorded music consumption: reconciling Bourdieu's theory of taste with facts', *Sociological Review*, 56, 78–101.

Luhmann, N. (1997), *Social Systems*, Stanford University Press, Stanford, CA.

Lukose, R. (2009), *Liberalization's Children: Gender, Youth and Consumer Citizenship in Globalizing India*, Duke University Press, Durham, NC.

Lusby, C., Autry, C. and Anderson, S. (2012), 'Community, life satisfaction and motivation in ocean cruising: comparative findings', *World Leisure Journal*, 54, 310–321.

Lynd, R.S. and Lynd, H.M. (1929), *Middletown: A Study in Contemporary American Culture*, Harcourt, Brace, New York.

Lynd, R.S. and Lynd, H.M. (1937), *Middletown in Transition: A Study in Cultural Conflicts*, Harcourt, Brace, New York.

Ma Huidi and Liu Er (2009), 'Social transformation: the value of traditional leisure culture of China revisited', *World Leisure Journal*, 51, 3–13.

Ma Huidi and NingZequn (2010), 'Survey and thinking on the leisure life of migrant farmers in China', paper presented at *International Sociological Association World Congress*, Gothenburg.

Ma Huidi, Zhao Peng, NingZequn and Li Xiang (2010), 'Survey of leisure life of senior people in China', in Modi, I., Ma Huidi and NingZequn, eds, *Leisure and Civilization: Interdisciplinary and International Perspectives*, China Travel and Tourism Press, Beijing, pp. 170–181.

MacCannell, D. (1976), *The Tourist: A New Theory of the Leisure Class*, Macmillan, London.

Maguire, J.S. (2008), *Fit for Consumption: Sociology and the Business of Fitness*, Routledge, London.

Mannheim, K. (1936), *Ideology and Utopia: An Introduction to the Sociology of Knowledge*, Routledge and Kegan Paul, London.

Marcuse, H. (1955/1987), *Eros and Civilization: A Philosophical Inquiry into Freud*, Routledge, London.

Markula-Denison, P. and Pringle, R. (2006), *Foucault, Sport and Exercise*, Routledge, London.

Marsh, P., Rosser, E. and Harre, R. (1978), *The Rules of Disorder*, Routledge, London.

Martinelli, A. (2007), *Transatlantic Divide: Comparing the United States and the European Union*, Oxford University Press, Oxford.

Marx, K. (1858/1993), *Grundrisse*, Penguin, London.

Marx, K. (1867/1965), *Capital: A Critique of Political Economy*, Lawrence and Wishart, London.

Marx, K. (1979), *Selected Writings on Sociology and Social Philosophy*, ed. Bottomore, T.B. and Rubel, M., Penguin, Harmondsworth.

Marx, K. (1989), *Readings from Karl Marx*, ed. Sayer, D., Routledge, London.

Marx, K. and Engels, F. (1845–1846/1965), *The German Ideology*, Lawrence and Wishart, London.

Marx, K. and Engels, F. (1848/1985), *The Communist Manifesto*, Penguin, London.

Maslow, A.H. (1943), 'A theory of human motivation', *Psychological Review*, 50, 370–396.

Maslow, A.H. (1954), *Motivation and Personality*, Harper, New York.

McGovern, P. (2002), 'Globalization or internationalization? Foreign footballers in the English league, 1946–1995', *Sociology*, 36, 23–42.

McKinlay, A. and Smith, C., eds (2009), *Creative Labour: Working in the Creative Industries*, Palgrave Macmillan, Basingstoke.

Mead, G.H. (1934), *Mind, Self and Society*, Chicago University Press, Chicago, IL.

Meadows, D.L., Randers, J. and Behrens III, W.W. (1974), *The Limits to Growth*, Pan, London.

Mennell, S. (2003), 'Eating out on the public sphere in the nineteenth and twentieth centuries', in Jacobs, M. and Scholliers, P., eds, *Eating Out in Europe: Picnics, Gourmet Dining and Snacks since the Late Eighteenth Century*, Berg, Oxford, pp. 245–260.

Merton, R.K. (1938), 'Social structure and anomie', *American Sociological Review*, 3, 672–682.

Merton, R.K. (1949), *Social Theory and Social Structure*, Free Press, Glencoe, IL.

Michels, R. (1962), *Political Parties*, Free Press, New York.

Mills, C.W. (1959), *The Sociological Imagination*, Oxford University Press, New York.

Moonkyum Kim (2010), 'The leisure transformation in modern Korea', in Erwei Dong and Jouyeon Yi-Kook, eds, *Korean Leisure: From Tradition to Modernity*, Rawat Publications, Jaipur, pp. 17–33.

Mouzelis, N.P. (1995), *Sociological Theory: What Went Wrong?* Routledge, London.

Mythen, G. (2004), *Ulrich Beck: A Critical Introduction to the Risk Society*, Pluto Press, London.

Mythen, G. (2005), 'Employment, individualization and insecurity: rethinking the risk society perspective', *Sociological Review*, 53, 129–149.

Nichols, G. (2004), 'Crime and punishment and sports development', *Leisure Studies*, 23, 177–194.

North, S. (2010), 'Strategies of leisure in Japan', paper presented at *International Sociological Association World Congress*, Gothenburg.

Ofcom (2015), *Adults' Media Use and Attitudes Report 2015*, Ofcom, London.

Pangburn, W.M. (1940), 'Play and recreation', *Annals of the American Academy of Political and Social Science*, 212, 121–129.

Parker, S. (1971), *The Future of Work and Leisure*, MacGibbon and Kee, London.

Parsons, T. (1937), *The Structure of Social Action*, Free Press, New York.

Parsons, T. (1951), *The Social System*, Routledge, London.

Parsons, T. (1966), *Societies: Evolutionary and Comparative Perspectives*, Prentice Hall, Englewood Cliffs, NJ.

Parsons, T. and Bales, R.F. (1955), *Family, Socialization and Interaction Process*, Free Press, Glencoe, IL.

Parsons, T. and Smelsner, N.J. (1956), *Economy and Society*, Routledge, London.

Peterson, R.A. (1992), 'Understanding audience segmentation: from elite and mass to omnivore and univore', *Poetics*, 21, 243–282.

Peterson, R.A. and Kern, R.M. (1996), 'Changing highbrow taste: from snob to omnivore', *American Sociological Review*, 61, 900–907.

Pfister, G. (2007), 'Sportification, power and control: ski-jumping as a case study', *Junctures*, 8, 51–67.

Piketty, T. (2014), *Capital in the Twenty-First Century*, Harvard University Press, Cambridge, MA.

Pronovost, G. (1998), 'The Sociology of Leisure', *Current Sociology*, 46, 3, 1–156.

Putnam, R.D. (2000), *Bowling Alone: The Collapse and Revival of American Community*, Simon and Schuster, New York.

bibliography

Rapuano, D. (2009), 'Working at fun: conceptualizing leisurework', *Current Sociology*, 57, 617–636.

Riordan, J. (1980), *Soviet Sport*, Blackwell, Oxford.

Riordan, J. (1982), 'Leisure: the state and the individual in the USSR', *Leisure Studies*, 1, 65–79.

Ritzer, G. (1993), *The McDonaldization of Society*, Pine Forge Press, Thousand Oaks, CA.

Ritzer, G. (1999), *Enchanting a Disenchanted World: Revolutionizing the Means of Consumption*, Pine Forge Press, Thousand Oaks, CA.

Roadburg, A. (1978), 'An Enquiry into Meanings of Work and Leisure', PhD thesis, University of Edinburgh, Edinburgh.

Roberts, K. (2009), *Youth in Transition: Eastern Europe and the West*, Palgrave Macmillan, Basingstoke.

Roberts, K. (2012), 'The end of the long baby boomer generation', *Journal of Youth Studies*, 15, 479–497.

Roberts, K. (2014), 'Youth and leisure in an age of austerity', in Nuere, C.O. and Bayon, F., eds, *El Papel del Ocio en la Construccion Social del Joven*, University of Duesto, Bilbao, pp. 17–31.

Roberts, K. (2015a), 'Social class and leisure during recent recessions in Britain', *Leisure Studies*, 34, 131–149.

Roberts, K. (2015b), *The Business of Leisure*, Palgrave Macmillan, Basingstoke.

Robinson, W.I. and Harris, J. (2000), 'Towards a global ruling class? Globalization and the transnational capitalist class', *Science and Society*, 64, 11–54.

Rolandsen, U.M.H. (2011), *Leisure and Power in Urban China: Everyday Life in a Chinese City*, Routledge, London.

Roux, B. Le, Rouanet, H., Savage, M. and Warde, A. (2008), 'Class and cultural division in the UK', *Sociology*, 42, 1,049–1,071.

Sala, E., Terraneo, M., Lucini, M. and Knies, G. (2013), 'Exploring the impact of male and female facial attractiveness on occupational prestige', *Research in Social Stratification and Mobility*, 31, 69–81.

Samdahl, D.M. (2010), 'Is leisure studies "ethnocentric"? It takes more than optimism: a view from Athens, Georgia, USA', *World Leisure Journal*, 52, 3, 185–190.

Sassen, S. (1991), *The Global City: New York, London, Tokyo*, Princeton University Press, Princeton, NJ.

Savage, M., Bagnall, G. and Longhurst, B. (2004), 'Local habitus and working class culture', in Devine, F., Savage, M., Scott, J. and Crompton, R., eds, *Rethinking Class: Culture, Identities and Lifestyle*, Palgrave Macmillan, Basingstoke, pp. 95–122.

Savage, M., Bagnall, G. and Longhurst, B. (2005), *Globalization and Belonging*, Sage, London.

Savage, M., Devine, F., Cunningham, N., Taylor, M., Li, Y., Hjellbrekke, J., Roux, B. Le, Friedman, S. and Miles, A. (2013), 'A new model of social class? Findings from the BBC's Great British Class Survey experiment', *Sociology*, 47, 219–250.

Schor, J.B. (1991), *The Overworked American*, Basic Books, New York.

Schütz, A. (1972), *The Phenomenology of the Social World*, Heinemann, London.

Sharma, V. (2006), 'The leisure principle for eradication of global hunger and a more prosperous world', paper presented at *The Phenomenon of the Culture of Leisure* symposium, Wroclaw.

Sharma, V. (2012), 'Introduction', in Dodd, J. and Sharma, V., eds, *Leisure and Tourism: Cultural Paradigms*, Rawat Publications, Jaipur, pp. 1–16.

Simmel, G. (1900/1990), *The Philosophy of Money*, Routledge, London.

Simmel, G. (1903/1950), 'The metropolis and mental life', in Wolff, K., ed., *The Sociology of Georg Simmel*, Free Press, New York.

Singer, P. (1983), *Hegel*, Oxford University Press, Oxford.

Skeggs, B. (1997), *Formations of Class and Gender*, Sage, London.

Skeggs, B. (2004), *Class, Self, Culture*, Routledge, London.

Sklair, L. (2001), *The Transnational Capitalist Class*, Blackwell, Oxford.

Skogen, K. and Wichstrøm, L. (1996), 'Delinquency in the wilderness: patterns of outdoor recreation activities and conduct problems in the general adolescent population', *Leisure Studies*, 15, 151–169.

Smith, A. (1776/1976), *An Inquiry into the Nature and Causes of the Wealth of Nations*, Clarendon Press, Oxford.

Snape, R. and Pussard, H. (2013), 'Theorisations of leisure inter-war Britain', *Leisure Studies*, 32, 1–18.

Sokho Choe and Hyejung Cheon (2010), 'Economic crisis and the change of work and leisure in Korea', in Erwei Dong and Jouyeon Yi-Kook, eds, *Korean Leisure: From Tradition to Modernity*, Rawat Publications, Jaipur, pp. 128–152.

Spracklen, K. (2009), *The Meaning and Purpose of Leisure: Habermas and Leisure at the End of Modernity*, Palgrave Macmillan, Basingstoke.

Spracklen, K. (2011), *Constructing Leisure: Historical and Philosophical Debates*, Palgrave Macmillan, Basingstoke.

Spracklen, K. (2013), *Leisure, Sports and Society*, Palgrave Macmillan, Basingstoke.

Spracklen, K. and Spracklen, B. (2012), 'Pagans and Satans and Goths, oh my: dark leisure as communicative agency and communal identity on the fringes of the modern Goth scene', *World Leisure Journal*, 54, 350–362.

Standing, G. (2011), *The Precariat: The New Dangerous Class*, Bloomsbury Academic, London.

Stebbins, R.A. (1992), *Amateurs, Professionals and Serious Leisure*, McGill-Queens University Press, Montreal.

Stebbins, R.A. (2001), 'The costs and benefits of hedonism: some consequences of taking casual leisure seriously', *Leisure Studies*, 20, 305–309.

Stebbins, R.A. (2005), 'Project-based leisure: theoretical neglect of a common
use of free time', *Leisure Studies*, 24, 1–11.

Steger, B. (1996), 'Hurried work, hurried leisure, and time to sleep: the
case of Japan', paper presented at *New Strategies for Everyday Life*
conference, Tilburg.

Sterchele, D. and Saint-Blancat, C. (2015), 'Keeping it liminal: the Mondial
Antirazzisti (Anti-Racist World Cup) as a multifocal interaction ritual',
Leisure Studies, 34, 182–196.

Stewart, B., Smith, A. and Moroney, B. (2013), 'Capital building through
gym work', *Leisure Studies*, 32, 542–560.

Stouffer, S.A., Suchman, E.A., DeVinney, L.C., Star, S.A. and Williams Jr, R.M.
(1949), *Studies in Social Psychology in World War II. The American Soldier,
Volume 1: Adjustment During Army Life*, Princeton University Press,
Princeton, NJ.

Sullivan, O. and Katz-Gerro, T. (2007), 'The omnivore thesis revisited:
voracious cultural consumers', *European Sociological Review*, 23, 123–137.

Tampubolon, G. (2010), 'Social stratification and cultures hierarchy
among the omnivores: evidence from the Arts Council England surveys', *Sociological Review*, 58, 1–25.

Tan Soo Kee (2008), 'Influences of Confucianism on Korean corporate culture', *Asian Profile*, 36, 1, 1–15.

Thomas, W.I. (1927), 'The behavior pattern and the situation', in *Publications
of the American Sociological Society: Papers and Proceedings*, 22nd Annual
Meeting, vol. 22, pp. 1–13.

Toennies, F. (1887/1955), *Community and Association*, Routledge, London.

Tsai, C.-T.L. (2006), 'The influence of Confucianism on women's leisure in
Taiwan', *Leisure Studies*, 25, 469–476.

Urry, J. (2014), *Offshoring*, Polity Press, Cambridge.

Varma, P. (1998), *The Great Indian Middle Class*, Penguin, Delhi.

Vitanyi, I. (1981), *The Goals, Methods and Achievements of Cultural Policies as
Reflected in the Social Development of Countries*, Institute for Culture, Budapest.

Vong Tze Ngai (2005), 'Leisure satisfaction and the quality of life in Macao,
China', *Leisure Studies*, 24, 195–207.

Wacquant, L. (2004), *Body and Soul: Notebooks of an Apprentice Boxer*,
Oxford University Press, Oxford.

Waiton, S. (2012), *Snobs' Law: Criminalising Football Fans in an Age of
Intolerance*, Take a Liberty, Dundee.

Wajcman, J. (2015), *Pressed for Time: The Acceleration of Life in Digital
Capitalism*, University of Chicago Press, Chicago, IL.

Wallerstein, I. (1979), *The Capitalist World-Economy*, Cambridge University
Press, Cambridge.

Wang Qiyan (2007), 'A comparison of Chinese and Japanese leisure modes', *World Leisure Journal*, 49, 142–154.

Warde, A., Martens, L. and Olsen, W. (1999), 'Consumption and the problem of variety: cultural omnivorousness, social distinction and dining out', *Sociology*, 33, 105–127.

Warhurst, C. and Nickson, D. (2007), 'Employee experience of aesthetic labour in retail and hospitality', *Work, Employment and Society*, 21, 103–120.

Warner, W.L. and Lunt, P.S. (1942), *The Status System of a Modern Community*, Yale University Press, New Haven, CT.

Weber, M. (1905/1930), *The Protestant Ethic and the Spirit of Capitalism*, Allen and Unwin, London.

Weber, M. (1922/1946), 'Class, status, party', in *From Max Weber: Essays in Sociology*, in Gerth, H.H. and Mills, C.W., eds, Oxford University Press, New York, pp. 180–195.

Welzel, C. (2013), *Freedom Rising: Human Empowerment and the Quest for Emancipation*, Cambridge University Press, New York.

Welzel, C., Inglehart, R. and Kingemann, H.-D. (2003), 'The theory of human development: a cross-cultural analysis', *European Journal of Political Research*, 42, 341–379.

Wessel, M. van (2011), 'Cultural contradictions and intergenerational relations: the construction of selfhood among middle class youth in Baroda', in Donner, H., ed., *Being Middle Class in India*, Routledge, Abingdon, pp. 100–116.

Willis, P. (1977), *Learning to Labour*, Saxon House, Farnborough.

Wouters, C. (2011), 'How civilizing processes continued: towards an informalization of manners and a third nature personality', in Gabriel, N. and Mennell, S., eds, *Norbert Elias and Figurational Research: Processual Thinking in Sociology, Sociological Review*, 59, s1, Sociological Review Monograph Series, Wiley-Blackwell, Oxford, pp. 140–159.

Wright, E.O. (1979), *Class, Crisis and the State*, Verso, London.

Wright, E.O. (2000), 'Working class power, capitalist class interests, and class compromise', *American Journal of Sociology*, 105, 957–1,002.

Yaish, M. and Katz-Gerro, T. (2012), 'Disentangling "cultural capital": the consequences of cultural and economic resources for taste and participation', *European Sociological Review*, 28, 169–185.

Yi-Chung Hsu and Yu-Cheng Hsu (2012), 'Work and leisure among Indonesian professional family caregivers in Taiwan: reality versus dreams', *World Leisure Journal*, 54, 337–349.

Yongkoo Noh (2010), 'Korean leisure policies', in Erwei Dong and Jouyeon Yi-Kook, eds, *Korean Leisure: From Tradition to Modernity*, Rawat Publications, Jaipur, pp. 34–58.

Yoshitaka Iwasaki, Hitoshi Nishino, Tetsuya Onda and Bowling, C. (2007), 'Leisure research in a global world: time to reverse the western dominance in leisure research?', *Leisure Sciences*, 29, 113–117.

Yu-Hao Lee and Holin Lin (2011), '"Gaming is my work": identity work in Internet-hobbyist game workers', *Work, Employment and Society*, 25, 451–467.

Zimdars, A., Sullivan, A. and Heath, A. (2009), 'Elite higher education admissions in the arts and sciences: is cultural capital the key?', *Sociology*, 43, 648–666.

Index